# THE AFRICAN AMERICAN
# WRITER'S HANDBOOK

BY ROBERT FLEMING

*The Wisdom of the Elders*
*The African American Writer's Handbook*

# THE AFRICAN AMERICAN
# WRITER'S HANDBOOK

## HOW TO GET IN PRINT AND STAY IN PRINT

## ROBERT FLEMING

ONE WORLD

THE BALLANTINE PUBLISHING GROUP

NEW YORK

A One World Book
Published by The Ballantine Publishing Group
Copyright © 2000 by Robert Fleming

www.randomhouse.com/BB/

ISBN 0-345-42327-5

Manufactured in the United States of America

First Edition: April 2000

10  9  8  7  6  5  4  3  2

*To my daughter, Ashandra, with my love and respect.
You have exceeded all of my expectations.*

# CONTENTS

# II. THE AFRICAN AMERICAN LITERARY HALL OF FAME                163

# III. LITERARY PATHFINDERS: THE OLD SCHOOL PROFILES          199

CONTENTS          IX

# ACKNOWLEDGMENTS

▲▲▲▲▲▲▲▲▲▲▲▲

There are always so many people to thank whenever one undertakes a project of this magnitude. I wish to acknowledge the following individuals for their special contributions to my work.

First, thanks to my longtime mentors and friends poet Russell Atkins, poet Norman Jordan, poet-artist Michael Harris, poet Anthony Fudge, and playwright Annetta Gomez-Jefferson for supporting me in finding my way as a writer in the early 1970s. To my friend Willard Jenkins, music critic aficionado extraordinare, much gratitude for your assistance in helping me land my first writing job at *The Scene* in Cleveland.

To my editor, Cheryl Woodruff, associate publisher of One World Books, for her invaluable editing and close supervision of this work, and her wonderful staff and associates: Allison Glismann, Gary Brozek, Nora Reichard, and Sheree Thomas. And to Linda Grey, former president of Ballantine Books, for green-lighting this project.

To my family, who have watched me develop from an apprentice of the Dark Art to a veteran practicing writer. A special thanks to my love and inspiration, Donna Hill, who continually astonishes me with each book. Finally, to my friends and advisers, Rosemarie Robotham, Charles Seaton, Marie Brown, David Jackson, Ishmael Reed, John A. Williams, Angela Harvey, Carlene Hatcher Polite, Nettie Jones, and the visionary herself, Gayl Jones.

# INTRODUCTION

In the last decade of the twentieth century, African American writers made an indelible mark on the American book publishing industry, placing their works in newly significant numbers with mainstream book publishers. With the new millennium now in its infancy, this transformation shows every promise of continuing to astonish. Forget the grim pessimism of the past. Discard outmoded fears about those stubborn barriers of ignorance, neglect and apathy, maintained through default by publishers who barely squinted in the direction of black books, often conveniently consigning them to an indifferent afterthought.

African American writers have *arrived*, proudly elbowing our way onto center stage of the national culture, and our creations are big business! The American publishing industry now acknowledges that there is a sizable black readership hungry for words and images by and about themselves—an ever-growing audience eager to support their authors as they meet that need with an increasingly commercial and literary output. As Cheryl D. Woodruff, associate publisher of One World, commented, "The African American market has exploded in the last six years and taken a quantum leap from relative infancy to surprising maturity. Averaging sales of more than 40 million dollars per quarter (more than 160 million per year), it is widely regarded as one of the fastest growing segments of the book-buying market. According to a recent Gallup survey, the African American market, 9.9 million readers strong, who purchase 39.7 million books in any given quarter, breaks down this way—57 percent of African American book buyers are women, 49 percent are college educated, and 35 percent are under the age of thirty-five. These readers are slightly younger and better educated than the population as a whole. In recent years the competition to serve this readership gold mine has heated up to an all-time high as auctions for top reprint and original authors have skyrocketed."

Today, national bestseller lists continually show a strong representation of black authors. Writing in every genre, they are surprising and challenging readers and reviewers through their imagination, craft, and applied knowledge.

How are these writers doing it? Whom do they know in the business to get these opportunities? Is there a secret formula for getting published? It seems everybody wants to be a writer living the glamorous life at the start of the twenty-first century, but there are precious few guidebooks tailored specially for the African American novice wishing to get his or her work into print. Getting published requires more than mere luck, a knack for the clever phrase, or generous relatives in high places. Writing well will satisfy the artistic and creative part of you, but placing that work with an established publisher and seeing the final product on the bookshelf will provide you with a golden opportunity to offer your particular vision to the world while paying the bills.

This book is the first of a new wave of reference guides targeting the black reader and writer in the rapidly morphing cyber-world of American publishing. Unlike anything currently to be found on the bookshelves, it is a how-to primer with a hint of soul. It offers the straight facts about how to get your work into print. For the African American writer, both novice and professional, this is an informative source to stack on top of your copies of Bowker's *Literary Market Place (LMP)*, the *Poets & Writers* guides, and the *Writer's Digest* reference volumes.

The core value of *The African American Writer's Handbook* is its demystification of the publishing world for the African American writer, reader, or anyone else considering or aspiring to a career in the industry. Books do not materialize through a mere gesture of Merlin's wrinkled hand in a mist of blue smoke. The young writer, or the novice of any age, full of ambition and dreams, must understand that a well-written, well-presented book—the finished product—is the result of countless hours of hard work—the writer's work, of course, but also that of collaborators, most of whom the author may never meet.

Once upon a time, getting published meant just delivering your work into the hands of an editor, by whatever means possible. But in an era of superagents, megadeals and blockbusters, the time-honored dream of that gem of a manuscript, unaccountably shining forth from the publisher's slush pile and illuminating the desk of its fortunate finder, remains among the rarest of modern-day miracles in the realm of real-life publishing.

Ask any popular African American novelist what is the most commonly asked question on his or her book tours and the reply will be: "Just how does somebody get published these days?" Unfortunately, competition for publication has soared as the number of writers has risen. And that number continues to increase. Countless manuscripts submitted by aspiring authors are rejected, returned to the sender for a lack of originality, poor grammar, and lackluster story lines. However, good writing will ultimately find a home with a publisher. Don't despair. In the succinct, commonsense opinion of John O. Killens, author of the novels 'Sippi and The Cotillion: "Folks want something new and well done." Today, as never before, luck and happenstance carry little or no weight in influencing the decision of wary editors to publish a manuscript.

Every writer wants to be read. Success in that quest today requires a business-minded sensibility and a well-mounted campaign to get and stay in print. That is where The African American Writer's Handbook is most useful. Anyone needing vital information on the dos and don'ts of the publishing business can turn to these pages, which reveal how the first-time writer can research the various publishing houses and their commercial needs even before submitting a book proposal.

Other essential elements within these covers will help you succeed as a writer, whether you write fiction or nonfiction. You will learn from the experts about a wide range of topics critical to the writer:

- the query letter
- the foolproof proposal
- multiple submissions
- agents and editors
- contracts and copyright protections
- sales, promotion, and marketing
- small-press publishing and self-publishing
- current trends in publishing
- Internet publishing resources

Beyond informing you on the basics, *The African American Writer's Handbook* explains the process of "making a book," from its genesis in the writer's original idea through its editing to the final packaging, marketing, and publicity. Other areas explored include advances and royalties, booksellers, grants and awards, vanity publishing, bestsellers, movie sales, tax tips, writing workshops and retreats, writers organizations, and writer reference publications. Unlike many other guides to book publishing now on the market, particularly those that unduly stress obstacles and pitfalls, this book is designed to arm you with nuts-and-bolts tools and insider information that will boost your confidence and expertise in your quest to publish your creative work. Every chapter of this book is aimed to support you in fully committing to your goal of publishing your manuscript.

An added plus for African American writers is the inclusion of highly informative and entertaining sections featuring profiles and interviews with established yet sometimes unknown writers, past and present, talking about the craft of writing and about their own unique journeys to publication. Their experiences become all the more valuable when one considers the scope of the talent involved: among novelists, people such as

Ann Petry, Toni Cade Bambara, Albert James Young, Carlene Hatcher Polite, John A. Williams, and Kristin Hunter Lattany; among poets, the likes of Dudley Randall, Naomi Long Madgett, and Haki Madhubuti—legendary voices presenting readers with much to consider in their words concerning craft, alternative publishing, and African American poetic tradition.

Publishing in the twenty-first century is a rapidly evolving, highly technical business, influencing almost every aspect of our society and world. With African Americans now numbering about 3.4 percent of the managerial and editorial workforce of the book publishing industry, chances are that an African American writer will work with a white editor. Writers of color with a steadfast commitment to Afrocentric publishing houses can find a worthwhile alternative to mainstream publishing in the black publishers listed with the National Association of Black Book Publishers. *The African American Writer's Handbook* candidly discusses the issue of low minority representation in the publishing industry and its impact on the quality and number of authors published and the kinds of books produced. Another related section offers a detailed look at the major publishers even as it seeks and finds insight among the smaller independents.

To assemble this book, I logged hundreds of hours of research time in libraries and on the Internet. I read every book and periodical I could locate that was relevant to the topics addressed in this handbook. Also, I spent countless hours and days interviewing authors, editors, and agents to gather the information presented here. Officials at various writers organizations opened the door to still other resources and alerted me to a host of important issues concerning authors. Their contributions helped to make this effort a much better book, exceeding even my expectations. Perhaps yours as well?

Ultimately, *The African American Writer's Handbook: How to Get in Print and Stay in Print* can be used as a tool for fashioning a lasting career as a writer by way of comprehensive and helpful information on the publishing industry in an era of intense competition and startling literary variety. What enables the productive, committed writer to sell his or her work is a profound understanding of the creative and economic demands of the publishing business. The aim of this book is to help make that sometimes long, yet rewarding, journey much easier.

PART I

▼▼▼▼▼▼▼

# THE ESSENTIALS

▼▼▼▼▼▼▼▼▼▼▼

▲▲

"To be responsible as a writer means that every word of mine will have been written truly, as truly as we knew how at the time of the writing. That is only the beginning, however, because writing, though done in solitude, is a social act. It needs the reader to complete it. Writing is a relationship in which we who write and you who read meet in the silent places of your soul. If I have written well and you have read well, we learn a little more about what it means to be wholly human."

—JULIUS LESTER
From *Falling Pieces of the Broken Sky*

▲▲

# THE PUBLISHING INDUSTRY TODAY

> "At its best, publishing is one of the crucial elements of our culture. It possesses the most potential for presenting the work of our best minds to the masses at a time when their creativity and vision are very much needed."
> —JOE WOOD
> Editor, The New Press

There has never been a better time for African American writers in the history of American publishing, with so many books coming from such a wide range of black creators on almost every topic imaginable. Black writers, for the most part, have made the critical adjustment to view the publishing industry as a business, understanding the need to merge their art with the demands of the consuming public. Although they want, like all writers, to get their work into print, they comprehend that the publishing industry is in a state of intense transition, that creativity and imagination will not guarantee a successful career when the level of competition among both publishers and writers has greatly increased. Still, a substantial number of African American writers are getting published and carving out an ever-growing share of the reading market.

Indeed, times have changed drastically for the publishing world. The formerly genteel pastime for gentlemen is now a high-risk, big-stakes business. Corporate publishers are wrestling with the pressing question of what to do with the present stagnancy of growth in overall readership in the face of competition for recreational space with the Internet, cable TV, movies, and video games. With increasing foreign ownership of American publishers, one fear has been that mergers will spell the end of the midlist author, who sells far fewer books than the marquee author. Half of the top twenty American publishing houses are foreign owned, comprising a 28 percent share of the market. The publishers say that they want to acquire good books that hold their own in the marketplace. But what sells? Few, if any, guarantees prevail in the publishing world; no book seems to be a certain sell-through, for even many of the brand-name authors have suffered dips in their sales numbers.

According to the 1998 Consumer Research Study on Book Purchasing, the unit purchases of adult books in 1998 fell 2.8 percent to 1.04 billion last year. The 1997 unit sales figures had moved up by less than 1 percent. Even mass-market paperback sales slid to a new low, tallying up the biggest drop in book units, nearly two-thirds of the decline. Hardcover sales also fell, but trade paperback sales held steady.

One theory is that there are books on every subject under the sun and too many books are being published. Some critics of the industry insist that a portion of the business's woes can be placed on bad judgment in title acquisitions, poor management, and an overemphasis on celebrity books, which often are purchased with huge advances. Publishing executives, aware of the complaints, have moved quickly to tighten their spending, keeping a closer watch on the editorial, production, and promotion departments—no more lavish parties or other costly job perks. Because it is now understood that two or three of these megabooks purchased with huge advances can affect the fortunes of an entire publishing house, the matter of author compensation is under closer scrutiny. However, not all in the industry are convinced that the present situation is as dire as many pundits would have us believe—that is, that the entire business is just minutes away from a total economic collapse. Some industry analysts say it's simply a major reassessment and readjustment in how the industry operates in a highly competitive society where leisure time is often impulsive or determined by discretionary income.

Many of those who monitor the publishing industry are optimistic, despite some significant changes:

· The consolidation of independent distributors and whole-salers and a loss of overall competition

· The shrinkage in the number of independent booksellers and fewer options for the discerning book buyer

· The growth and dominance of the large bookselling chain stores in almost every major national region

· The consolidation of the major publishing houses, resulting in fewer outlets for writers and agents, and a reduction in publishing slots

· The widespread view within the industry of the author as a business commodity and no longer as a mysterious, glamorous artist, leading to a major policy change in the publicizing and promoting of published writers.

With over 63,000 books published yearly, no one will tell you that all of them are volumes of quality or substance, or possess real commercial potential. The new push in the industry is to locate, cultivate, and grow new markets among the nation's very diverse readership. Some efforts have been hit-or-miss, such as to exploit the exploding Latin market, but other markets have shown some promising results—the Asian and African American audiences, along with the lucrative gay readership. And the editors are scouting for new readers in previously silent communities, hoping to bring them cost-effectively into the mainstream.

While article after article proclaims that the industry is no longer about publishing what is good but instead is focused on what can show a profit, it would be foolish to regard every book printed as a product of greed or to think that publishers care for nothing beyond achieving the largest possible market share. Among many of the publishing houses, there exists a staunch commitment to publishing books that make a difference, to taking artistic and commercial risks. Some true prestige is added into the industry when a house finds a work that is both literate and highly commercial. In fact, many houses use the large profits of their front-line, bestselling authors to bankroll more challenging titles that promise a limited audience. This approach is also taken for the benefit of first novels, poetry from new voices, and nonfiction for a specific niche market.

The fear is that limited consumer demand may end the days of publishers as advocates of provocative, cutting-edge art, despite these supposed glory days of a sound economy and more disposable income. Will the ongoing merging of the large mainstream publishers really transform the business and lift its artistic sights? Will reorganization and downsizing help matters? Will the reduction of overhead costs, the merging of departments, and the slashing of staff really help to sell more books? What will happen to the books of dialogue, debate, and discourse? Will bigger equal better?

Unfortunately, the hardcover may cease to be the spine of the publishing business, especially if the electronic book catches on. Still, there are those readers who will never tire of buying and handling the traditional format of a book, despite the conveniences of technology. For the worker bees of publishing—the people who edit, design, and produce the books—nothing can ever replace the joy of witnessing the evolution of an unedited manuscript to a handsomely printed book. They fear they're witnessing the passing of a Golden Age where the art and craft of book editing, design, and production will be soon forgotten.

The problem here is that the book, a product born of the creativity and imagination of the writer, must rely on the buying habits of the reader. Yes, even your number-one bestsellers do not produce the kind of box-office revenue that hit films generate, but something will be tragically lost if the profit motive completely dominates the acquisition process of the publishing world. Many fewer titles will be published, and the bar of quality may be lowered to accommodate popular appetites. But commercial trends are fleeting and fickle.

However, one thing is certain. No matter what adjustments are made within the publishing industry, the future of books is not as precarious as some naysayers would have you believe.

Two real indications of health within the industry are the rapid growth of various regional bestseller lists throughout the country and the Oprah Book Club phenomenon; both trends show that people are continuing to read books in significant numbers. Publishing has become the realm of the commercially targeted book, which is a good thing in that more areas of the American reading public are being serviced than ever before. And African Americans, who are among these targeted groups, are seeing more diversity in the range of books being offered. Yes, black writers are becoming more visible throughout the evolving publishing business. We must work even harder to make our presence felt all throughout the industry — as writers, editors, publicists, sales personnel, management, and publishers. The time is right for a greater push in all of these areas. In the final analysis, good books are still published and continue to find their way into the hands of those people who love them.

## A PARTIAL LIST OF
## MAJOR AMERICAN PUBLISHERS

This select list of the more important publishing houses can assist you in targeting the appropriate company for your submission or query. Many of the bigger houses publish books under several imprints, so it's essential to research them to find the best home for your work.

**Trade Hardcover Houses**
Addison-Wesley
Ballantine
Bantam Doubleday Dell
Basic Books
Beacon Books
Carol Publishing
Crown
DoveBooks

E. P. Dutton
Farrar, Straus and Giroux
The Free Press
Grove/Atlantic
Harcourt Brace
HarperCollins
Henry Holt & Co.
Houghton Mifflin
Hyperion
Alfred A. Knopf
Little, Brown & Co.
Macmillan Publishing Co.
William Morrow & Co.
The New Press
W. W. Norton & Co.
Pantheon Books
Penguin Putnam
Random House
St. Martin's Press
Scribner
Simon & Schuster
Times Books
Villard
Walker & Co.
Warner Books

**Mass-Market Houses**
Avon
Ballantine/Del Rey/Fawcett/Ivy
Bantam
Berkley
Dell
Harper
New American Library/Signet/Onyx
Pocket
Warner
Zebra

▲▲

*"It is one of the tragedies of life that one cannot have all
the wisdom one is ever to possess in the beginning. Perhaps, it is just as well to be rash and foolish for a while. If
writers were too wise, perhaps no books would be written
at all. It might be better to ask yourself 'Why?' afterwards
than before. Anyway, the force from somewhere in space
which commands you to write in the first place, gives you
no choice. You take up the pen when you are told, and
write what is commanded. There is no agony like bearing
an untold story inside you."*

—ZORA NEALE HURSTON
From *Dust Tracks on a Road*

▲▲

# THE WRITER'S CRAFT

Before a book can be published, it must be written, and that is not an easy task. Many people dream of being a writer, the large advances, the signings, the movie deals, the TV tie-ins, the parties, the premieres, all the glory and trappings of fame and fortune. Unfortunately, the majority of writers do not live the Good Life or enjoy the fabled glamorous existence often connected with the celebrity writer. For many, writing is a way of life, a profession without the limelight, a job to keep food on the table and a roof over one's head. Yes, this commonplace reality differs greatly from the glittering fantasy one sees in films and on television.

Most established writers speak of the need to write almost as if it were an addiction, a compulsion beyond their control, a natural extension of their true selves as much as breathing or eating. They say it's more than the incredible rush of emotion that comes from seeing your work in print for the first time or reading your words published between the covers of a book. It's something more than that. Often the need to write is a combination of factors, possibly the same characteristics of the personality that moved you to fill the pages of a diary or to write sappy poems that you never showed to anyone or to toil thankless hours rewriting copy at the high school newspaper.

In preparing for the quest to bring your book to print, it's essential that you understand your motives for starting a writing career. Without a doubt, your parents or your significant other may not share this hunger that compels you to stare at a blank sheet of paper for hours or to tap away on the keyboard of your computer in your room deep into the night without a break.

With all of the sacrifice and hard work a lifetime membership implies, what are your reasons for wishing to join the Holy Order of Writers? Figure that out first before quitting your day job or investing in a top-of-the-line computer. Don't register for those expensive creative-writing classes before you understand your choice, because you will not become wealthy overnight. Writing, for the committed, is not a frivolous hobby but serious business.

SITTING IN a Paris café in the late 1950s, Richard Wright divulged to William Gardner Smith, the author of the popular post–World War II novel *The Last of the Conquerors*, Wright's surefire formula for a successful book. First, he said, the writer must be concerned with the total impression he wants to make on the reader. That impression must underline every word, sentence, paragraph, and chapter of the work. Next, generous portions of story, bearing such essential elements as surprise, suspense, movement and characterization, must be added. After producing a blazing first draft, the writer would take three drafts to sharpen the plot, setting and atmosphere, and to shed all excess verbiage before applying the final polish. A book was finished when there was nothing left to fix, concluded Wright before leaving.

Once you've decided why you want to write, read, study, and absorb the work of the writers recognized as masters of their craft for their fine literary style. The next step is to select your specialty, your preferred genre, your area of greatest reading interest. Go to the library or a bookstore and look around.

Ask yourself the following questions as you consider the start of your new writing career:

1. What type of book do you like to read most?
2. Who are your favorite authors?
3. Whose writing style do you admire most?
4. In what areas do you have some expertise or work experience?

This is a good start for a beginner, but the dedicated writer, with skills and an uncertain project in mind, must go further in understanding his temperament and abilities. Are you a novelist or someone who would be more comfortable writing a biography of jazz pianist Bud Powell, a travel guide of scenic Rio de Janiero, a study of the Geechee folklore and customs, or some other form of nonfiction? While browsing at the megastore, see what books are in demand and get a good idea of the quality of your competition. Keep in mind that because there are fewer titles being published today, your work must be marketable. If you want to be published, you must write something that sells.

If you think your life story, like that of activist Angela Davis or baseball slugger Willie Mays, might make an excellent memoir, be sure that it contains something fresh, original, and fascinating for the reader. It is not often that one can read autobiographies of the caliber of the Delany sisters, Malcolm X, Billie Holiday, or Piri Thomas. Indeed, there are stories so important, so inspiring that they must be told, people so singular in character and deed that they must be analyzed and remembered in print, and events so monumental that they must be faithfully recounted on the page. Be brutally honest with yourself about what you have to offer to the literary world. Do not delude yourself or sell yourself short.

J. CALIFORNIA Cooper's richly textured novels are frequently praised for their strong, enduring women, but she insists they're only a reflection of real life. "They have to work hard but they get out there and make it," the wise griot of *The Wake of the Wind* notes. "That is what the stories are written for, telling people to put their minds on their business, their options, their choices, and to see that they have some."

Along with autobiographies and memoirs, there exists an extensive range of categories that fit neatly within the realm of nonfiction. Review the list and determine which category best suits your ability:

- biography
- autobiography/memoir
- travel
- inspirational
- self-help
- business and personal finance
- humor/satire
- true crime
- cookbook

No matter whether a writer is working on a nonfiction project or shaping a novel, the urge must be to push your imagination and abilities to their limit, to probe your topic or characters to their emotional and spiritual depths, to question not only the ways of the world but your role and place in it. That excavation of information or search for truth in your writing can produce astonishing moments of surprise and revelation not only for you but for the reader as well. Although every novelist wants his or her work to reach the widest audience possible, there is a telling difference between commercial and literary fiction, with the emphasis often coming both in how the story is told and in the characters depicted.

MARGARET WALKER says that her landmark novel, *Jubilee*, took ten years of research and nearly thirty years of writing before it was complete. The heart of the inspiring, epic story of black survival and the terrors of slavery and Jim Crow came from a bedtime tale told to the young Margaret by her grandmother.

Commercial fiction often emphasizes the storytelling aspects of fiction, with much stress placed on using known formulas to reach the widest audience possible. The popular works of E. Lynn Harris and Terry McMillan are the best-known examples of this type of novel. In literary fiction, great care is taken to craft the narrative with style and nuance, using intricate plots and complex characters to attract a more sophisticated and demanding reader. When readers think of literary novelists, names such as Toni Morrison, Bebe Moore Campbell, Charles Johnson, Ernest Gaines, and Tina McElroy Ansa come immediately to mind. These writers delve deeply into the emotional and psychological lives of their characters.

None of this talk about literary novels is to denigrate the value of good storytelling, for to re-create a fictional biography of a person's life from beginning to end is no easy feat. Nothing can be harder than putting the most effective words and sentences on the page to influence and manipulate the thoughts and emotions of a reader. In commercial fiction as well, the author possesses the goal of creating the best book possible for the reader, accomplishing that aim with a final product that reads easily and effortlessly.

In fiction, both commercial and literary, there are several key genres, all demanding a certain mastery of language and narrative voice. You may find some of your favorites among the following:

· mystery novels
· romance novels
· Western novels
· horror novels
· fantasy novels
· science-fiction novels
· children's/young-adult novels
· thrillers

What does it take to be a good novelist, other than a skill with language and imagination? Returning to our discussion about literary versus commercial fiction, both require the persistence and discipline to sit down at the desk, shut out all distractions, and focus and concentrate for long periods of time.

Most novelists keep notebooks full of snatches of ideas, random thoughts, intriguing turns of phrase, and general observations about how people think and speak. While some writers may wrestle with finding time to work, others approach the task with eagerness, joy, and much anticipation. As the saying goes, a writer writes, and nothing interferes with that process once it has started.

NIKKI GIOVANNI, a poet and educator whose militant fire has not dwindled over the years, once spoke candidly about why writers continue to write even after a book becomes an unqualified financial success. In her words, you're only as good as your last book. "God wrote one book," she told an interviewer. "The rest of us are forced to do a little better. You can't live forever on that one book. No matter how interesting, or how great, or how whatever, you are forced to continue, to take a chance."

A novelist maps out his plot, its action and dialogue, its characters with all of their conflicts and contradictions, the ideas and themes of the work, and overall content. Using a severe analytical eye, he homes in on the form and structure of the narrative, checking for any rough spots or snags that may break the spell of the novel. If he wants to improvise along the way, he is careful not to let that spontaneity get in the way of the story line.

Patience must be a chief trait of the novelist, for rushed, forced writing will result in a self-absorbed, selfish book that will distract the reader, leaving no room for him to participate in the unfolding of the story. Some writers will even read the work aloud to ensure that the narrative flows smoothly and cleanly. The flow, rhythm, and sound of the text is important in conveying the power of the story. Don't be afraid to rethink your ideas or to revise wherever the narrative seems uneven or ineffective. It is very rare that a novelist will get everything right in a novel on the first try.

Always keep your audience in mind. They must identify

fully with your characters and their fictional experience, because if the readers lose interest in their choices, actions and stories, then it is highly unlikely that the book will be read to completion. Write according to your own pace. There is no artistic mandate that insists that you produce a novel a year. If you are serious about your art, you will remain a student of words, language, and ideas throughout your career. Never become complacent or overconfident about your ability. Continue to study and read, searching for new ideas, themes, and techniques. Cultivate friendships with accomplished writers, for there is much to be learned in those exchanges.

WRITING CAN be a dangerous business, and you must be prepared. The Pulitzer Prize–winning novelist James Alan McPherson, of *Elbow Room* fame, recalls that another renowned scribe, Ernest Gaines, author of *The Autobiography of Miss Jane Pittman*, always placed a gun on his desk when he began to write.

Organize your work. Plan a writing schedule with all of your tools in place. Establish a routine or a ritual if you must. Stick to it as you would an exercise regimen. Learn to utilize your time wisely. Allow nothing to interrupt the time you have set aside for your writing. Once you have started a project, stick with it unless it lacks the quality and passion you find essential to your work. Often a writer can begin a bad habit of routinely beginning and stopping a novel at the first sign of difficulty. The history of publishing is full of one-book wonders, writers whose creative well ran dry as soon as they finished the one book in their system. Some writers never arrive at that level. They quit when the going gets tough. Every writer runs into a rough patch when the writing can become arduous, slow, even torturous, but dedication and commitment to the process will ultimately win out. Stick with it. Don't give up. Good writing takes time, discipline, and a professional attitude to create something of lasting value.

Readers often romanticize the life of the writer, forming their opinions from Hollywood, Broadway, and other segments of the media. Connie Briscoe, the best-selling author of *Sisters & Lovers* and *Big Girls Don't Cry* answering an inquiring reporter concerning the freedom that comes from her book revenues, quickly added: "You have a certain amount of freedom in terms of when you will work. I say a *certain* amount because at some point, if you want to keep your fans you have to produce. You must sit down and write."

Lastly, remember that each book you write is another building block toward a long, productive career. Don't expect a miracle overnight, a huge bestseller and instant fame. The writing careers of those authors who have become household names took years to build, going through peaks and valleys of both successes and setbacks, before producing the esteemed body of work.

So get started, begin writing, and let nothing and no one deter you from achieving your dream. You'll be amazed at what you can accomplish. Imagine getting paid for something you love doing. Imagine seeing your work displayed in a bookstore for sale. Well, it's possible if you just believe!

Maya angelou recalled how she almost turned down a life of letters. In 1967, the writer James Baldwin took her to a dinner party held at the home of the cartoonist Jules Feiffer. The guests swapped stories after their meal, and Maya, in rare form, stunned the others with her tales. Feiffer's wife later called an editor, who phoned Angelou to ask her about writing an autobiography. Angelou repeatedly said no, despite the editor's continued offers. Only when the editor issued a challenge that it was nearly impossible to write an effective autobiography did Angelou yield. The result was the writer's classic first book, *I Know Why the Caged Bird Sings*.

▲▲

*"There is no such animal as 'Art for Art's Sake.' Like I have said many times before, all art is propaganda, all propaganda is not art. Art is social and political, takes a position for humanity or against. Art is functional. . . . In the great white institutions of learning, one is taught that there is nothing new under the sun; everything has been said before, it is from now on merely a question of form, craft, or rephrasing. But my great-grandmother used to say: 'The half ain't never been told.' It is probably true that Western man has nothing more or new to say to humankind. It is time (long overdue) for black men to speak, to create a new vision for mankind, a vision oriented to man, not to things."*

—JOHN O. KILLENS
From *Amistad 2*

▲▲

# THE LEGACY OF AFRICAN AMERICAN LITERATURE

> "I have however deep concern with the development of a literature worthy of our past, and of our destiny, without which literature certainly, we can never come to much. I have a deep concern with the development of an audience worthy of such a literature."
>
> —STERLING BROWN
> From "Our Literary Audience" (1930)

At the start of the twenty-first century, African American literature now is generations old, with a stellar list of writers and thinkers forming a legacy that would make any people proud. That achievement has not come without its measure of difficulty, sacrifice, and suffering. From its humble beginnings with Olaudah Equino, Phillis Wheatley, and Jupiter Hammons, black literature seems to have taken on a back-breaking share of social responsibility and moral conscience in its many texts, from the early slave narratives to the fictional proclamations of race pride through the protest novels to the current explorations of African American culture and relationships.

When the poet and critic Sterling Brown made the above-quoted statement in 1930, African American writers were not commonplace nor were they deeply appreciated, not even in their own community. The lack of popular support has never stopped black writers from being creative or productive, so a long legacy of fine work exists as a foundation for those who follow. The multitalented W. E. B. Du Bois, Paul Lawrence Dunbar, and James Weldon Johnson all continued the quest of building on that memorable start with artistic contributions, in every aspect of the literary field, during the early years of the twentieth century. Very few writers can match their prolific output in quality, variety, or creativity. Their pioneering efforts set the stage for the tremendous eruption of imaginative black voices in the Harlem Renaissance of the 1920s, introducing such writers as Countee Cullen, Langston Hughes, Alain Locke, Zora Neale Hurston, Wallace Thurman, Nella Larsen, Jessie Fauset, and Claude McKay. Collectively, they saw art and literature as effective race-building and race-affirming tools, the ideal means to gain more recognition for African Americans in their ongoing fight for equality and fuller access in this society. Unfortunately, only a small number of the key writers from that crucial period survived the onset of the Great Depression and the passing of the publishing world's brief infatuation with black culture.

All that changed with the overwhelming 1940 success of Richard Wright's *Native Son*, the first novel by a black author to become a Book-of-the-Month Club Main Selection, selling over a quarter of a million copies in three weeks. This type of popular reception caught American publishing completely off guard, and the search was on to find another black author to duplicate the groundbreaking feat. While the majority of the "protest" novels printed were less than impressive, quite a few of them were notable, such as William Attaway's *Blood on the Forge* (1941), Carl R. Offord's *The White Face* (1943), Chester Himes's *If He Hollers Let Him Go* (1945), Ann Petry's *The Street* (1946), Alden Bland's *Behold a Cry* (1947), and William Gardner Smith's *Last of the Conquerors* (1948). Understanding the dynamics of the American publishing marketplace and reading audience, some African American novelists experimented with fiction containing a black view of a white world, using white characters to provide another manner of analysis into the mainstream culture. Several of the most accomplished efforts came from the pens of Ann Petry (*Country Place*), William Gardner Smith (*Anger at Innocence*), and Richard Wright (*Savage Holiday*). Writers Willard Motley and Frank Yerby would take a similar approach to their novels but for different, mainly commercial, reasons.

As the postwar period of the 1950s began in earnest, there was a hope among many blacks that the old Jim Crow ideology that ruled America would wither, especially given the growing preoccupation with communism and atomic warfare. In the words of Chester Himes, this view was summed up: "White folks got a lot more to worry about than us." Some African American writers grew tired of the noble pleas and grumbles of so-called protest fiction and started to see it as an impediment to the evolution of black literature.

William Gardner Smith was one of the writers calling for an expansion of focus, themes, and artistic imagination, making that imperative a key argument in his 1950 article, "The Negro Writer: Pitfalls and Compensations": "It is often hard for the Negro writer to resist polemicizing. He is driven often to write a tract, rather than a work of art. So conscious is he of the pervading evil of race prejudice that he feels duty-bound to assault it at every turn, injecting opinion into alleged narration and inserting his philosophy into the mouths of his characters."

However, the revival of black nationalism in the 1960s only rekindled the fires of protest and militancy in the literature as more radical, aggressive minds took center stage. Much of this new anger was directed at the black middle class, which many militants saw as being silent partners in their oppression by white America. Amiri Baraka termed "Negro Literature" mediocre in a 1966 essay, saying it lacked the power and authenticity of black music, which evolved from the masses and not the middle class. Like a gathering storm, the powerful emotions arising from the civil rights campaigns of Little Rock, Birmingham, Montgomery, Selma, and the Mississippi "Freedom Summer" invaded the written word. This more critical view of segregation was shared by an increasing number of writers as a series of novels reflected this repudiation of the old literary traditions through an angrier, more candid stance: Richard Wright's *A Long Dream* (1958), James Baldwin's *Another Country* (1962), William Melvin Kelley's *A Different Drummer* (1962), John O. Killens's *And Then We Heard the Thunder* (1963), Ronald Fair's *Many Thousand Gone* (1966), Margaret Walker's *Jubilee* (1966), and John A. Williams's *The Man Who Cried I Am* (1967). All of these books built on the stylized excellence of Ralph Ellison's masterwork, *Invisible Man* (1952), with its rich use of metaphors and symbols, to a more directly combative assault on the evils of racism. While in some cases not as technically accomplished as Ellison's mythic novel, these novels showed the lethal accumulation of frustration and rage felt in a black community that was now seeking writings that expressed those sentiments as did these two seminal works: James Baldwin's *The Fire Next Time* (1963) and *The Autobiography of Malcolm X* (coauthored by Alex Haley, 1965).

With the emergence of the Black Arts Movement of the 1960s, the influence of Malcolm X, Frantz Fanon, and the self-definition and self-determinist aims of cultural nationalists dominated. Key figures in this call for a return to more revolutionary art and more community activism were Amiri Baraka, Larry Neal, Addison Gayle, and Maulana Ron Karenga. Small presses sprouted overnight in many black communities, and writers staged street performances and readings, seeking to politicize people at a grassroots level. While riots gripped several major American cities, poets such as Sonia Sanchez, Nikki Giovanni, Haki Madhubuti, Etheridge Knight, and Carolyn Rodgers expressed that discontent for the little man and woman.

As poet, critic and playwright, Larry Neal detailed the aims of this cultural aesthetic in his classic 1968 essay "The Black Arts Movement": "The Black Arts Movement is radically opposed to any concept of the artist that alienates him from his community. Black Art is the aesthetic and spiritual sister of the Black Power concept. As such, it envisions an art that speaks directly to the needs and aspirations of Black America. In order to perform this task, the Black Arts Movement proposes a radical reordering of the Western cultural aesthetic."

However, that black aesthetic itself came under attack in the 1970s, when a young band of literary outlaws headed by Ishmael Reed, Al Young, Quincy Troupe, Steve Cannon, and Cecil Brown sought to widen the definition of black literature by returning to a neo-Hoodoo view of African American life, using elements of blues and folk in their work. Gayl Jones's *Corregidora* (1975) and *Eva's Man* (1976) also astounded black readers with their honesty, artistry, and raw sexuality. Their influence was felt significantly among young writers and artists of this period, only to decline somewhat during the conservative 1980s.

With the 1990s, and a further lessening of black America's militant mood, writers turned to a more intimate, more domestic examination of the social and cultural relationships of black men and black women. Novelists such as Toni Morrison, Terry McMillan, Bebe Moore Campbell, Alice Walker, Connie Briscoe, and E. Lynn Harris tackled sexual and gender issues in their work and found bestseller status, awakening American publishing to a readership starved for more positive, personal images of itself. The tremendous success of McMillan's *Waiting to Exhale* (1992), selling an impressive three million copies, influenced a whole generation of writers that some critics call "the children of Terry": Lolita Files, Benilde Little, Sheneska Jackson, Omar Tyree, Eric Jerome Dickey, Franklin White, Donna Grant, Virginia DeBerry, and Van Whitfield.

Needless to say, there are other writers who continue to progress on their own literary journey, choosing to stress craft and conviction over sentiment and romantic angst. Along with Gayl Jones's much heralded return with *The Healing* (1998), a host of gifted voices exist, waiting for even wider recognition: Diane McKinney-Whetstone, Shay Youngblood, Tina McElroy Ansa, Paul Beatty, Charlotte Watson Sherman,

Maxine Clair, Helen Elaine Lee, Brian Keith Jackson, Faye McDonald Smith, Florence Ladd, A. J. Verdelle, Tananarive Due, Nalo Hopkinson, Linda Raymond, Rosemarie Robotham, Lionel Newton, Alexs D. Pate, Dawn Turner Trice, Sandra Jackson-Opoku, Colson Whitehead, David Dante Troutt, Kim McLarin, Colin Channer, and Phyllis Alesia Perry, among others.

While names may have been left out from the above list, one thing is clear, and that is that the African American literary legacy is alive and well. New names are appearing weekly in America's bookstores as younger writers add their talents to our rich and vital canon. In the words of editor Cheryl Woodruff: "Future generations will look at this time as one breakthrough moment. The eyes of history are upon us. We have to be mindful of our creative legacy, our artistic traditions, and realize that those who follow us can only build upon what we have produced."

▲▲

"I think the only function of the black writer in America now is just to produce works of literature about whatever he wants to write about, without any form of repression or any hesitation about what he wishes to write about, without any restraint whatever. . . . And it is conceivable, since black people are creative people, that they might form on the strength of these creations an entirely new literature that will be more valuable than the output of the white community. Because we are a creative people, as everyone knows, and if we lend ourselves to the creation of literature like we did to the creation of jazz and dancing and so forth, there's no telling what the impact will be."

—CHESTER HIMES
From *Conversations with Chester Himes*

▲▲

# THE QUERY LETTER: FIRST CONTACT

Getting your foot in the door at a publishing house is not as mysterious and difficult a quest as some would have you believe. An essential tool toward attaining this goal is an effective query letter, your formal introduction to the people who hold your fate as a writer in their hands.

## THE LETTER THAT SELLS

The query letter is your initial pitch to an editor for your manuscript or project. Imagine yourself to be a salesman of a product or service, permitted a scant three to five minutes to sell your wares before a skeptical board of directors. The clock begins ticking the moment you enter the room. Each word and gesture must count, not one wasted breath may be taken. Such must be the impact of your query letter, enthralling the reader from its very opening.

Be brief. No editor will invest time in reading a letter that rambles on and on, never convincingly stating its goals or intentions. As your one big shot at snaring the attention of an editor who can acquire your manuscript, your letter must be dazzling, bold, and informative—a tall but not impossible order. The future of your project depends on how well you outline your work, its content and structure, its consumer appeal and strengths in the market. Leave little to mystery and nothing to chance.

## THE ART OF THE PERSUASIVE QUERY

By industry standards, a query is nestled on one page, maybe two, but not more than that. Be sure to single-space the text, employing your best use of English in the writing. This is not the place for bad grammar, misspellings, or typos of any kind. While the letter should embody your excellent writing skills throughout, it must also expressly assert your zeal and your ability to rewrite, edit, and revise. These attributes are the most vital of a writer's gifts—and they are the publisher's imperative. The final product must be flawless. Pay special attention to its content. Articulate any significant themes or ideas from your book that might entice an editor to take a second look at your project. Explain why that project is important to you, why it is commercial, and why you can be counted on to deliver a final product that will reflect favorably on the publishing house.

Generally, the query letter is used to pitch ideas for nonfiction books to publishers. In the case of fiction, you might titillate the editor with a cleverly phrased synopsis of the novel, supported by a few stellar sample chapters. Don't brag about your word wizardry in the cover letter accompanying your submission. Let the work speak for itself. Submit only your finest efforts. If you have doubts about the intrinsic appeal or importance or timeliness of a topic, or if the quality of your writing is not top-drawer, put that piece back into your file cabinet because a mistaken choice could be at once your first and your final chance to open a relationship with that editor. Occasionally, an editor smitten by a partial submission of a novel may request to see the finished manuscript, wondering if the spectacular prose, superb plot, and nuanced characterizations are sustained consistently in the author's completed work.

## A SIMPLE, WINNING FORMULA

Remember that the orderly and efficient rendering of information and the brevity of it are critical components of any effective query letter. Here is a well-tested formula:

· Use a concise, businesslike style for your letter.
· Establish a connection quickly between the editor and yourself. If you have been referred by someone who knows the editor, mention that fact in the opening paragraph of the letter.
· Be economical with words in summarizing your project or manuscript.
· If summarizing the plot of a novel, describe the major characters, conflicts, and valuable selling points of the work.
· If summarizing a nonfiction project, detail your topic or subject, the book's market potential, and its target audience.
· Include a brief author's bio that presents your education, your particular qualifications as a writer, and your special abilities to deliver the project and sell it to an audience.
· Ask the editor whether an outline and sample chapters should be submitted or, rather, a completed manuscript. A SASE (self-addressed, stamped envelope) for the return of your materials should be enclosed.
· Conclude the letter by thanking the editor for his or her time. Also, be certain to include your contact information: phone number (both home and work), mailing address, fax number, and E-mail address.

## STAY TIMELY

When composing a query letter for a nonfiction project, check the subject or topic for freshness. News items and issues become stale fast in this computerized Information Age, and no editor or publisher wants to be stuck with a book on a subject whose importance is past, or thousands of copies of a book that will not sell. As crucial as originality and fine craft are to a project, being current, or better yet, visionary in electing a winning topic cannot be overrated. The hottest of literary trends come and, sooner or later, go. (Who wants to read another book on Monica Lewinsky now?) However, there are exceptions to this publishing rule about ever-changing fads and trends. Tell-alls about the Kennedy clan, fresh accounts of the love life of Princess Diana, or new "revelations" about Marilyn Monroe's mysterious death will continue to sell regardless of the value and quality of each new book.

Whatever your subject, give close consideration to the proposed delivery date of your project, since the publisher's lead time for a book can often be a year or more. Keep in mind that the public can be fickle, changing the focus of their interest at warp speed.

## GOOD PRESENTATION IS YOUR PASSPORT

Editors seldom possess any downtime, their hectic schedules requiring the most efficient management of their work hours, so any communication mailed to them must be precise, clutter-free, and neat. No coffee stains or faded Xerox copies. Stay away from clichés, boasting, or rap lyrics. The tone of the letter should be conversational, without any Ivy League posturing or Etonian pretension. Save your best quotations of Hamlet or Henry James for the appropriate venue. Unless the publisher is affiliated with a university press, avoid the stiff academic pose and go with a warm, engaging tone that will not alienate a commercial publisher. With time at a premium, assist the editor in the task of understanding your query by placing the most important elements of your pitch at the top of your letter. If the opening paragraphs are a yawn, the letter may be discarded before its real treasures are reached in its closing sections. And probably the worst offense you can commit is to address the editor in an arrogant tone.

At the end of the query, make the direct pitch for the sale of your idea by giving a delivery date for the completed work. Do not make an unreasonable estimate, which would only alert the editor to a possible con job on your part. Why promise the moon if you know that delivering it is an impossible task? On the other hand, there is no need to be shy about tooting your own horn. Editors worry about writers who lack confidence in their skills. Intrigue the editors. Bewitch them with your best work, your best query.

## ADDITIONAL ITEMS TO ENCLOSE

When a query letter hits its mark, it makes an eloquent case for both you and your project, promising a product that delivers both artistically and commercially. If there is additional material to be enclosed with the letter, put your name on all items. Among the things you might wish to send with the query are a résumé, photocopied clips of articles or reviews of previous works, and a self-addressed, stamped envelope (SASE) for the return of your package. Remember that many publishing houses no longer accept unsolicited manuscripts, due to the heavy volume of submissions. Call first and inquire. Do not waste your time by blindly sending your work out to a publisher without a contact name. Finally, always thank the editor for taking the time to read your query.

## PATIENCE IS A VIRTUE

Be patient. Don't pester the editor with additional letters asking why the process is taking so long. Above all, don't drive the editor crazy with excessive telephone calls about the status of your submission. Be patient. Don't worry. Your answer will come. Be positive. Just think: In the best-case scenario, the editor, swept away by your query letter, calls or writes you to say a meeting is in order. They want to see you, to talk to you. What a major talent! You have mastered the first hurdle with grace and style, and the art of the deal continues through the live presentation of your pitch—the next critical step in the quest to getting published.

Consider this: If you were fantastic on paper, you will be that much better in person. And it began with a well-written, thoughtful query letter.

## SUMMARY: THE EFFECTIVE QUERY LETTER

· Construct a one- or two-page query letter, using an economical businesslike writing style.

· Summarize your fiction or nonfiction project carefully and skillfully.

· Always list the strong selling points of your project, target market, and consumer interest in topic or subject.

· Note any special qualifications, expertise, or awards earned as a writer to show what you can bring to the project.

· Ask the editor what manner of submission should be made if there is interest in the work: an outline and sample chapters or the completed manuscript.

· Always thank the editor for taking the time to read your query.

# CREATING THE FOOLPROOF PROPOSAL

Hundreds of thousands of people submit work each year to American publishing houses with the hope that it will be chosen to appear between covers. Among them, only a small number are selected for the privilege of seeing their words in print. Don't call overworked editors to pitch ideas. Instead, sell your work in writing. The better the proposal, the higher your chances of making the final cut in the publishing process.

## THE PROPOSAL VERSUS THE QUERY

Like your query letter, your proposal must be as finely composed and written as possible, the better to overcome the huge odds presented by the heavy volume of submissions piling up in baskets in the editor's office. Your query took up two pages at most, but your proposal will be more expansive, sometimes using as many as twelve to fifteen pages to convey your information. Research and preparation are essential in planning your engaging proposal. Think your subject over before committing it to paper. Research it well. Even brilliant writing cannot dress up a poorly conceived project. Spend time to know your audience and your target market. Remember that your editor will think about all of these factors before giving a green light to your idea.

## NONFICTION PROPOSALS

Fiction and nonfiction require two different approaches at this stage in the quest for publication. Most nonfiction projects gain acceptance by publishers after their review of a submitted proposal, so preparation and research again hold a crucial place in your winning a positive response. So much of your future as a nonfiction writer lies in your ability to convey in the proposal the richness of your ideas for your project. Before sitting down to create your ultimate sales pitch, ask yourself the following questions and answer them as honestly as possible. If the publisher becomes interested in your work, you may well be asked to respond to them in a meeting where there will be no room for hesitation and indecision.

· Why is your proposed project important and timely?
· Why should a publisher be interested in this project?
· Is there an audience for this proposed book?
· Are other timely, up-to-date books on this subject already on the market?
· How will your book be different from others on the subject?
· What special qualifications do you have to write this book?

After some soul-searching, you can proceed with the task of putting together the proposal to persuade the editor to buy your book. Put your all into the proposal. Do not assume that it will be read leisurely and carefully if it is dull, long, and wordy. Do not think that the editor will automatically presume you are the person to do the job if your skill, artistry, and creativity are not reflected in some way in your proposal.

## ETIQUETTE FOR THE PROPOSAL

Make sure to include a title page with your proposal, providing your name, address, and home and work phone numbers. A fax number and your E-mail address are also comforting to the publisher, who may need to get revisions back in a speedy manner during the closing days of the publishing process. Clear, clean copies are a plus. No one wants to read a smudged page of text. Don't rush this preparation process. A proposal that has received a few extra hours of care can be the deciding factor between acceptance and rejection. An effective proposal convinces both agents and editors that your book is worth their interest. When you feel certain that your proposal is perfect, set it aside overnight. If on the next morning you gasp "Who wrote that?!" you are back to the drawing board. If it still looks effective, send it.

## THE NONFICTION PROPOSAL CHECKLIST

The components of the nonfiction proposal are numerous, with each element as important as the next:

- cover letter
- title page
- overview of project
- author's biography, stressing special writing qualifications and publishing experience
- target audience and marketing strategies
- analysis of competing titles and their sales figures
- table of contents
- chapter outline
- sample chapters
- length of manuscript and projected date of completion
- supporting documents, photographs, illustrations, and charts

## FICTION PROPOSALS

Fiction proposals generally require less research and preparation than do nonfiction offerings, since you are not pitching a biography, a wide-ranging collection of essays, a technical manual, or your investigation of a topic scientific or historic. Most publishers require a complete manuscript before they will consider any possibility of publication. However, they will accept proposals from established writers who have a proven record in the marketplace. But there are exceptions to every rule, and some publishers have accepted proposals from new and promising talents. What follows is a list of the components of the traditional fiction proposal:

· A one-page, single-spaced cover letter is sufficient for a fiction proposal, with sample chapters.
· The opening paragraph contains the book title, book length, fiction category, and type of plot.
· The second paragraph discusses the marketability of the book, gauges its competitive strength against others of its type, and tells why it would be a good buy.
· The third paragraph gives a more detailed summary of the book, major characters, action and conflicts, and states other selling points. Avoid interpretation.
· The fourth paragraph offers more about you, the author, your writing experience and publishing history.
· You conclude with contact information (phone number, address, E-mail address, and fax data) and a sincere thank-you.

## PROPOSAL DOS AND DON'TS

Handwritten submissions are forbidden, verboten, completely unacceptable—like showing up for a formal evening wearing tennis shoes. Everything (except the cover letter) must be typed and double-spaced. Double-check each sentence for grammar and spelling. Nothing breeds rejection letters like sloppiness and haste. Stress in your résumé any specialized area of expertise you may possess.

In describing your project, less is more. Don't write the book here. Many aspiring writers forget that too much information early in the proposal can lead to data overload and the glazing over of the editor's tired eyes, which then leads to the editor tossing your hard work into the rejection pile. Save your abbreviated analysis and insights for your outline or chapter summary. Do not repeat yourself. Use detail and anecdote if they can accurately support the key themes of your project.

If the timeliness of your subject is important to the potential sale of your book, emphasize that fact and buttress it by citing information such as recent books in your genre that were commercial successes or received critical acclaim. Sometimes, timing is everything: Hitting a literary trend at its peak can determine whether a book soars or sinks. Compare the previously published works with your book, noting the significance of your project and its ability to blaze new ground. Dazzle the editors with your preparation and homework.

With fiction, the journey to print requires a greater commitment. Most agents or editors require a completed manuscript, especially from first-time authors, before coming to any agreements. Veteran novelists may need only two or three sample chapters to get a publisher's consideration. Novices should never promise more than they can deliver. If your novel is not completed, a substantial portion of the work, possibly sixty pages or more, might suffice.

## THE FICTION PLOT SUMMARY

Nothing sells fiction like a powerful story, complex characters, a well-detailed setting, and briskly paced action. Put extra care into your fiction proposal. In no other area of publishing does such intense competition prevail. Start your pitch in your cover letter by asserting why your novel will be an valuable addition to the publisher's lineup, especially if it is a genre or mainstream work where there exists faithful audiences eager for new talent and fresh voices.

In your plot summary, an explanation of the novel's major themes and character interaction must be rendered in clear, insightful paragraphs. There may be room here for a brief detailing of subplots of consequence and their relationship to the main plot, along with the resolution of the novel's major conflicts. Try not to be abstract with your plot; keep it accessible. And the sample chapters should feature some of your most compelling writing. Show your editor that you can tell a story with supreme style and grace. Even if your novel stems from an old, familiar formula, you must find a way to give it a new twist, one that grabs the reader's attention and never lets go.

With both nonfiction and fiction proposals, submit only neat, readable copies. Give an estimated page count and projected delivery date for your manuscript if you are including only sample chapters. Do not forget to label with your name all supporting documents to your proposal and cover letter. Ensure success by giving your agent and publisher your latest contact information, by both answering machine and voice mail. Submit your best offering and leave nothing to chance.

## SUMMARY: THE FOOLPROOF PROPOSAL

· The proposals for fiction and nonfiction must give book title, book length, and category.

· Indicate the target audience and the book's competitive strengths against others of its type.

· If the proposal concerns fiction, you need a brief but informative plot summary.

· If it is a nonfiction proposal, you must detail the book's intentions and goals, along with your special qualifications to write it.

# COPYRIGHT PROTECTIONS

## A LEGAL PROTECTION

Copyright law offers a shield of protection to the original creations of authors. It gives the writers the opportunity to enter their works into the marketplace without any concern of losing their right of ownership. Whether it's a poem or an essay or a novel, no one can publish your work without your permission. As the author of the work, you have the right to choose where it may be published.

Under the tenets of copyright guidelines, only you can generate and distribute copies of your writing. Furthermore, all "original works of authorship" are covered with copyright protection for an author's lifetime with an additional fifty years included. Please note that copyright law does not protect titles, facts, or ideas.

Anytime you produce anything from your typewriter or computer, it's immediately protected by copyright law. No registration with the U.S. Copyright Office is needed to protect your work from poachers. Some writers register their work for more comprehensive protection to acquire a copyright date in case of an infringement lawsuit.

## HOW TO REGISTER YOUR WORK

· Call, write, or visit the website of the Copyright Office, and ask for Form TX or the Application for Copyright Registration for a Nondramatic Literary Work. This form registers all unpublished or published fiction, poetry, nonfiction, text-books, reference works, and periodicals if they appear in a book, magazine, anthology, chapbook, or newspaper.

· Once this form is completed, send it with a copy of the work and $30 to the following address: Library of Congress, Copyright Office, Register of Copyrights, 101 Independence Avenue S.E., Washington, D.C. 20559.

## FOR FREELANCE WRITERS

In the world of the freelance writers, you can work with others on projects or even write an assignment for someone else. Or there might be a case where you might want to transfer your exclusive right to a work to another person. Both situations require careful planning and should be performed through a written legal arrangement.

Finally, if there is a fine point of the copyright law that confuses you, don't assume it's an insignificant matter. Get additional information and request forms by writing to the Copyright Office, calling 202-707-9100, or visiting its website (http://lcweb.loc.gov/copyright). Forms can be downloaded from the site.

# SUBMISSIONS: ONE OR MORE

CHARLES JOHNSON, author of the novels *Dreamer* and *Middle Passage*, says he once wrote six novels in ten years at ten pages a day. However, his superbly crafted novel *Oxherding Tale* took five years, during which he produced 2,400 pages of well-researched prose in order to complete the treasured 250 pages that comprised the completed manuscript.

· Realize that if you are out there on your own, attempting the daunting task of placing your manuscript without benefit of an agent, the first thing you need is a strategy.

· Follow a well-prepared scheme to avoid the usual fate of unsolicited manuscripts in the slush pile. Beginning the submission process without a carefully considered plan is inviting failure, rejection, and heartache.

· Be aware that a huge manuscript, the size of Baldwin's *Just Above My Head* or Mailer's *Harlot's Ghost*, will only frighten an editor if it arrives unannounced, like an uninvited guest at a dinner party. Unedited epic works invariably get the quick rejection shuffle in this era of harried editors, overtaxed assistants, and demanding publishers.

· Avoid form letters with your submission. "Dear Sir" or "Dear Ms." is nothing short of the kiss of death. Do your homework. Find out the name of the editor you wish to contact and personalize your submission.

· Go to the library and look up the publishing house of the editor whom you want to read your work. Many of the editors and their respective houses have been profiled in *Publishers Weekly*, the book industry's leading publication.

· During your investigation, call the editor at the publishing house to see if she or he is still there. Also, confirm the spelling of the editor's name. Introducing yourself by way of an error in that situation is an embarrassment you will wish to avoid.

· Request a catalog while you're talking with the editorial assistant. It will give you an idea of what books are being acquired by the publishing house's various imprints.

· Don't stop with just one publisher. Make a list of likely candidates. Go to your local bookstore, either a superstore or an independent, and note the titles, authors, and imprints that have published books on topics similar to the subject of your manuscript.

· Locate the names of the editors and agents on each book's acknowledgment page, for these contacts are vital to your submission plan. List several names, so you can continue your quest for publication despite such setbacks as unusually long delays or sudden rejections.

WALTER MOSLEY, author of the bestselling Easy Rawlins mystery series, endured the pain of seeing his manuscript rejected fifteen times before it was sold. That manuscript was his astonishing debut novel, *Devil in a Blue Dress*, which was made into a popular film.

# MANUSCRIPT ETIQUETTE TIPS

· Never send a manuscript that is not neat and legibly typed.

· Use a white, sixteen-pound-weight, standard bond paper—one sturdy enough to withstand handling by numerous people in the editorial process. Avoid printing on erasable paper and onionskin sheets, which may smudge.

· Avoid dot-matrix computer script. No editor wants blurred vision from trying to read print that causes optical illusions.

· Double-space all text and leave a respectable margin at each side of the page.

· Use a separate cover sheet. Place your name, address and phone number, along with all fax and E-mail information, at the bottom of the page.

· Center the title and subtitle of your book halfway down the cover page.

· Always retain copies of your manuscript, in case the original is misplaced in transit.

· Don't forget to spell-check all text. Proofread your manuscript very closely. You are assured of a rejection letter if your work reads like an assignment recycled from English 101.

· Place your last name and the page number in the upper-right-hand corner of each page.

· Before mailing your manuscript, purchase a durable binder, one that, though it may not accommodate the size of your materials with perfect ease, will endure repeated readings without dismantling.

· Always mail your manuscript in a sturdy box that can withstand the abuse of careless postal clerks. Secure the box with a strong tape at the corners as well as along the middle seam.

· To guarantee its return, include a stamped, self-addressed bag mailer. If you want an alternative to the federal mail route, explore the rates and services of Federal Express, the U.S. Postal Service's Priority Mail, or any of the other established mailing firms. Aspiring writers on tight budgets can shop around for the most economical rates.

# THE TRUTH ABOUT AGENTS AND WRITERS

## WHY HAVE AN AGENT?

Many published writers will say that finding an agent was their most important decision in reaching the goal of getting into print. To become truly successful in the business of words, you need to have an agent working for you in the editorial suites of the major-league publishing houses. Here, the stakes are high, and weak or ill-timed decisions by the author can carry long-lasting consequences in a still-evolving writing career. Finding a qualified advocate who is best suited for you and your work requires patience, research, and self-knowledge.

· Talk to other writers about their agents, or note which agents are thanked by the author on the acknowledgments page in books that you enjoy and respect, then compile a list of the likely candidates, and investigate their success rate in the marketplace.

· Check out the client list of your candidates.

· Go to the library and browse old copies of *Publishers Weekly* for any past articles mentioning the accomplishments of these agents.

In other words, take your time and research your choices, because a poor decision in this matter may hamper your career rather than enhance it. Only representing yourself could probably produce worse results.

Some veterans in the writing business will advise you to hire an agent located in the greater New York City area, near the nerve center of the nation's publishing world, not one from the Midwest or West Coast. One writer with a few books to his credit once said to a newcomer at a Manhattan party: "You want an agent available for lunching with the publisher and editor, and not one who must conduct all of her business over the phone from miles away. It defeats your purpose to have someone representing you from half a world away." There may be some truth to this statement, for proximity does indeed have its advantages; but nothing beats an effective agent with a gift for chat, persistence, and a good product to bargain, whether based near or far.

In a high-tech world, geography takes a backseat to the other intangibles of the writer-agent-editor relationship, with the advent of the fax machine, cell phone, and E-mail. Your agent is never really out of reach. Of more significance than distance, other criteria should play an even greater role in selecting the person who will represent your interests in the frenzied publishing arena. Before setting out on your search for an agent, you should ask yourself some fundamental questions, objectively measuring the quality of your writing talent and your commercial appeal.

· How good am I?
· Will my writing evolve into something greater than what it is now?
· Is there an audience for my writing?
· How serious am I about my writing career, about investing the time and energy needed to grow it into a substantial part of my life?
· Is this a hobby or a vocation?

Faith Childs, an agent and a former labor relations attorney with a thoroughbred client list that reads like a chart of Who's Who in literary black America, stresses that the writer must also bring some positives to this new union. "You read the work before you see the person. With most people, you know the measure of the writer before the meeting. I'm not an alchemist, but I know it's in the fingers. If someone has unrealistic expectations, I will not assist them in their delusions. If you want to be famous, rob a bank. You do not become a writer to become famous. Let's face it, most writers don't even earn out their advances."

## A MATTER OF TRUST AND RESPECT

The next critical phase in the selection process begins as you make a list of the criteria to be used in sizing up all candidates in your agent sweepstakes. First and foremost, you want someone you can trust and respect. If your meeting with the prospective agent makes the hairs on the back of your neck stand on end, and just doesn't feel right, then continue your search elsewhere. Keep in mind that whoever you choose as your agent will handle all of your earnings from the publisher. A disreputable agent can wreak havoc with your finances, opening the door for untold clashes and possible legal conflicts. Choose wisely.

Marie Brown, an agent and former editor with thirty-one years of experience in the publishing business, spells out the basic requirements for a good relationship between the writer and his representative. "A writer wants someone who knows the book industry well. The writer's writing and aesthetic should be compatible with the agent's taste, so there are no artistic conflicts later. Most important, the personalities and social styles of the pair should match because this is such an intimate relationship. A writer needs to feel that the agent will go that extra mile."

Returning to the topic of economics: Your agent keeps an eye on sums of money owed to you by publishing houses for past or current work. When pressure on a publisher is needed to speed up an overdue payment, that is assumed by the agent, who can prod the editor into forcing the house's accounting department into responding faster. Your agent knows the various personalities of the editors and other key personnel at the company, so little time is wasted on pursuing channels that will not produce results.

"In the old days, the primary relationship was between the writer and editor, with the agent as the outsider," says Molly Friedrich, super-agent rep for the bestselling authors Terry McMillan and Frank McCourt, among others. "Now, the good agent is as essential as a good editor. Representing yourself is like having a fool for a client, as someone once said. It's very hard. Sometimes when you're offered large sums of money, you get emotionally embroiled without someone else looking at the situation objectively."

Loyalty is something that can never be overrated. You want someone who will not desert you when the hard times come, when the next book slumps in sales. While some agents like the personal, friendly touch in their relationships with writers, other insist that the union be kept strictly business, nothing soft and fuzzy. Their take on the pairing is that it is utterly financial and based in business, unsentimental and nonfamilial. If you need a shoulder to cry on or sisterly advice, seek out a sibling or significant other for that support, not your agent. In such matters, professionalism always counts. No agent wants to acquire the role of baby-sitter or therapist while working with a client. There might be little that your agent can do when the first wave of rejection letters or bad reviews come in a torrent, causing you to act out after your fragile ego shatters.

"If I know the reviews will be devastating, I will tell the author not to read them," says Carol Mann, a veteran agent with Shelby Steele and Marita Golden as clients. "A good agent wants to spare the author pain and suffering. You work to salvage the situation, and try to keep the author on track so enthusiasm for the work and productivity does not decline. It's important for an agent to support authors as much as possible."

## FINDING THAT RIGHT FIT

As crucial as the trust issue may be, you need someone who believes totally in your present work and in your ability to create a lasting body of writing. Your agent should be your chief advocate in the ongoing skirmishes to get you the largest possible royalty advance for your books, accepting nothing less than your efforts deserve. Agents fight harder for something they feel strongly about.

Furthermore, a good agent, who is enthusiastic about an author, can generate a presales buzz on a manuscript that can result in a higher advance and sometimes in a full-scale bidding war during an auction, bringing in a six- or seven-figure deal. Editors, on the lookout for the next "hot" thing, often judge a book's potential by sensing the agent's zeal for a project. If an agent seems merely to be going through the motions about a manuscript, the publisher may conclude, Why buy it?

"You have to be careful with the money issue," says Victoria Sanders, an agent with a straight-shooting approach to the business. "I'm very aware of building a career with a publishing house and an editor. You need to be committed to seeing a writing career in the long term. Nobody wants to be a one-book wonder."

Advances are increasing at such a rapid pace that some authors consider a five-figure advance a failure. Yes, big contracts exist, but they are the exception rather than the rule. Every publishing decision starts with the all-important questions of profit and loss, the bottom-line issues. It's very hard to convince a publisher to back a book for hardcover publication that might sell only 7,000 copies. Writers producing books that will stand out in the marketplace usually get the larger checks. It's never hard to sell something that is original or cleverly derivative.

Every agent understands the importance of getting the publisher's support in promoting and marketing a book, and that support is extended most frequently when there is a significant financial investment in the project. All agents worth their salt realize that no one loses out in a good sale, not the writer nor the publisher nor the agent, whose fee, now 15 percent of the contract amount, is much better in a lucrative deal than with a standard cookie-cutter contract where neither writer nor agent benefits.

"With every writer I try to get as much as I can up front," says Jane Dystel, a respected New York agent who counts Lorene Cary, David Troutt, and Jewell Parker Rhodes among her clients. "The objective is to get the publishing house to commit as much as possible to your writer and that means money, especially in terms of promotion. The more money paid by the house, the more attention it gives."

After an initial success, your agent should sit with you at some point to map out the best writing choices in building on this promising foundation toward a long-term, productive career. Beware of agents who lack the experience to offer credible advice. Inquire into their track record and determine how successful they've been in the marketplace. The more experienced agents, having racked up years of experience in sparring with editors and publishers, will come up with a plan to fully exploit your talent and potential. They know which editors will try to pay the lowest advance possible for a book, regardless of its value. Your agent's mission is to ensure that you get paid what you are worth and nothing less.

That may also mean advising you, the writer, to say no to projects that have very little commercial appeal or prestige, projects that could damage your reputation. Although every writer wants to support himself from his work, no one desires to be seen as a hack. In the beginning of a career, during the salad years, a writer may accept questionable assignments to fulfill his requirements as an apprentice, but as time progresses, it becomes increasingly important to select carefully the project that will bear your name. And the astute agent will say: "Pass this one by, it's not for you." When both the writer and agent click as a partnership, the results can be financially rewarding and artistically satisfying.

## SOMETHING MORE ABOUT
## CONTRACTS AND EXPENSES

In the glory days of publishing, every agreement was signed
and sealed with an honest smile and a warm handshake. It was
a time when a person's word was his or her bond, when agreements did not need the assistance of a lawyer and an accountant. Today, most decisions come with binding contracts,
spelling out the goals and intentions of the writer-agent-editor
partnership. The agent contract, for instance, will articulate
the time span of the alliance, all put in writing; but some do
not set limits for closure, making it possible for either party to
walk away at any time.

No legal decree states that an agent must handle all of a
writer's work. This determination of when to represent a work
(or not) depends mainly on the services offered by the agency.
Many of them handle only full-length manuscripts, while others will accept articles, essays, short stories, and even poems to
pitch to publishers. Needless to say, such issues and choices
are things you should discuss at the very start of your relationship with your agent. Also, speak openly about the agent's
commission on domestic and foreign sales, and determine just
what the parameters of his role as middleman with the publisher would be.

During that initial session, clarify how the accounting area
of your partnership will be undertaken, and precisely what additional office expenses (e.g., mailings? photocopies?) will be
charged against your incoming revenues. Some authors' reps
will charge for the time spent with you in hammering out a
suitable proposal or revising a manuscript with high potential.
Time is money to an agent, so there is a price for every precious minute given.

While the effort to place a manuscript continues, agents
will keep a record of all submissions and correspondence on
the status of the project during the agenting process. Periodic
phone calls to agents for updates can be expected, but very
few of them have the time for daily chats with their clients.

Don't be afraid to ask about your manuscript if the agent has not responded with news in a reasonable time. That's your right, but don't abuse the partnership with unneeded calls and letters.

As a novice author, you want to understand what your agent will try to get in a successful book sale, since a publisher may take advantage of a young writer with an inexperienced representative. Sometimes a fresh-faced agent may bargain away foreign, audio, and first-serial rights for a book with limited commercial clout. But often, a publisher will take a chance on a writer whose work shows enough earning potential to break through the midlist barrier of 15,000 copies, and then the advance can be sizable. The publisher usually goes with a "hard/soft" deal where the contract also cedes trade and mass-market paperback rights to the house along with the hardcover sale.

In a typical sale, a hardcover publisher may take command of the rights in the contract:

- trade hardcover rights
- trade paperback rights
- mass-market paperback rights
- book club rights
- limited-edition rights
- sequel or next book option
- condensed version rights
- textbook edition rights
- anthology and textbook permissions

In most instances, the following areas would be controlled by the author and the agent, and separate negotiations would take place with interested parties:

- film and television rights
- audio rights
- foreign rights
- merchandising rights

- first-serial rights
- electronic rights
- stage rights
- multimedia rights

All of the money acquired from the sale of these subsidiary rights is considered ancillary income, or revenue made outside the principal royalty advance. Much of the income gained here by your agent further indicates an essential reason for attaining an effective representative, since this revenue would be lost if the author were acting on his own. And often, the amount of money can be significant if your property is commercially attractive. For example, your royalty advance may total $150,000, yet your agent can make another $200,000 from film and foreign rights alone. You will not mind paying your agent the 15 percent fee charged for every subsidiary sale or option made, especially if the additional income is hefty.

Most often, publishers will not go that extra mile to sell subsidiary rights for authors, most notably foreign rights. This is where your agent has the advantage. By working with a subagent knowledgeable in the inner workings of the foreign publishing world, your agent can rely on him to act as a reliable representative for your work abroad. Subagents take usually 10 to 15 percent off any advance payment or royalty from the overseas sale, and the remaining amount is sent to the domestic agent, who takes another 15 percent. Still, this is not a bad deal since it is money that would not have been forthcoming without the assist of the agent and the subagent.

"Subagents are specialists," agent Faith Childs explains: "In order to make money, subagents must place their books with a verve and passion equal to that of the primary agent. They understand that some American material doesn't translate commercially in certain foreign markets, so it's important that these agents have a superior knowledge of their business."

## THE RACIAL DIVIDE: BLACK VS. WHITE AGENTS

One ongoing debate in the writing world among African American authors centers on the issue of choosing an agent based on racial solidarity, discarding other major considerations such as commercial success and closer ties to a predominately white publishing industry. Go with the brother and sister, support your own, is often the word heard among many black writers. Still, others insist that financial concerns must come first when selecting a representative, because writing must be treated as a business. The question, for those who say practicality is key to this critical decision, becomes, Can the black agent produce the big deal and the big dollars?

"It's not the agent but the material that sells," says Jane Dystel, a white agent. "I'm looking for good writers, period. I don't choose my clients according to race but according to quality of the writing. Some authors may get the larger advances just based on timing and getting in at the start of a trend. This current trend will not bottom out because there are quality books being written and an educated African American audience. The trash will fall away."

Another white agent, Victoria Sanders, has a no-nonsense approach to the race issue's role in the selection progress. "If a writer prefers to have a black agent, they should choose one," she says. "I don't think color is essential in the business, but if it is an issue for the writer, then it should not be ignored."

For African American agents, the subject of race is intertwined with the bigger question of racial preference and economics in the almost lily-white publishing industry. Black agents need the support of the African American literary community in order to survive. White writers rarely use the services of the black agents, choosing to go with marquee names among the agencies. Now, both black and white agents vie for the best and the brightest talents among the growing pools of African American writers, currently plying their craft in more genres than ever. None of them remain out-of-bounds, like golf and hockey once were for the black athletes. Wherever the money can be made, there are black writers working in that venue, skilled, articulate, and refreshingly intellectual.

"It's true that white agents can go in and get more money, having more entrée to places where we can't go," says Marie Brown, dealing bluntly with the situation. "Our plight is damaged even further when black writers often leave their black agents to go with white agents once their careers take off. A black agent may work extremely hard to build such a career only to have this defection happen, and it can be a real disappointment. Many writers are easily seduced by the big deal. The relationship between a black agent and a black writer is deeper because of the bond of racism felt daily by both people. That type of bond does not exist in the same way for the white agent and black writer. We know one another in a way no one else can."

One complaint among some black writers is that white agents lack the spiritual tie or emotional investment in the African American community, so money often becomes the central concern over other issues, such as quality and relevance. Who cares what images or messages are pumped back into the Hood or to Middle America? It's not simple. True, sometimes a black agent is the only one willing to take a chance on an untried writer. For this alone, black agents deserve our support.

"One of the reasons that there is a lot of inferior writing from black writers sold to the houses is because many white agents are not concerned with the quality of the work as much as the amount of the sale," says Denise Stinson, a veteran agent who represents Nathan McCall, Pearl Cleage, and Omar Tyree. "In the long run, this disregard for quality and craftsmanship hurts black writers in specific and African American literature in general. Black agents understand the role of building a legacy in selling quality work."

Also, on the political side, having a black agent will not change the view of black America held by Joe Six-Pack, because it is all about dollars and competition. The war is strictly business. Black agents are battling quite successfully for their share of the author's market, going head to head with some of the more established agencies in the country. Whether the basic question for you here is political or economic, ultimately the choice is yours, always keeping in mind what your career needs.

## GETTING A DIVORCE FROM YOUR AGENT

When do you sever the knot between your agent and yourself? If your agent does not live up to his role as your representative, then it's time to go elsewhere. If your agent is constantly unavailable and weeks pass without contact, it's time to start looking for another one. If every word from your agent is negative, it's time to reevaluate your relationship. If communication between writer and agent is often mean-spirited, aggressive, and sometimes even rude, it's time to end the association. If the trust is gone, it's time to go.

Be sure that you are not pressuring your agent to sell a work that is not worthy of you. Sometimes your agent may be swamped with calls and other demands from other clients. Remember that you are one of many clients on your agent's roster. Trouble can often be avoided by spelling out the parameters of your relationship before the first agent agreement is signed. Many agents may retain authors on their list that they would love to dump, but can't because the writers may have been successful at one time but went into a slump, or the writers signed back in the agent's salad days. And sentiment prevents a cold, clean break.

When the separation comes, it should be professional, with as little drama as possible. Courtesy should be shown by both parties, bringing a miserable situation to an end. No rough stuff. Settle things with your old agent before circulating any work to a new representative. Be adult. Part ways respectfully.

# QUESTIONS FOR A NEW AGENT

1. Does your agent believe in your talent and share your artistic vision and commercial goals?

2. How well does your agent know the book industry?

3. How successful has your agent been in negotiating lucrative deals with the larger houses?

4. Do you feel comfortable with your agent? Does the social style and personality of your agent match yours?

5. Is your agent capable of selling subsidiary rights in foreign markets?

6. Is your agent easily accessible? Do your phone calls and letters get a timely response?

7. Will your agent go the extra mile to place your work successfully?

8. Is your agent honest and candid with you?

9. Is your agent trustworthy and someone you respect?

10. What are your agent's views on revision and rejection? Is your agent someone who can be counted on in the long run?

LANGSTON HUGHES, who never had a huge bestseller, was often asked what price a writer paid for a semi-successful career. He quipped to a reporter in 1955: "How have I written so many books—and one as long as my latest manuscript? By not doing anything else much in my life. Is writing fun? Sure! Is it lucrative? Yes, if you're Frank Yerby or Ernest Hemingway. As for me, when young writers ask me if it is possible to make a living from writing, I usually answer, 'Yes, but not necessarily a good living.' I haven't got a Cadillac. I don't own a house. I haven't got a wife or a television set. All I got is a lot of books—with another one on the way."

# THE CONTRACT QUIZ

**Q:** Why can't I just sign the contract when I receive it from my publisher?

**A:** Every contract, regardless of the length of your relationship with your publisher, should be examined closely. This is a business arrangement and it should be treated accordingly. Contracts can be as different from one another as kittens in a litter. Never rush into signing the contract without giving it proper study and appraisal. Discuss matters thoroughly with your agent. If you don't have an agent, review the contract with a publishing lawyer or a veteran author with experience in contract negotiations.

**Q:** What are some of the things I should consider when I approach contract talks?

**A:** The first thing you should ask yourself is whether you are getting full compensation for your work. Do not accept any contract that leaves you feeling underappreciated or underpaid. Also, determine whether all of your rights as a writer are protected, lest your work be exploited without your input. In fair business dealings, both parties should be satisfied with the terms of the agreement.

**Q:** Is there ever an occasion when I should take a hard-line stance with my publisher?

**A:** Choose your battles wisely. Do not confront your publisher on issues that are meager financially or of little significance. In most cases, seek to find a middle-ground solution, one favorable to both sides. However, remember that the publisher is always attempting to close a deal that will be in his best interests. If you find a clause or condition covered in your contract that you cannot accept, be professional and patient in your discussions to resolve the issue. Most publishers understand how far to push any bargaining situation; rarely will they let matters reach a total impasse, where talks are no longer possible. Still, be firm if the issue is something very important to you. Your career may hang in the balance. If there seems to be no room for compromise in the contract negotiations, you may be forced to seek another publisher.

**Q: Before talking with my agent about the contract, what should I do?**
**A:** Approach this situation as you would any business matter. Go over the contract before speaking to your agent. Familiarize yourself with all clauses of the document so that even the most minute provision, which might be buried in the fine print, does not escape your attention. Such preparation will enable you to ask all of the right questions as you discuss the contract in depth with your agent.

**Q: Should I be frightened of the option clause?**
**A:** No. Most publishers include an option clause as a way of encouraging author loyalty. A publisher may feel that considerable time and money have been invested in building an author's career, despite the house's seeing only modest marketplace success from the writer's books. Hoping to earn larger profits, the publisher is betting on the author's ability to do well in the future. An option clause requires an author to take his or her next book to that publisher, guaranteeing that house first look at that prospective property. Still, the option is lost if the author and publisher fail to agree on contract terms for the new work. Then the author can shop the manuscript to another house for a higher financial return.

**Q: What can I do if the publisher tries to use the option clause to hold me even if I'm dissatisfied with my treatment at the house?**

A: Some authors panic when they see the option clause inserted in their contracts. Although those writers may be unhappy with the publisher's handling of their books, which happens most often in the marketing and promotion of them, they will say nothing and will sign whatever is placed before them. Remember: The terms of any contract must be agreed upon by both parties, and your signature on a contract means that you are pleased with its terms. You cannot be forced to sign a contract against your will. If during negotiations you wish to exit the relationship, simply ask for top dollar for your new manuscript. The publisher will sometimes refuse to pay that amount. Once that refusal is made, you are free to pitch your work elsewhere. Also, be aware of a common practice of some publishers who word their two-book contract to sound like the traditional boilerplate contract with an option clause. You can be trapped in a two-book situation if you don't pay attention to detail. Read your contract carefully, because the deal is done once you sign it.

**Q: Can there be repercussions if the publisher feels I've played hardball in the negotiations?**

A: A bad relationship with a publisher can produce hazardous consequences for a young writing career. When the publishing partnership no longer works, books can be released into the marketplace with a halfhearted marketing and promotional push from the publisher. Indeed, playing hardball can have a definite downside. As an author, you should seek only fairness and respect in your contract talks. If that is accomplished, there is no reason for the situation to turn ugly.

**Q: What if another publisher offers me a bigger payday?**

A: You may want to weigh that offer carefully, thinking about all relevant factors in moving to another house, especially if your affiliation with your current publisher has been long and productive. It's a competitive business, and some publishers will do anything to land a good writer with potential to score a big success. However, good editors and supportive publishers are hard to find. The bottom line is to evaluate where you are in your career, because short-term gains and huge advances can sometimes be counterproductive in the long run. A good, profitable working relationship between an author and an editor is rare. In a case like that, why switch? If it's not broke, why fix it?

# ELECTRONIC RIGHTS

Using advances of the Internet and its ever-proliferating developments in electronic publishing technology, the publishing world is enlisting in a profound cycle of change. Every writer will be impacted by these shifts that are transforming the book business in the era of the E-book (electronic book).

## ELECTRONIC RIGHTS AND HIGH-TECH ACCESSIBILITY

First, be aware of your rights as an author in the realm of computer-related technology, where your work can be reproduced, displayed, and exchanged. You want to retain control over who may obtain the right to reproduce or download the text of your work once it has been stored electronically. Whether it is released as a CD-ROM or as an E-book, you want to govern the issuance of all your work that readers may be able to obtain through subscription databases and on-line services. Imagine subscribers downloading your writing through a service like America Online or Yahoo! or CompuServe, using it for their own design or passing it around—absent your approval and appropriate royalties.

You want to monitor the reproduction of all or part of your work through all types of interactive and multimedia products. Some literary agents are particularly troubled by the new ability of publishers to print economically single copies or small print runs of a title for customers, by a process called print on demand, thus maintaining publishing rights on relatively slow-moving titles—forever. Another trend, already established—the on-line sale of books—allows consumers to order work direct from publishers and from certain book chains, to be read on E-books. Despite some ghosts not yet exorcised from the system, E-books are the wave of the future and will certainly give the traditional book some serious competition down the line.

Despite hopes that these advances will yield new audiences for authors and their ideas, writers are worried about getting adequate compensation for their work that is displayed and read on E-books and computer screens. They wonder about the income lost when their work is displayed in a nonrevenue-generating setting such as a home page. The other concern is that an E-book can never go out of print, since it is stored electronically, and that reality may prevent the authors from ever regaining rights to their work in that medium.

Some publishers who require control of electronic rights will, in time, permit those rights to revert to the author. This reversion is often written into new contracts; but some publishers are invoking use clauses in older contracts to retain electronic rights, citing the fine print concerning "information storage and retrieval" as providing a legal opening for such action. However, court challenges have resulted in rulings against publishers in some cases, citing that technology for which electronic rights were granted was not in existence at the time the original book contract was signed.

## THE RISE OF THE E-BOOK

With less money needed for text storage and production of E-books, which do not require paper, printing, production, or warehousing, expenses incurred by the publisher are much reduced. Thanks to those economic concerns, there is talk of increasing the royalty percentages for authors in electronic formats.

Always involve your agent in talks regarding your electronic rights. Make sure that your representative or consultant is current on the latest developments involving authors and electronic rights, because once those rights are granted to a publisher, an author will find it hard to control how his work is used on the Internet. Be exacting. Your future earnings could be at stake.

# WHAT AN EDITOR DOES FOR YOU AND YOUR BOOK

## THE EDITOR AS SHEPHERD

From the outside, the editor's job appears glamorous—lavished with perks, and all-powerful—when in reality it is anything but that. While the editorial position may be one of the most interesting in the publishing industry, sitting behind that desk carries a lion's share of responsibility, disappointment, and daily challenge. The pressure to produce winners for the nation's bookshelves is unrelenting, with competition among the editorial staff often operating at fever pitch.

## THE ROLE OF THE MODERN EDITOR

Where do the publishing houses find these people? Editors come from diverse social and cultural backgrounds, their intellects and imaginations formed from a host of educational backgrounds, from progressive liberal arts colleges to high-powered university publishing programs. In modern publishing circles, the job of editor has evolved into a post where buying manuscripts and baby-sitting eccentric authors are only two aspects of their many duties. Editors, as we will see, do many things that were not covered in their job descriptions just ten or fifteen years before the year 2000. There is less emphasis now on posh lunches and swank cocktail parties, and more stress on producing books that make money. Still, ask most editors about their reason for seeking out that profession and the answer is usually the same: "I love BOOKS."

The editor, whom most writers meet, may acquire a book after a discussion over lunch or following ongoing talks with the agent, but once the contract has been signed, the work has only just begun. Due to the huge volume of submissions, editors are forced to prioritize their reading, reviewing agented manuscripts first, and then the vast quantity of unsolicited material. Often, they employ freelance readers to spot the submission with enough style and substance to be given a more thorough examination. The reader's report will detail the manuscript content, whether fiction or nonfiction, going into its structure, strengths, and weaknesses. Although such reports are sometimes influential, the final verdict remains that of the editor. If the manuscript shows exceptional merit, the editor will tag it as a project for further review, possibly for a quiet evening's evaluation. Most editors sacrifice large blocks of their—theoretical—recreational time, spending much of it reading manuscripts, catching up on paperwork, and writing correspondence.

While working on manuscripts, they confront other duties, too, including collaborating on book jacket design and text design, and writing jacket copy. Editors shepherd their books from acceptance to final production, maintaining a close watch for anything that might derail the project. After all, it is the editor who touts the book's merits at the initial editorial presentation before the publisher, and who later captains a presentation for the sales, marketing, and publicity people. The editor, as much as the agent, becomes the book's leading advocate during the publishing process, promoting it with an almost religious zeal, fighting to see that it gets its fair share of the budget and of artistic care. The editor's enthusiasm for the book must infect the support staff in other departments, making converts of everyone, in the quest to create a bestseller. Periodic calls to the author and agent keep everyone current on its progress.

"Not only does the editor acquire or pursue a young writer's work, he also nurtures, guides, inspires, promotes, markets, and shapes the writer's work inside and outside of the house," explains Carol Taylor, a former editor at Crown. "The editor is the book's chief spokesman and will have to answer many questions about the nuances of the topic, market, or marketing efforts. Therefore, if a writer is lucky enough to be acquired by an editor whose vision for the book complements and inspires his own, he has already won a great deal of the many battles he will have to fight during the production and publishing process."

The books come from submission or solicitation into the editor's office, each by a single act—but before the production process is completed, the entire publishing house will be involved, and even invested, in the distinctive commodity that appears on the bookshelves. Many chefs have a hand in the baking of this pie. It's a collaborative effort much like producing a TV program or filming a movie. The editor consults constantly with the author on rewrites and revisions, making certain that all key elements come together as a cohesive whole. When the developmental work and line editing of the manuscript is finished, the editor turns it over to the managing editor, who assigns the manuscript to a freelance copyeditor for a tight check against bad grammar, factual errors, repetitions, and other miscues. A final production cost estimate is run, based on the copyedited manuscript, and a retail price is determined along with a final production and publication timetable. Most books take nearly a year to finalize from final manuscript to bookstore release—which can seem like forever to a new author.

## THE ALCHEMY OF EDITING

How important is editing? Since anyone with a computer and a little time can create a manuscript, the input of the editor in some instances becomes a matter of extreme necessity. The quality of submissions varies wildly, so taking a chance on a writer with artistic potential and no commercial track record is something done less and less frequently in publishing today.

Given the decline of the midlist book, one expected to make no big stir in the marketplace regardless of merit, publishers and editors bent on staying in business will opt instead for the sure thing or something close to it. A lunch with an engaging writer may fire up sublime thoughts of bestsellers and such; anyone can talk a good book. But what of producing one? Even when a book is delivered on schedule, there remains much fine tuning, sometimes preceded by broad tuning, to be done. Editors can work on as many as twenty titles a year, not counting reprints and special projects. Many books must be constructed from the raw material that may constitute a submission, requiring the editor to act as a necromancer of sorts, sensing the real power of the work buried beneath layers of overwrought words and faulty structural choices.

"The editor's role is a facilitator's role," says Janet Hill, a seasoned editor at Doubleday. "As an editor, you try to get to the jewel hidden within the manuscript. Sometimes it's hard for a writer to see the work because he's been working so closely with it. However, the editor, experienced in this type of thing, sees what's good and what's bad."

Editorial artistry occurs during the crafting, texturing, and layering of a work, be it fiction or nonfiction, when the editor works with the author on adding dimension and depth to the manuscript. The reality is that a large percentage of editors become coconspirators in a way, collaborating with the writer to give the original artistic vision its full sway. A young writer might be tempted to surrender totally to the sometimes awesome influence of the editor. Don't! Don't be intimidated by the alchemy of editing. Remember that it is your book and *you still retain final control over what is published carrying your name*. The editor listens and attempts to understand what the author is trying to say, looking not at what is on the page, but at what can be brought there to further enhance the book's impact.

## REVISIONS AND THEIR MEANING

Textual changes, whether revisions or rewrites, are always needed; there has never been the perfect manuscript, completely untouchable. Revisions come from editors as suggestions made after their reading of submissions, first as ordinary readers open to the work's every whim. Later, the approach becomes more clinical, repairing lapses in story, style, structure, and symbolism. The editorial process becomes transformed into a craft that is more than just rearranging sentences, pruning dependent clauses, and adding commas.

No editor can force a writer to accept revisions that feel like a violation of the overall work. You, as the author, have the right to question everything. On the other hand, several editors say they've worked with authors who said no, refusing to hear any persuasive talk about productive changes, and whose refusals hurt their books.

"Editorial criticism must be rooted in something real," says Valerie Wilson Wesley, a former editor and writer of mysteries. "You don't have to be a good writer to be a good editor. I've encountered editors who were writers who rewrote [my] work, and that's intolerable. I hate that approach because sometimes you're rewritten badly. Good editors can edit your work to the point where it is seamless. It's a gift. You're lucky when you find that."

Sometimes the editor takes the chance, believing the lunch table hype about a manuscript's potential, and is forced to construct a sellable book from a huge collection of pages filled with overwriting and confusion. Previously, an editor enjoyed some leisure in fashioning and honing a book. Today, the attitude is less forgiving of manuscripts requiring disproportionate amounts of time and attention to reach standards discussed before the signing of the contract. Current standard contracts contain clauses that allow publishers to reject "unacceptable" manuscripts, works that are of inferior or unpublishable quality or that fail to deliver the promised work.

That does not mean there are not editors who invest whatever energy is needed to support a submission they believe in.

"When I was at a certain house, I bought a midlist book, a spiritual-based title, which no one expected to sell in large quantities," says Adrienne Ingrum, an eighteen-year veteran in the industry with editorial and executive stints at Grosset, Putnam, and Crown. "I signed it up with a $5,000 contract, knowing it would not make a lot of money. It became a labor of love. I edited four drafts of the book and someone senior complained—why was I spending so much time on the book? The book did respectably in stores, but that is the current attitude. Everything is so rushed now."

## PICKING WINNERS

As one axiom of the publishing business states, bestsellers and other popular books make the money that permits publishers to spend on titles that find smaller audiences; for example, such items of prestige as a novel by an obscure Eastern European author, an illustrated history of Chicago architecture, poetry from Tibetan sages, a paean to the south of France. The publishing business has often been called elitist and aristocratic, an industry that thumbs its nose at the tastes of the common man while rushing to satisfy them. Truthfully: An editor needs a few marketplace winners now and then in order to retain artistic freedom and sufficient budget to continue as a competitive player.

If an editor passes on a number of good books that later turn up flush under rival publishers' imprints, questions will be asked. If he or she acquires a flock of turkeys, that editor will soon be out of a job. More than anyone else at the publishing house, the editor is responsible for making a manuscript into a market-ready book, and the failure of that effort will be held against him or her alone. If a work comes in with an assured voice and solid research, if it is beautifully structured, if it carries current or timeless interest and poses no overdemanding challenges, then the editor can feel confident that, well tended, it will hold its own among the competition.

## THE CRAFT OF LINE EDITING

One current debate about the quality of books being produced centers on the issue of line editing and copyediting: whether contemporary manuscripts are scrutinized and polished sentence by sentence. Sometimes lackluster books, both fiction and nonfiction, arrive in stores splendidly packaged but structurally confused and poorly executed, having been only marginally conceived. Critics also say that too many books—period—are being published. Inevitably, these factors together have written a recipe for slipping standards and waste. The recipe needs serious revamping.

Even the noted publisher Walter Hines Page once said that "all publishers make many more mistakes in accepting books than in delivering them." With many houses understaffed and under pressure to compete commercially, fatigued editors occasionally let a book slip through the radar before completing the necessary pruning and polishing, whether because of writer resistance to revisions, work overload, or a flood of weak product needing too much attention before a rapidly approaching publication date.

"Some editors do not have the strengths of line editing and conceptual guidance, two important editorial ingredients," adds Ingrum. "In the old days, editors cared about what was on the page. Now, some do not, and that shows in what is coming to the bookstores."

Compounding the problem, economically stressed houses have cut their editorial ranks at a time when more books are being published. Statistics released by R. R. Bowker indicate a significant decrease in editorial staffs over the past decade, in contrast to a substantial 42 percent increase in titles being published. Editors must deal with a shorter turnaround time on publication schedules, permitting less time for actual line editing and for close scrutiny of final texts. Nor has the musical chair approach to editorial positions helped matters, with fewer editors enjoying secure employment at houses undergoing ownership transitions and/or downsizing through mergers or outright purchase. Thus, authors often find themselves dealing with a constantly changing cast of editors while working on manuscripts. Such inconsistency often undermines the finished product.

To their credit, many editors concede that more and more errors are getting through the safety net. Making the situation even more troublesome is the reality that in growing numbers, books are being written by people who are not professional authors, but celebrities or notable personalities. Accustomed to coddling and compliments, they may work with an established author or hire a ghostwriter. Yet, sabotaging that initiative, often they will allow their inflated ego to cripple the final product by adding puffery and other trivia or withholding elements essential to understanding their life, and thus the book. The reader buying that book may or may not know any of this. He does know once he has delved into that biography or novel or collection of essays he bought, that it lacks consistency, clarity, and personality.

## LONGEVITY

The real test for the editor and the writer comes when the consumer brings the book home. Most publishers take judicious chances, especially with fiction, in the hope that if success doesn't score that first time out, then the second release will be the home run. They seek the new talent that will capture a portion of the market and have a long-lasting career that will reward their initial investment in the unproven author. Danger lurks when the newcomer flops badly or, worse yet, flees the house that discovered and nurtured him for a larger advance elsewhere. The writer signs for a huge sum with another publisher, and the gamble taken by his first supporter is lost.

## THE SEARCH FOR THE COMMERCIAL BOOK

No matter how many times they have been burned by poor artistic decisions, publishers continue to back promising writers. They believe that good authors will always be found, that first-rate ability will not be long denied. Everyone in the business understands that relationships between the writer and the reader can be as fickle as young love. Occasionally, even the most accomplished author, with his lengthy track record of blockbusters, falls short of his target sales estimates and finds himself scrambling to reinvigorate his career by reinventing the winning formula. One way he accomplishes this is to find new areas to explore in his work and, with the assistance of the editor, to fashion a project that will once more catch the eye of the reader.

Readers have never been so restless. They become bored quickly and, like a growing infant, need constant stimulation and fresh challenges. Also, the competition for their attention has never been so fierce, with TV, cable films, video games, and computer sites all vying for their time. Whereas the established author is given a little leeway for successes of only minor proportion, the novice writer often does not have that option. If the newcomer has flat sales, despite a brief promotional push, and the book does not "earn out" its advance, that author faces a harder time in getting his next book published, or even considered.

Negotiating a decent advance may be an exercise in futility. As a writer — one hoping to publish more than just one book — clearly you owe it to yourself to make sure that your first effort is the best one you can offer to the reader at that time.

Regardless of the qualifications of your editor or the prestige of your publishing house, the commercial fate of a writer can be very uncertain. Sometimes the second book finds its audience; sometimes it misses the mark. Most frequently, the writer fails to produce a second book of artistic and commercial worth and vanishes from the scene. The number of "one-book wonders" in the history of publishing is astonishing, only underlining how difficult it is to maintain a profitable, productive writing career over the years. Being an author is not as easy as it may look.

## THE FICTION AND THE NONFICTION OF IT

Question any editor about the differences in editing fiction and nonfiction, and the answers can go on for several hours, depending on the person's love for words and ability to chat. More often than not, editors prefer working with fiction. It permits a greater chance for true collaboration and fewer restrictions between the two key partners. Editors try to avoid problems by buying only finished novels, deliberately skirting the complications of too many rewrites or blocked authors. Such a cautious approach is not needed toward the nonfiction manuscript, which can be submitted in a partially completed form, especially if authored by an established writer with an impressive record of competent, successful books. Yet even then, the danger exists that a book purchased on the basis of sample chapters or an outline will not be submitted as acceptable.

The demands are more clearly defined for the editor working with nonfiction: More specialized knowledge is required. If you're going to edit a book on film or architecture, it's best to have a fundamental understanding of the field. Since editors usually possess a strong liberal arts education, they are quick studies on a wide range of topics, and, if the work calls for expert input, the manuscript may be vetted, or examined, by a professional in the particular field.

Editing fiction is wholly different. "With fiction, it's all totally subjective," says Rosemarie Robotham, formerly a senior editor at a leading publishing house and currently an editor-at-large at *Essence* magazine. "Editing fiction is not about following a set criteria of whether it's good or bad. It's about whether the work of fiction affects me deeply, whether it has an impact, because each writer has a different vision. It's about whether it can be made to work or whether it already works."

Possibly the difference between fiction and nonfiction, in the eyes of the editor, comes not only in the artistic standard of each category but in their marketability. Nonfiction can sometimes have a short shelf life, for its topic may be much more immediate. A reader of nonfiction must be sold on the subject. For instance, a Civil War buff will buy another book on the battle at Bull Run or the Andersonville detention camp only if it contains new data or fresh revelations. Otherwise, he will pass it by. That criterion does not fit for fiction, since a reader will often take a chance on an old story with familiar themes if it is told in beautiful, interesting prose.

The word *commercial* no longer carries the baggage it once did. Every editor, every writer, wants a novel that will sell, understanding that there is still a large audience for a good story with full-blooded characters and a well-developed plot. This is not to say that the literary novel, when superbly written, cannot find a sizable readership. Many recent entries on the national lists of bestsellers indicate that it can succeed handsomely.

Most first-time novelists benefit greatly from the editor's keen pencil, largely because they come from diverse backgrounds, some of them not necessarily tied to writing. Upon selecting these new talents, the editor and the publisher know they will be lucky to sell 6,000 copies on the novel's maiden run; yet such a projection does not affect the dedication often shown to perfecting the work of a novice. The editor's art is achieved here when the tone and the vision of a novel are enhanced without any violation of those key elements. No change is to be taken lightly. Experienced editors can get into the author's head, comprehend the scope of his imagination, anticipate his moves, and speak in his voice. They can find the "idea" of the novel with laserlike precision, seize upon it and reinforce it with supporting literary choices.

"When a good editor is finished with the work, the writer should say 'Damn, I'm good,' " Robotham explains. "The editor's touch should be almost invisible to the reader. In fiction, this merging of editor and writer must gel, or the results can be disastrous. A good editor should get ego satisfaction from seeing the final work be the best it can be. The book is the writer's work; the editor is the silent partner. It's the writer's book, and he should take the bows and receive the praise."

If the editor emerges as the unsung hero in publishing, that subdued renown resonates only as long as a winning streak prevails. The business end of the house maintains an ever-vigilant eye on the successes and the failures. Should an editor take something unproven and make it work, he or she is a star. If it doesn't pan out, the consequences can be grave and that job could be lost, depending on the size of the financial investment. This dollars-and-sense reality leads so many editors to play it safe—never to buck the odds, to submit almost slavishly to the winning formulas. Most industry watchers say that editors need to assimilate something of both those perspectives, the cautious and the maverick, in order for publishing to retain its delicate balance of art and commercial appeal.

Formulas are indeed essential, to both fiction and non-fiction. However, renegade editors are today seeking to set trends with new fiction, finding fresh hybrids of styles instead of catching the end of a commercial wave to make a deeper dent in the market. They're not making the big money, but their efforts go a long way in keeping publishing respectable and interesting. Other editors are combing the slush piles, seeking to find the next Bebe Moore Campbell, Margaret Atwood, or Anne Rice. Or the next John Updike, Ralph Ellison, or Ishmael Reed. Still, it's always better to start the new wave rather than trying to ride out the old.

Some editors, unfortunately, choose to opt for the fiscal advantage rather than for high literary quality, racing to beat the competing publication of other books of a similar topic with a title of lesser quality. Remember the many "self-help" books and the recovery book clones at the height of their popularity in the late 1980s and early 1990s? It was a fad that made the houses a great deal of money. But it fizzled quickly, catching some of them by surprise. The motto of so many editors remains this: Go with whatever works now and make the sale.

The popular belief has always been that women read fiction while men go for nonfiction—the books about real-life war, politics, and sports; about competition, courage, and bloodletting. Fiction, which looks at those topics and endless others through a different lens, has ever been the better seller. And since the advent of CNN and all-news cable programming, nonfiction sales figures have slipped further. Such books as Stephen Ambrose's memorable revisiting of grueling World War II campaigns or David Halberstam's sterling account of the early civil rights sit-ins take a backseat to quickie titles by Hollywood call girls or to lowbrow tell-alls by former lovers of politicians and royalty. Books about celebrity and assorted vices have muscled in on shelf space formerly allocated to straightforward recountings by historic figures of pivotal events.

Without a doubt, editing substantive nonfiction is hard work. Every fact, theory, and opinion must be carefully assessed and dissected. Sources must be checked for credibility and motive. The editor must monitor the author's tendency to lapse into a confusing jargon or academic shop talk that would glaze over the eyes of the reader. If the book deals with a topic that has been the subject of many titles, such as the John F. Kennedy assassination or the fall of Saigon, the editor's responsibility is to monitor the text and see that it covers new ground. Sometimes there may arise a tug-of-war resistance from an author of nonfiction when he is asked to simplify the material, but the good editor knows how to achieve clarity without having to endure too many tantrums.

Since nonfiction today uses many of the techniques of fiction, the editor must be assertive in monitoring the author who might cross the line into a murky area where lawsuits lurk. Besides, rare indeed is the author gifted enough to create a "nonfiction novel" of the magnitude of Truman Capote's *In Cold Blood* or Norman Mailer's *The Executioner's Song*, two acclaimed contemporary examples of the mingling of usually distinct literary forms; or of some hybrid on the order of Michael Herr's peerless Vietnam War chronicle, *Dispatches*. In the hands of amateurs, products of the now-familiar New Journalism techniques can be embarrassing and even unreadable. Thus the editor must become a stickler for the organization and presentation of information, mandating that the material unfold coherently. There is no room in nonfiction for hysteria or emotional theatrics: The editor must rein in the author so that the tone of the work throughout is objective. And, most important, good nonfiction must never contain gaps in its narrative, research, or facts. All three are big taboos.

"I'm looking for an idea that is new, and someone adding to existing conversations about the important topics of our time," said the late Joe Wood, of the New Press, a full-scale nonprofit publishing house, founded in 1992 by former Pantheon chief André Schiffrin. The New Press has made a name for itself with an expanding list of premier titles of political and cultural analysis. "Good, cogent writing is key. The nonfiction that interests us is produced by people who are bucking the status quo, who are looking at things from another point of view. We're in a country that prides itself on being anti-intellectual. This is reflected in our lack of emphasis on education: We subsidize large corporations to stay in cities while we cut funding for schools. The market for serious books is limited but still profitable. We publish intellectually challenging, serious books, and they find a market."

According to Wood, the profit margin at the end of the 1990s for top-drawer nonfiction was not as high as it was at the end of the 1970s or the 1980s, and may not rebound to those levels, given the profound changes in consumer tastes. Whether or not the changes in readership for this market may be long term or even permanent, the desire for informative, well-written nonfiction will always exist.

## CAN JUST ANY WORDSMITH EDIT BOOKS
## WRITTEN BY PEOPLE OF COLOR?

An editor can be a generalist, someone capable of editing a book on any topic under the sun, or she or he can be a specialist, skilled in making the prose of a science-fiction or mystery manuscript sing. Every editor wants to live up to the high standard of the craft set by such legendary figures as Maxwell Perkins, Helen K. Taylor, Ken McCormick, Jean Colby, Harold Strauss, Helen Harter, John Farrar, L. Rust Hills, William Targ, and Sol Stein. Currently, editors remain eternally hopeful that they'll get the opportunity to collaborate with the author of an exceptional work with an extraordinary new voice—one that will let the two coconspirators fully engage and further expand their abilities as they produce that literary labor of love.

Since 1992, the percentage of African American authors getting published has increased steadily. That positive trend is now a surge, posing new challenges for the largely white editorial staffs at the big publishing houses. Only a few of the major houses employ African American or Hispanic editors in any notable capacity. According to a recent *Publishers Weekly* article, you could count on two hands the number of people of color in editorial positions, if you included summer help. This deficiency has many black and Hispanic writers wondering and debating whether their books are being effectively served by white editors, who have so little firsthand experience with ethnic culture.

"It's like a country club setting where everyone is white, from money, and highly suspicious of anyone or anything that doesn't reflect their culture," said one editor, who was extremely nervous about being quoted. "They say the reason more blacks, Hispanics, and Asians are not hired as editors is that they lack the training and talent. Not so. Most nonwhites never even get their foot in the door at these places, and those who do burn themselves out trying to prove that they are worthy. This is an industry that sees itself as politically left, intellectually progressive, so many in the business are blind to the problem. Essentially, this is a white business."

One anecdote told by some black editors is supposedly based on an actual incident: A white editor polishing a book on the African American experience approaches a black editorial assistant with a word she doesn't know. "Is it black English, some sort of slang?" the white editor asks tentatively. The assistant examines the page of print carefully, reading it several times before answering evenly: "It's a typo." That may earn a chuckle, but the underlying truth of this humorous aside is not very funny.

It's not funny if you're a writer and the soul of your book is lost due to editorial miscues born of cultural confusion. The bestselling author Terry McMillan tells how the publisher of her second book, *Disappearing Acts*, sought to change her female character to a more gritty, earthy woman because it was thought that a black audience would not accept someone who "sounded white and lived off a trust fund." The novelist later left that publisher when an editor pressed for further alterations, this time with the leading black male character.

And sometimes the cultural factor may have not an active effect, but one of benign neglect. "I've published only two books with major houses," says Paul Beatty, a noted African American poet and writer of the acclaimed novel *The White Boy Shuffle*. "On my poetry, I didn't get much help. With my novel, it would have been nice to get some feedback as well, but that was all right. A few cultural nuances may have been missed. However, I read books that are not so well edited. I think the job of editor has changed. They're more like talent scouts. It's like being a social worker with a large caseload. Someone's work will fall through the cracks."

Working with an African American editor does not guarantee that your book will always be treated as you want it to be, that everything will be done to your satisfaction. Race does not automatically ensure competence, or even compatibility.

But often it can present a comfort zone that many writers find very welcome. Some of them say it allows a kind of cultural shorthand to be communicated between the author and the editor, since fewer things, cultural and aesthetic, will need explaining.

"I believe that there is a deeper level of empathy, understanding, and synergy that happens when I am editing and marketing a black book," says Carol Taylor, recalling her editorial experiences. "But this should be common sense and should apply to any market or ethnicity. However, it seems to be easier for many people to understand and accept why a gay editor would be more likely to successfully edit and publish a book geared to a gay audience, even if only because of his ties to that market and world, but it is less feasible [to those same observers] that a black editor would be needed to edit a book geared toward a black audience. Does that mean I am saying that only black editors can publish successful black books? Obviously not, but it does imply that with their collaboration, cultural mistakes that could kill black books are less likely to happen."

Stereotypes, both racial and economic, have traditionally plagued editorial thinking in addressing African American and other minority fiction. Will the black reader accept a character, created by an African American writer, who is a scientist, politician, or architect? Can a Hispanic audience identify with a fictional character who is a theatrical director or a United Nations diplomat? Yes! With Terry McMillan, Bebe Moore Campbell, Connie Briscoe, and others popularizing financially upscale black characters, the demand for fiction showcasing middle-class lives has been demonstrated in a resounding success at the bookstore cash register. Despite this trend, the number of African American editors with influence has not dramatically increased, leading many of the more popular black novelists to protest.

"The publishing business controls many of the social and cultural attitudes we see in this America," says Walter Mosley.

"Many of the publishers and editors who dominate the decisions and choices made in the industry still view some segments of the American book market as a niche market, not worthy of full consideration or equal opportunity. This industry has made a large profit, millions of dollars, from our readers and yet there are not many of us in those editorial offices. Maybe it's time for us as writers and artists to support our own publishers and bookstores. Give something back to our communities and support one another."

Mosley, an outspoken activist for more black editorial and management opportunities in publishing at all levels, put his money where his heart was by taking his unpublished manuscript, *Gone Fishin'*, to Black Classic Press, an African American house, in 1996. He also waived his usually large advance and donated to BCP his paperback, audio, and foreign rights. His generosity strengthened the financial picture for that small publishing house, opening the door for BCP's greater investment in young writers and for modernization of the company's facilities.

Paul Coates, the publisher of Black Classic Press, termed the project a success when he saw the positive public reception to Mosley's commitment to independent black publishers and to their rising editorial influence. Mosley's gesture was one significant step. May other steps follow.

Whether they do or do not, and whether you, the writer, do or do not work with a black editor, strive to make the editing process a positive, productive experience for you and your partner. Above all, stand your ground where you must; yield where your editor has a point. Remember that the book comes first. Tension in the author-editor relationship disrupts the chemistry needed to create an exceptional title. You can do without that barrier.

## WHEN YOUR EDITOR HAS GONE

What do you do when you are notified that your editor has left your publishing house just as your project is getting under way?

For an author, this could be the worst news possible, but don't panic. The publishing industry, in an era of mergers and business turbulence, is quite aware of the large employment turnover and will likely lose little time in introducing you to your new editorial guide. Editors come and go. Writers may feel anxious upon the departure of a trusted editor, and often seek to follow their ally to the new house of his or her employment. It can be hard to re-create a bond similar to the earlier one with the acquiring editor, the person who originally contracted the book.

Naturally, the incoming editor will sometimes show a deeper commitment to authors already on his list than to those newly inherited. Every experienced author knows how very much solid support from an editor can matter in the harried moments of delivering a truly finished work, finely polished and on track for production. You need that true-believer zeal in order to push the project through the rough times. Let the new editorial relationship take its course. Give it a chance before walking away from it.

If it becomes unacceptable, then seek an escape from the pairing that will leave as few scars as possible. Frequently, publishing houses, notably the larger ones, may attempt to block an author from defecting — especially if the collaboration has been highly profitable. The same degree of resistance is rarely shown in the fiscally marginal area of midlist books, where the moneymaking authors do not sell enough books to affect the fortune of the house. Many publishers permit the writer to follow the editor to a new home; most, however, frown on the practice.

Where the author is courted to stay with the house, the official line becomes that the publisher remains committed to the writer's work regardless of whatever personnel changes occur, and that the new editor will continue that unflagging support. Yes, but: There could be complications. Writers knowledgeable about the rapidly changing business remember the 1997 cancellation of more than 100 books under contract by HarperCollins. The bold financial move frightened agents and writers alike, causing them to wonder if that act foreshadowed a new trend. Of the 106 titles axed, 36 were deemed unpublishable (of poor quality, if you will), and another 70 tagged late. Authors, worried about this wholesale rejection of in-house (contracted) manuscripts, began asking agents what it meant in regard to loyalty and the return of advances.

Following the HarperCollins cancellations, news emerged that Simon & Schuster and Doubleday were initiating similar policies of cutting titles. The publishers say it's a natural occurrence, a pruning of deadwood and old projects with no chance of earning a sizable profit. Falling book sales, meager profits on blockbuster hopefuls, and a greater stress on the fiscal bottom line have moved some editors to consider imposing harsher contract terms. The manuscript must be delivered on time (by the date specified in the contract) and in minimum need of repair.

The National Writers Union continually complains that the "lateness" issue is subjectively applied, since some writers seem not to suffer penalties from missing their publication deadlines. The more established, big-name author often gets extensions for years on his contract, thanks to a publisher's hope, anticipation, or belief that the final product will be worth the wait. Suddenly, your publisher can decide that your manuscript is too late to justify publication, even if the violation is one of just weeks or months. Some writers' advocacy groups, such as the National Writers Union and the Authors Guild, insist that this cancellation of the book contract for lateness is essentially a business ploy, designed to trim budgets. The publishers reply that there has been no major rise recently in cancellations or rejections.

What happens if your book is canceled? Get a full explanation of this decision from your editor and publisher, and then consult with your agent. Decide whether all of your questions have been properly answered. Inquire about your options, and explore whether a sale to another house is possible. Some houses may want a partial or total repayment of the advance, while others will ask for a reimbursement from future sales. Let the issue come to a conclusion without high drama or bitter words. Work out all details graciously, without rancor, everything low-key, because no one wants a full-out battle that could harm potential talks with another house.

# SALES, PROMOTION, AND MARKETING

## FROM THE PUBLISHER TO THE SHELVES

How do those books get from the publishers to the stores? Who convinces the book buyers to acquire what new releases or older titles? Well, before the entire process of distribution begins, the magic of sales and promotion must go into effect. Each of the major publishing houses has its own sales force, of varying size, with territories to be covered. Each territory is visited by a sales representative who pitches the publisher's offerings with every new publishing season. Some houses, rather than employing salaried sales representatives, use commissioned personnel who sell books for several clients and cover a vast area and several types of stores.

## THE SALES CONFERENCE

Before the sales blitz starts, the editorial, marketing, and publicity departments of the house gather for a sales conference, which occurs three or four times yearly. It often lasts three or four days. In the past, some publishers experimented with an electronic conference system, using filmed presentations, but they discarded that mode. The conferences, attended by the editor-in-chief and other key members of the editorial hierarchy, are used to invigorate the sales and promotional departments, to pump them up about the current line of books. Many publishers now invite representatives of influential independent booksellers, large chains, and wholesalers to fly out to some exotic locale for the Big Pitch. Wisely, the publisher seeks to generate a positive buzz around its upcoming book releases. The sales staff and marketing reps sit as the editors present their books, detailing their merits and suggesting approaches for breaking them out in the market. Frequently, one of the more bankable authors, a franchise writer, is asked to address the group to lend an air of celebrity or glitz to the festivities; or audio/video presentations for key authors may be offered, along with several pep talks, to the troops. Every editor strives to get the sales staff energized about his or her books, in particular, knowing that the drive and commitment of those salespeople can spell success or failure for the new releases.

## ANATOMY OF A SALES REP

Veteran sales representatives listen intently as titles are presented by the editorial personnel. They look for a hook to sell the book, something to make it memorable among the hundreds of books coming into the stores. Each sales rep has a number of accounts in a territory and a quota of books to be sold; each will be armed with catalogs, book covers, photos of authors, and the desire to get their yearly bonus, which is based on their sales profits minus returns (volumes that failed to sell in the stores). These are the people who will persuade booksellers to maintain a supply of your books on their shelves even if there is a leveling off in sales demand.

Their quotas are geared to their territories and to the topic of the book and its individual attributes: in sum, to its projected sales potential. Logically enough, the most expensive books, along with other titles that have generated a buzz within the house, are given the larger quotas and receive the biggest sales commitment. The publishers keep an eye on advance sales for a book as the first indicator of the response of the buying public to the title. If a title heats up, quickly finding an audience, the sales staff push for even more product to be rushed to key stores to exploit the rush.

## A SHORT SHELF LIFE

Despite all hype, adrenaline, and love of the product, publishers know that in the perennial glut of the marketplace, some books will never make it off the ground, will never find their audience. Books and their authors and publishers suffer this fate most painfully in the big chain stores where a new book has only ninety days to grab a readership before it is banished from the shelves. After that time, new titles come in and the unprofitable books are returned to their publishers. The taste of the reader is unpredictable. A book can have all of the sales, marketing, and promotional punch of the house behind it and still fail in the stores. However, there are surprises and just as often a book, for no apparent reason, will take off, its sales will soar.

## THE AFRICAN AMERICAN BOOK BUYER

Sales within the African American book-buying market have been estimated at more than $258 million annually, according to a current report by the Chicago-based Target Market News, an African American market research firm. But there is a large untapped segment of the African American audience that has not been reached.

"The publishing industry does not know how to market black books," says Manie Barron, an associate editor at Random House who spent five years in sales and marketing. "For the most part, it's following a formula: If this is successful for $x$, let's use it for $y$. Many audiences are not reached by the industry, but some houses are starting black departments and reaching out to black bookstores. Still, so many of our black books are not getting the marketing or promotional budgets they deserve."

The cookie-cutter approach also has some agents riled. Publishing veteran, agent Marie Brown, says that the essential criteria for a good book have not changed but the selection process has been modified, holding financial profit paramount. "Most books receive no real advertisement budgets, so nobody knows they're out there," she notes. "The burden for success of a book really falls on the author's shoulders. He has to be sales-man, promoter, and marketer—everything."

Agent Carol Mann agrees. "The industry has changed in recent years, and there are both fewer houses and indepen-dent booksellers. Writers must ensure that their first book is as good as possible. It can make or break your career. You can't expect the publishers to carry the weight for you. There is not a science to making a book sell. Just hard work."

That hard work doesn't mean getting on TV with Oprah or buying a huge ad in *The New York Times* or *The Washington Post*. It means a full-scale campaign to sell your book to the public. Some publishers, such as One World, have dedicated their efforts to nontraditional marketing campaigns, with pro-motional activities targeted to beauty salons, community ex-positions, and black book clubs. As budgets for publicity and promotion tighten, innovation and creative ideas are essential.

"With the publicity and promotion budgets slashed, it's not enough to rely on reviews and author tours," says Beverly Robinson, a twenty-one-year veteran and director of publicity at Ballantine's One World imprint. "The author's role is im-portant, but many books sell without much direct author in-put. Tours don't necessarily make a book successful. In an age when crowds of *New York Times* bestselling authors can greet two to three readers at bookstore events, we must all face the fact that there is no single bestseller formula. If the book's con-tent does not deliver, the connection won't be made. If the re-views do not pan out, that doesn't help. A book works in the market when several factors come together, and timing is most critical of them all."

The issue of timing becomes particularly vital when, as happens not infrequently, two (or more) houses publish simi-lar books at the same time. The first such book to hit the mar-ket has the sales advantage, because the presumptive copycat title (which may actually have been the first one signed up by a publisher) is always seen as having commandeered an already rolling bandwagon.

Several other factors are considered in the marketing and promotion of a title: originality, timeliness, attractiveness of the package, strength of the marketing hook, a possible movie or television tie-in, and the commercial appeal of the book itself.

The age of the Internet now being well upon us, we see more Web emphasis in book promotion and marketing, with author websites, book excerpts, chats with readers, and other on-line interviews. Such efforts are increasing as the publishers scale back budgets for tours and other traditional modes of sales campaigning.

One sure thing remains—the ravenous appetite of African American readers for good books. "That hunger is increasing," says Emma Rodgers, owner of Black Images Book Bazaar. "Our readers want more and more, and that void must be filled. I expect the selection of books from our writers will become richer, deeper, and more layered as our writers venture out into previously unexplored areas of fiction such as adventure, horror, legal and medical thrillers, and political thrillers. Once our writers put out quality, entertaining books in those areas, the sales will go through the roof. The readers are waiting, the challenge is on our writers to be bold and imaginative."

# SELF-PROMOTION:
# FINDING THE AUDIENCE
# FOR YOUR WORK

Mainstream publishers will frequently give substantial support to publicize the work of more established writers, but new authors may not receive the benefit of a significant promotional budget. If this should happen, there's no reason to panic. First, you should ask yourself several questions about your book and yourself. Who are the readers for my work? Where do they read or buy? Is the appeal of my book local, regional, national, or international? Remember, you should not depend on your publisher to do all of the work when it comes to getting your book into the hands of your readers.

Beverly Robinson, of Ballantine's One World imprint, says the publicity and promotional efforts by publishing houses have become much more focused, with more emphasis on getting a higher return on their dollar investment. "Most houses have cut back on publicity, and everyone is required to make their efforts more cost-effective. Since many books get very modest budgets for publicity, you have to do the best you can with what you have by becoming very creative. For this reason, author participation in publicizing the book directly to its potential audience is critical to ultimate success."

That's a point that must be repeated: An author must get involved in the promotional process if his book is to have any chance of success. To make your book a success, you must consider all of your potential publicity and promotion options even as you start to research your work, whether it's a novel or nonfiction. No one wants to write a book that will never be published or read. Since competition for readers is very fierce, with more new titles finding their way to bookshelves every month, try to write your book for the widest possible audience. Check out the competition. Explore other books in your genre or area of expertise. Study the most successful offerings in your domain and examine how their authors and publishers promoted and marketed them. Look for any unusual or special promotional hooks used in their campaigns. Do your homework. Visit both chain and independent bookstores to ask the sales staff what books are selling and *why*. Log on to Amazon.com and other Internet book outlets to monitor signs of durability in the literary marketplace.

By starting your publicity effort before the release of your book, you can begin to gather the kind of media contacts needed for a highly successful launch. If your book possesses a timely element or originality, don't forget to publicize those qualities. Work in conjunction with your publisher's publicity and marketing divisions so you do not duplicate work unnecessarily at your own expense. Keep in mind the long lead time required for the print publications, especially the biweekly and monthly magazines. Remember that most books have only three months to find an audience before they're yanked from bookstore shelves. So be prepared to publicize your work from the moment your agent makes the sale.

The reason for the early emphasis by an author on the promotion of his work is often due to the inexperience of the mainstream publishing industry in reaching the customers who sometimes are uncomfortable in bookstores. "When editors evaluate manuscripts, they analyze the text, the writer's history, and media profile," says Adrienne Ingrum, former vice president at Crown and Putnam and current publishing consultant. "A manuscript can be fixed but an author's public presentation is key. The writer must sell his product. A black writer has to reach the person who doesn't necessarily go to the bookstore but reads. The big publishers often do not know how to do this."

Book tours are a necessary part of the literary life, but they can be long, grueling, and exhausting. Some authors love the road, the hotel food, endless radio and TV interviews, the same questions at book signings and readings asked over and over by newspaper reporters and the public in countless towns and cities. Gwendolyn M. Parker, author of the acclaimed novel *These Same Long Bones*, candidly recounts her first impression of a national book tour: "The truth I had to face in the morning was that I could no more imagine myself actually doing what was so blithely described by my publicist than I could imagine myself lying astride a car in a bikini in an auto show."

Reaching the audience calls for ingenuity on the part of the writer, who must seek out every new avenue of communication, including those on the Web. Along with using E-mail to contact potential customers and fellow authors, continually update your master mailing list to booksellers, reading groups, and distributors. Plan your publicity campaign with military precision. Whenever you're invited to a speaking engagement or other media appearances, mention your book, but do it in a manner that seems natural and not like you're selling a new vacuum cleaner.

To further capitalize on promotion opportunities, always carry copies of your finished books with you. It's always highly effective to drum up individual and group interest in your work and any future events you have scheduled. Also, contact editors at newspapers, magazines, and TV or radio stations to publicize upcoming reading events with a pitch geared to promote the most intriguing sections of your book that appeal to specific audiences, be they feature sections, sports, business, or entertainment.

Be certain to autograph your book, for this increases its value and desirability. Many stores will let the author autograph copies sold after the reading for customers who could not attend the event.

The savvy writer finds ways to get articles in the newspapers and magazines that have nothing to do with the book section. Speaking of the media, writing articles or op-ed pieces for major newspapers, magazines, and other publications will keep your name in the public eye, making it easier to market your work. The gatekeepers of electronic and print media are always on the watch for fresh faces to serve as authorities on various contemporary, newsworthy topics, so boost your book sales by becoming extremely knowledgeable in your field. If your book concerns a topical issue, immerse yourself in the latest information on that topic and market yourself as a recognized expert in the field. As a major source in a specific field, you may be able to garner key invitations as an established authority for your local or regional news outlets. Don't forget to ask the media gatekeeper to mention your book and show the cover. Such basic tactics can help your sales soar.

"Many of my clients find radio and phone interviews more effective than the old traditional methods, along with on-line Web chats and interviews," says Simone Cooper, a freelance publicist with many years of experience in the publishing arena. "Although publishers are committed to publicizing books, the cost of tours has become prohibitive, so they are seeking other ways to promote their authors. The city-to-city tour is not as important for authors as it once was."

Controversy surrounds the issue of travel and touring, because in a recent survey by *Publishers Weekly*, many booksellers still view readings and signings as the best ways to build a readership. In so many ways, nothing gets the word out about your book like a visit to those places writers are invited to appear—bookstores, clubs, libraries, civic associations, writer organizations, conferences, seminars, and professional events.

"Promoting a black book is totally different than the effort for a white writer," notes Jacqueline Jacobs, a promotions staffer at Warner Books. "You do not see many ads for books in the black media, so that makes touring and personal appearances more important. A black writer has to go out and make the rounds of the black bookstores and reading groups. He must connect with the audience to feed the interest for his work."

Reputations are made on the road, touring. Many successful writers, like Iyanla Vanzant and Maya Angelou, developed workshop and seminar formats that have served to widen their audience. If you're considering the professional speaker's route, hire a professional publicist to book your appearances and handle all of the critical details of mounting your road-show campaign.

When setting up a presentation, explore with the event's organizer the possibility of preselling your book so it can be distributed as a part of the promotional package. Negotiate the sale, keeping in mind that the greater exposure, especially at one of the more popular expos, may be worth receiving a smaller immediate profit. Give the organizer a break on the cost and it'll pay big promotional dividends down the road. Also, be prepared to give a full-court press. Print news releases, postcards, brochures, bookmarks, or some other form of consumer handout that can be passed along to the customer at the scheduled event. All of these promotional materials should carry the title of your book, your name, the name of the publisher, the publication date, price of the book, and your mailing address.

Yes, your challenge as an African American writer is to deliver the message of your work to your potential readers. Publicity and promotion. If you make the time and effort, the payoff will be not just financial, but invaluable feedback from your audience. "Once your audience knows you, they will support you," Jacobs concludes. "Some publicists say New York is the toughest place for a writer to break into, but it can be done. Any city or region can be worked by a writer if the right amount of effort is made. One thing is certain: If we don't go out and support our authors, then the publishers will decide that we are not reading them."

Harriet wilson's novel, *Our Nig*, published in 1859, is considered the first novel by an African American writer to be printed in America. The writer, who endured her share of personal tragedies, understood the need for a supportive audience: "In offering to the public the following pages, the writer confesses her inability to minister to the refined and cultivated, the pleasure supplied by abler pens," she wrote in the book's preface. "I sincerely appeal to my colored brethren universally for patronage, hoping they will not condemn this attempt of their sister to be erudite, but rally around me a faithful band of supporters and defenders."

# CRITICISM IN PROPER DOSES

Are you frightened of criticism? Does some honest assessment of your work chill your soul and propel you headlong into writer's block? Who decides what is good or bad? Who knows what real talent is? How can you tell if the criticism you receive is legitimate? Is criticism essential to your growth as a writer?

Criticism, like opinion, is a very subjective art form. It can be practiced by anyone with a pen or a mouth. There are very few guidelines for criticism and a professional license is not required. Unnerving, isn't it? Anyone can pass judgment on the work of another, but for the fledgling writer, poor, abusive, or ill-conceived criticism can have a permanent damaging effect. "Who told you that you are a writer?" "Do you really think that this is writing?" Two thumbs down, and you're finished. The best teachers and critics never make dire predictions or sweeping appraisals of a young apprentice's talents or potential. Nor do they announce the demise of an established writer's talent because of a slip in the quality or frequency of the product.

If a writing-workshop instructor or editor pronounces your work dead on arrival, weigh their opinions carefully if you truly believe in your writing and your abilities. James Baldwin, author of *The Fire Next Time* and *Another Country*, worked ten years on his first novel, *Go Tell It on the Mountain*, before it found its way to publication. Another success story, Terry McMillan, discounted early warnings from her editors that her debut novel, *Mama*, would reach a limited audience, and assembled a tour of black community bookstores to peddle her book to thousands of appreciative buyers. She made her luck,

and she made her book happen. In another time, critically acclaimed author Jean Toomer let the fickle praise of puzzled
white critics and the lack of response from a baffled African
American book audience for his experimentally lyrical *Cane*
silence his distinctive voice. He never published again with a
mainstream house in his lifetime. Who knows what wonderful
volumes of prose Toomer could have produced if he had
turned a deaf ear to the furor surrounding his book?

▲▲

> *"It will be argued, and I think with truth, that his charac-*
> *ter, Bigger, is made far too articulate, that he explains*
> *much too glibly in the latter part of the story how he came*
> *to meet his fate. . . . Later he has romanticized and ratio-*
> *nalized himself into the declaration that 'What I killed for*
> *must've been good!' . . . Mr. Wright does spoil his story at*
> *the end by insisting on Bigger's fate as representative of*
> *the whole Negro race and making Bigger himself say so.*
> *But this is a minor fault in a good cause. The story is a*
> *strong and powerful one and it alone will force the Negro*
> *issue into our attention."*

—From the March 3, 1940, review of Richard Wright's
novel *Native Son*, which appeared in *The New York
Times Book Review*

▲▲

In reality, the role of a competent and responsible teacher
or critic is to share his experience and expertise about the art
and craft of writing with the novice without ego or reproach.
No grandiosity or needless personal attacks are appropriate.
Remember, there are standards for "good writing." Langston
Hughes, who often worked with young writers, always advised
them never to accept criticism or instruction blindly, to form
their opinion about what was applicable to them, to integrate

carefully into their craft the lessons learned. He admonished young scribes to not be robots or blind followers. "Be independent in your thinking," he warned, "and always question, question, question."

In fact, the worst thing a teacher or critic can do is to be dishonest or get caught up in his or her own power drives. An egotistical or insincere teacher can undermine a young writer's confidence and destroy his or her future development. Since writers work in isolation, separated from the outside world, they often have a tendency to take criticism of their work much too seriously. Also, know the limitations and biases of your critics. Check their credentials, the quality and artistry of their books. Upon my arrival in New York in 1975, I attended a writing workshop where the teacher, a noted novelist and essayist, slammed the writings of a young student so hard that she wept and ran from the room, never to return. She gave up, inspiring the teacher to comment wryly: "If you can't stand the heat, stay out of the kitchen."

▲▲

*"The reader who is familiar with the traumatic phase of the black man's rage in America will find something more in Mr. Ellison's report. He will find the long anguished step toward its mastery. The author sells no phony forgiveness. He asks none himself. It is a resolutely honest, tormented, profoundly American book."*

—From the April 13, 1952, review of Ralph Ellison's novel *Invisible Man*, which appeared in *The New York Times Book Review*

▲▲

Constructive criticism is always good. Dorothy West, who founded the innovative Harlem Renaissance literary magazine *Challenge* in 1934 and wrote the pioneering novel *The Living Is Easy*, once said it was unwise for authors not to read criticisms. Very true. It is important to understand that criticism in its most productive forms is essential to attaining mastery of your craft. And don't be afraid to make mistakes. In a sense, there is no such thing as a mistake, for every miscue made only contributes to the art that a writer brings to the page. Remember that failure, in so many ways, is more than success.

The good teacher or critic knows how much to criticize, knows where to draw the line so the student will hear what is being said. Overkill harms. Too-harsh criticism only falls on deaf ears, and the moment of opportunity is lost. Temper the criticism.

Avoid mentors whose worldview dictates that an African American writer cannot learn anything from reading white authors or from listening to white critics. National Book Award winner Ernest Gaines addressed this controversy head-on in the Fall 1972 issue of *Black Creation*: "I don't care what a man is. I mean, a good artist is like a great doctor. I don't care how racist he is. If he can show me how to operate on a heart so I can cure a brother, or cure someone else, I don't gave a damn what a man thinks. He has taught me something. And that is valuable to me." The message here is that a young writer should read everything and listen to everybody with something to say, always understanding that the quest for knowledge is not defined by the source's race or personal beliefs. Read Albert Camus, Ernest Hemingway, Charles Dickens, Willa Cather, Jane Austen, Mary Shelley, along with Wright, Killens, Petry, Morrison, and Ellison. Read and absorb, for the answers to the puzzle of artful writing can be found anywhere.

And always question, question, question.

PERHAPS NO book ever caused such furor upon its publication as did Richard Wright's fiery work *Black Boy*, whose scathing attack on Jim Crow rocked the nation. The Wright controversy reached into the hallowed halls of Congress, where southern bigots condemned the author and his book. On June 7, 1944, U.S. Senator Theodore Bilbo of Mississippi blasted *Black Boy* on the floor of the powerful political institution: "The dirtiest, filthiest, lousiest, most obscene piece of writing that I have ever seen in print . . . It is so filthy and dirty but it comes from a Negro, and you cannot expect any better from that type."

Since writers regularly read some manner of criticism, you as a writer should familiarize yourself with the work of the best critics and analyze how they evaluate writers and their work. Beware of skeptics who pan everything. Pay close attention to critics who are able to apply a flexible standard of literary excellence to writing, drawing upon an eclectic pool of sources and influences rather than just the usual yardsticks of the Western literary canon. A good measure of criticism of African American literature would not only include the limited aesthetic of American writing but incorporate works from African, Caribbean, and Asian cultures as well. A significant number of blacks distrust the Western literary canon of ideas because it has not served them well. Much of the criticism they see ignores or reduces the complexity of African American life to new versions of outdated stereotypes or judgments that do not reflect the black aesthetic. The criteria for good criticism allow for subtle shifts in both society and culture. What was not acceptable yesterday may be quite acceptable today. Ultimately, criticism can be a very positive tool for writers if applied appropriately. It should not be feared but welcomed.

▲▲

"Song of Solomon *isn't, however, cast in the basically re-alistic mode of most family novels. In fact, its negotiations with fantasy, fable, song, and allegory are so organic, con-tinuous and unpredictable as to make any summary of its plot sound absurd; but absurdity is neither Morrison's strategy or purpose. The purpose seems to be communi-cation of painfully discovered and powerfully held convic-tions about the possibility of transcendence within human life, on the time-scale of a single life.*"

—From the September 11, 1977, review of Toni Morrison's novel *Song of Solomon*, which appeared in *The New York Times Book Review*

▲▲

# OF BESTSELLERS AND BESTSELLER LISTS

▲▲

*"I do not write for a special audience. I write and trust what I've said may strike a responsive chord in someone else. During my career as a writer, my so-called public has changed several times. I've found that my audience changes with my own changing outlook. I do not seek for an audience; I let the audience follow me, if it is interested."*

—Richard Wright
From *Conversations with Richard Wright*

▲▲

What is a bestseller? Our grandmothers probably considered bestsellers to be the Bible, the Montgomery Ward catalog, and the all-purpose Sears Roebuck catalog, of which an estimated 12 billion copies have been distributed since its maiden run in 1896. And maybe the *McGuffey Reader* was in there somewhere.

## BLACKS AND BESTSELLERS

Blacks and the subject of race have always been fodder for the American literary world, providing the central themes for three pivotal bestsellers published before 1940. The first of these seminal works, Harriet Beecher Stowe's *Uncle Tom's Cabin*, published in 1852, was often termed "the little book that started the War Between the States." Stowe, who was white, would never admit that her tale was based on a popular seventy-six-page pamphlet—a slave narrative written by Josiah Henson, who helped more than one hundred of his fellow slaves escape to Canada. Instead, when a reporter asked Stowe about the book, she said: "God wrote it, I merely wrote it down." The critically acclaimed book, hated by slaveholders in its day, was later used by some white Americans to formulate several of the racial stereotypes employed to falsely define the social and cultural characteristics of blacks. Stowe's fictional meditation on the horrors of slavery was the first novel to utterly grip the imagination of a nation while selling over 1 million copies.

The second of these provocative works, Thomas Dixon's racist novel *The Clansman*, was so popular that many of the nation's bookstores were forced to wait weeks, even months, for its arrival. Again, blacks occupied center stage on the American scene. When filmmaker D. W. Griffith wanted to use the controversial story as the basis for his 1915 epic film *The Birth of a Nation*, the director struck a deal with Dixon that earned the author several million dollars for his damning view of the darker race; earlier, Griffith had been unable to pay Dixon the agreed figure of $7,500 for the story. Some say this was the first real Hollywood book deal. However, it was an unfortunate day for African Americans. The movie, with its bigoted scenes of black aggression against whites, triggered a series of race riots that resulted in widespread property damage and deaths in black communities.

The last of these popular racial bestsellers was Margaret Mitchell's *Gone With the Wind*. Published in 1936, it won a Pulitzer Prize the following year. For decades, that lengthy novel of the Old South's fading glory days remained high on the all-time bestseller list, bolstered by the overwhelming popularity of the Selznick MGM film classic starring Clark

Gable and Vivien Leigh. Blacks were galvanized not so much by the book as by the movie that featured Hattie McDaniel's portrayal of the no-nonsense Mammy who drank hard liquor with Gable and won a Best Supporting Actress Oscar, a first.

## RICHARD WRIGHT'S NATIVE SON AND THE PROTEST BOOM

Although there was demand for African American literature during the fabled Harlem Renaissance, nothing prepared the publishing industry for the explosion of sales accompanying Richard Wright's *Native Son*, a tragic protest novel of black rage. Within six weeks of its publication in 1941, the book sold a quarter of a million hardcover copies, an impressive figure even today. It became a hot-ticket item, due not just to word of mouth on the streets: Nearly every publication in the country ran some manner of notice about Wright's no-holds-barred work. Also, *Native Son* was a Main Selection of the Book-of-the-Month Club, and it rocketed to the top of national bestseller lists, remaining there for over two months. Wright was lionized internationally following this stunning and, to some, almost unbelievably successful debut.

The forties saw other African American writers burst onto the national literary scene. Willard Motley's first novel, *Knock on Any Door*, was a bestseller in 1947 and was later transformed into a hit film starring Humphrey Bogart. A *New York Times* book critic raved: "An extraordinary and powerful new naturalistic talent herewith makes his debut in American letters." By the 1960s, the novel, with its lead character Nick Romano, was in its seventeenth printing, having sold more than 1.5 million copies. Two other Motley novels, *We Fished All Night* (1951) and *Let No Man Write My Epitaph* (1958), received respectable notices but did not reach the commercial heights of his first work. Several black critics wrinkled their noses at Motley because he wrote about poor Italians, Irish, Jews, and Poles trapped in murderous slums, but never about blacks. Like Wright, Motley knew poverty intimately, having lived in a cold basement apartment in Chicago for many years while writing his bestseller. It later financed his escape from the United States to Mexico. There he wrote his last novel, *Let Noon Be Fair* (1966).

Another bestselling African American author, Frank Yerby, made it to the national bestseller lists in the 1940s and 1950s with a middlebrow mix of pulp fiction, adventure yarns, and costume dramas. His early work was erratic in quality until 1944, when he wrote the short story "Health Card," a blistering attack on racism that brought him sizable national attention and the O. Henry Award. Yerby shrewdly practiced a schizophrenic approach to his fiction after hitting that peak in his career, reserving his shorter stories for the concerns of blacks while developing his novels with chiefly white characters and less controversial themes. It was a strategy that worked. His first novel, *The Foxes of Harrow* (1946), shot right up the bestseller lists. The Old South bodice-ripper sold millions of copies, was translated into over a dozen languages, and became a popular 1951 film. Yerby kept up his winning ways with succeeding novels such as *The Vixens* (1948) and *The Golden Hawk* (1949), covering a wide range of themes and historical events. Over his lengthy career, the Yerby touch was stamped on more than thirty novels that totaled more than 50 million copies sold and served as the basis for several Hollywood films.

## THE CONTEMPORARY ILLITERATE MYTH

While the works of James Baldwin, Ralph Ellison, John O. Killens, and Ishmael Reed enjoyed much critical acclaim, the plum of a soaring commercial blockbuster eluded them in the 1950s, 1960s, and 1970s. No doubt all of these writers wanted the financial security of a huge-selling book, but publishers of their day did not actively market their tomes to America's nonwhite audience. The unwritten belief among several houses was that a sizable literate black readership was not achieved until the late 1980s, despite the unparalleled popularity of Alex Haley's 1976 international blockbuster, *Roots*. Black people don't read books, said some whites in the industry.

ALEX HALEY worked twelve years on his popular novel *Roots*, which served as the basis for the acclaimed television series that attracted a record 80 million viewers. Success was a mixed blessing for the soft-spoken writer. He enjoyed meeting with heads of state and adoring crowds, but the star treatment left him unprepared for the price of celebrity. Haley observed, "No matter how much you have, you can eat but one meal at a time, drive but one car at a time, live in but one house at a time, sleep in but one bed at a time, with one woman. Money cannot buy one extra hour of life. . . ."

## THE POWER OF THE BLOCKBUSTER BOOK

All writers, no matter what their race or creed, want to see their works appear at the top of national bestseller lists in *The New York Times*, *The Washington Post*, *Los Angeles Times*, *USA Today*, *Library Journal*, and *The Wall Street Journal*. A position on the *New York Times* list is the most coveted, for it signals an anointing from the publishing elite in New York City, the mecca of publishing.

In the past, a look at the national bestseller list revealed the same names—white names—Michael Crichton, Robert Ludlum, Robin Cook, Anne Rice, Lawrence Sanders, Mary Higgins Clark—with a Stephen King formula thriller always to be found somewhere in the mix. Some of King's spine-tingling novels have remained on the lists as long as thirty-five weeks before running out of steam. Publishers pray for a book with the kind of staying power shown by John Berendt's gothic true-crime stunner, *Midnight in the Garden of Good and Evil*, which has lingered at the top of national lists for over four years. Authors newer to the scene, including Charles Frazier, with his Civil War epic *Cold Mountain*, and Frank McCourt, through his sobering memoir *Angela's Ashes*, give aspiring scribes hope that their work can also find a home at the top of the heap. Some independent bookstores and writers' organizations have questioned the validity of bestseller lists, since their tabulations are usually compiled from a select number of outlets, much along the lines of a random Harris poll sample.

## THE AFRICAN AMERICAN BESTSELLER

What does this have to do with African American readers? Quite a lot. Since the days of Richard Wright's smashing literary success, an increasing literate black readership, supported by a solid base of black-owned bookstores, has opened the formerly white-dominated bestseller lists to African American talent. In 1992, books by three black women held positions near the top of the lists nationwide—Terry McMillan's *Waiting to Exhale*, Toni Morrison's *Jazz*, and Alice Walker's *Possessing the Secret of Joy*. McMillan's highly popular love saga achieved a crossover appeal, much to the delight of her publisher, and stayed on the *New York Times* bestseller charts for an astounding thirty-eight weeks. E. Lynn Harris's third novel, *And This Too Shall Pass*, spent nine weeks on the *New York Times* bestseller list, a rarity for a black male author.

In 1998, the American Booksellers Association said that 9.9 million African American adults were regular book buyers, even at a time when the cost of hardcovers has made such a purchase a consumer luxury. Yet, despite those rising prices, black readers continue to support their favorite authors—as these recent *Publishers Weekly* figures indicate: Toni Morrison's *Paradise* (more than 800,000 copies sold), Bebe Moore

Campbell's *Singing in the Comeback Choir* (more than 150,000 copies sold), and Alice Walker's *By the Light of My Father's Smile* (more than 125,000 copies sold). Morrison's *Paradise*, which examines several key racial and gender issues, was a fixture on the nation's bestseller lists for many months in early 1998.

However, much support for these books originated from a faithful core of African American female readers, who paid little attention to well-placed reviews, backing the "sisters" as well as other briskly selling African American authors such as Connie Briscoe, Eric Jerome Dickey, Omar Tyree, Benilde Little, Susan Taylor, Lolita Files, Van Whitfield, Colin Channer, and others.

Still, African Americans have been considered a niche market for publishers, despite their having spent $355 million on books in 1998; that figure continues to soar, according to book industry data. Book purchases for whites, on the other hand, have gone flat, showing only nominal growth. What the book industry has been slow to admit is that there is considerable interest in African American books by a growing nonblack readership, despite the national debate on multiculturalism. The notion that "whites don't buy or read books written by blacks" rings false when the numbers of whites acquiring many of the leading African American books are tabulated. Increasingly, white Americans seem eager to enjoy the wealth of experience in other cultures.

The history of the popular African American book in the commercial literary marketplace has been a rocky one, fraught with often poorly packaged, weakly promoted products, that were sometimes dismissed as being of inferior artistic quality. Only in recent years has there been a push to right this wrong. From the inception of the bestseller lists, in 1895, to the present, that instrument for measuring the popularity of writers has prompted criticism and controversy because it has ever failed to use talent and mastery as the yardsticks for proclaiming certain works worthy of acclaim. A spot on the A list frequently has little or nothing to do with skill or superior artistry, but much to do with the size of the publishing house and its ability to distribute and market its product.

## CONTROVERSY CONCERNING THE LISTS

Many booksellers and consumers use the current bestseller lists, both national and regional, to decide what is worthy of their attention. Some writers and industry critics have complained that books not on the bestseller lists get short shrift and are often pushed aside on shelves to make way for the big sellers or heavily budgeted items earmarked for top billing. In publishing, the amount of money targeted to market a book is critical. With a book budget, size does indeed matter. The budget often determines which books find their way to the bestseller lists, and is based on the amount of funds set aside for promotional tours, the number of books printed, ads placed in publications, and media appearances secured. Critics have long stated a belief that slots on the major bestseller lists can be bought with the right amount of revenue—much to the chagrin of publishers, who uniformly deny such claims.

Another serious criticism is that in their analyses of book sales, the tabulators of bestseller lists do not consider canvassing purchases made through Christian outlets, mom-and-pop stores, specialty shops, newsstands, price clubs, much of the independent market, and most black-owned outlets. Some wonder why wholesalers' book sales are counted by several of the influential lists when wholesalers do not sell direct to the public.

Pointing to the inherent deficits of the lists, many black writers say that opportunities for cracking them are close to nil. Some book lovers in the black community have sought their own remedies to this problem.

Rapidly gaining prominence in book circles is the Blackboard list, an African American bestseller list developed by Faye Childs in 1991 and supported by the American Booksellers Association. The Blackboard monthly list of the top five fiction and nonfiction sellers, which has caught the eye of most mainstream publishers, gathers its sales information from seventy black stores and retailers in thirty cities. The Blackboard list appears monthly in *Essence* magazine and in the American Booksellers Association's periodical *Booksellers This Week*. It is not unusual to find copies of both of these black-oriented publications on the desks of agents and editors throughout the industry.

## A CHALLENGE TO THE NEW YORK TIMES BESTSELLER LIST

The *New York Times* bestseller list, an institution for sixty-nine years, is now facing its biggest challenge: the recently established list from Barnes & Noble, the giant national chain of a thousand stores. While the chain, with $3 billion in sales, will continue to post the *NYT* list, it will now offer its version, still giving discounts of 30 percent for paperbacks and 40 percent for hardcovers on both lists. Most booksellers and publishers feel the new list will not pose a serious threat to the long-standing influence of the esteemed newspaper's weekly anointing of the chosen books for its Sunday book section. Although B&N's action sends a signal to the newspaper that it has growing clout in the evolving publishing industry, no one at *The New York Times* believes that B&N's action will force *New York Times* officials to rethink how its list is compiled. Critics at the newspaper insist the new list could pose questions about B&N's marketing and promotion of various favored titles in its stores to support its in-house publication. In any case, time will tell if this new list will pay dividends for the confident book chain and display the kind of staying power the *New York Times* list has already proven to have.

## THE ROUGH ROAD TO BESTSELLERDOM

Alas, the road to bestsellerdom is not an easy one. A publisher can neither predict which books will achieve that goal nor purchase a niche for his product on the lists. Some big books capture the public's attention quickly, generating huge sales over six or seven weeks, then tapering off to almost nothing. In many cases, the brisk sales can come in the first three weeks after the book's release before a decline, usually a sharp one, occurs. In 1997 alone, 50,000 books were published, but only about ninety books in both fiction and nonfiction categories earned bestseller status. The "magic number" for this revered perch in the book industry has changed drastically since, in the 1970s, the big sellers moved 12 million copies or more.

Today's figures reflect the intense competition for the hearts and minds of consumers, as TV, film, and on-line entertainment vie for share in the market. A current bestseller is considered a winner if it smashes the 100,000-copy mark. As the nineties closed out, the numbers for industry profits were depressed across the board, with the average book, whether a first novel or a nonfiction work from a new author, routinely selling at a peak of 6,000 to 7,000 copies. A large mainstream house often will not take a chance on a book that might not sell at least 15,000 copies. Both publisher and writer desire the book with "legs," a product that continues to sell at a constant rate through many printings. Unfortunately, that is not the lot of most books, which end up as returns or unsold merchandise for the publisher to accept at a loss.

Only a small percentage of writers make it to the top rung of commercial publishing with their book. Bestsellers are a rarity, so most writers are content to make just a comfortable living from their work. The practical writer, for the most part, maintains his livelihood by holding down a standard nine-to-five, keeping his eyes on the prize while pursuing his literary goals. Only a select few will ever produce a profitable bestseller. The sound approach to reaching your writing objectives is reflected in a bit of golden advice often given by the noted poet and essayist Audre Lorde in her renowned writing classes: "Plan your writing career. Be practical. Do not expect fame and fortune overnight. Set reasonable goals. Don't give up your day job or your dreams."

# OF BOOKSELLERS AND DISTRIBUTORS

## THE BOOKSELLERS AND BOOKSTORES

One of the major players in the surge of African American literature in the marketplace has been the assistance of black bookstores. Despite some important store closings, independent black booksellers are repositioning themselves to handle a rapidly changing market, where large chains are now stocking African American titles in large numbers and offering discounts at their superstores. Overall, this trend has caused a significant drop in the market share of business conducted by independents, down from 19 percent to 16.5 percent of the nation's book trade in recent years, according to industry figures.

Jacqueline Jacobs, a staffer in Warner Books' promotions department, states that the importance of the independent stores, especially the African American outlets, cannot be overemphasized. "We need our black bookstores because the chains do not stock our books beyond their short shelf life," she says. "The owners and staff at African American bookstores treat the books by our authors with loving care. Some of the best books I've read have been recommended by black booksellers."

Like all bookstores, the independents face the challenges posed by other distractions vying for the consumer's recreational time and dollar such as movies, movie rentals, cable TV, the Internet, and video games. Often the book buyer does not go to the usual store but to nontraditional outlets such as specialty shops, beauty salons, and churches.

A recent *Publishers Weekly* article put the number of booksellers specializing in African American titles at close to 400 outlets, but Emma Rodgers, owner of Black Images Book Bazaar, says that total could be much higher if you count stores that sell other items. The fate of black booksellers in an increasingly competitive business is tied directly to the types of books being published successfully. While African Americans are buying more books, that may not be true for many other segments of the population, as purchases of adult books fell 2.8 percent, to 1.04 billion, last year, according to the current Consumer Research Study on Book Purchasing.

Since an increasing number of books are being purchased on-line, through subscription book clubs and catalogs, and from nontraditional outlets, the challenge for publishers and booksellers is now to harness the growing African American market. The large chains, which now control nearly 26 percent of the book consumer market, have embarked on a one-stop shopping approach to attract new customers, offering would-be book buyers lots of guilty pleasures beyond reading, such as live music, food, and uninterrupted reading time in a comfortable setting. The major bookseller chains include Barnes & Noble, Borders, Waldenbooks, and Books-A-Million. In 1998, their sales increased 0.2 percent while independents lost 0.6 percent of sales, according to the current book purchase study.

For publishers, that added plus of having a staffer in an independent store "hand-sell" or personally endorse a book is what gives these outlets their special significance. Still, the critical position of the superstores cannot be ignored, according to Carol Taylor, former Crown editor and editorial consultant. "Superstores offer a wide selection, diverse services, deep discounts, accessibility, and a level of comfort that is impossible for independents to match. These days publishers believe that the best way to sell books is to get them in the superstores, the mall bookstores, and the price clubs.

Subsequently these stores now dictate print runs, advertising budgets, and even a book's chance of being acquired."

At a recent symposium, Leonard Riggio, CEO of Barnes & Noble, the world's largest bookstore chain, said the success of the chains indicates the health of the publishing industry overall. "With all of the media forums out there—cable TV, movies, video games, computer software, on-line experiences—in the past ten years, the percentage of the discretionary dollar spent on books has gone up by 35 percent," Riggio said. "People are in bookstores, and they're not just drinking coffee. They're buying books. And they're buying across a wider spectrum. . . . So I don't see the gloom and doom."

Clara Villarosa, owner of the Hue-Man Experience Bookstore in Denver and the first African American board member of the American Booksellers Association, is cautiously optimistic but feels that sound business practices hold the key to success for the independents. "Unfortunately, we're in a culture of convenience, everything's about saving time. Buying a black book at a black bookstore is not a priority. For this reason, black bookstores are closing and will continue to close. You can count the stores across the country that are expanding on one hand. The African American bookstore is under siege. To survive, we must adapt. To survive, we need the support of our community."

## LEADING AFRICAN AMERICAN BOOKSELLERS

African American Bookstore
Carl Webber
Gertz Plaza Mall
162-10 Jamaica Avenue
New York, NY 11432
718-658-2821
cmweb@earthlink.com

Afro-American Bookstop
Michelle Lewis
5700 Read Boulevard, #275
New Orleans, LA 70127
504-243-2436
fax: 504-243-2255

Afrocentric Bookstore
Desiree Sanders
333 S. State Street
Chicago, IL 60604
312-939-1956
fax: 312-939-1961

Apple Book Center
Sherry McGee
7900 West Outer Drive
Detroit, MI 48235
313-255-5221
fax: 313-838-3117

Bestseller Bookstore
Patrick Payne
43 Main Street
Hempstead, NY 11550
516-564-5103
fax: 516-564-4607

Black Bookworm
Sonja Williams Babers
605 E. Berry Street, Suite 114
Fort Worth, TX 76110
817-923-9661

Black Images Book Bazaar
Emma Rodgers
230 Wynnewood Village
Dallas, TX 75224
214-943-0142

Books for Thought
Felicia Wintons, Store Mgr.
10910 N. 56th Street
Tampa, FL 33617

Cultural Collections
Juliette Armstrong, Mgr.
730 Belmont Street
Brockton, MA 02301-5602

Eso-Wan Books
James Fugate, Store Mgr.
3655 S. La Brea Avenue
Los Angeles, CA 90016
213-294-0324

Haneef's Bookstore
Hanifa Shabazz, Marketing
    Mgr.
Freedom Plaza
911 Orange Street
Wilmington, DE 19801
302-656-4193
fax: 302-657-2106

Heritage House
Stephanie Coleman
901 S. Kings Drive
Charlotte, NC 28204
704-344-9695
fax: 704-344-9655

Hue-Man Experience
Clara Villarosa
911 Park Avenue W.
Denver, CO 80205
800-346-4036/303-293-2665
fax: 303-293-0046

Karibu
Brother Simba
3500 East/West Highway
Hyattsville, MD 20782

Marcus Books
Blanche Richardson
3900 Martin Luther King Jr.
  Way
Oakland, CA 94609
510-652-2344
fax: 415-931-1536

Nkiru Books
Brenda Green
76 St. Marks Avenue
Brooklyn, NY 11217
718-783-6306
fax: 718-783-6245

Phenix Information Center
Joann & Faron Roberts, Store
  Mgrs.
334 North E Street
San Bernardino, CA 92401
909-383-2329
fax: 909-383-2331

Pyramid Bookstore
Akbar Watson, Mgr.
544-2 Gateway Boulevard
Boynton Beach, FL 33435
561-731-4422
fax: 561-731-0202

Roots & Wings
Eleanor Boyd, Mgr.
1345 Carter Hill Road
Montgomery, AL 36106
334-262-1700

Shrine of the Black Madonna
  Bookstore
Maia Thomas
946 R. Abernathy Boulevard, SW
Atlanta, GA 30310
404-752-6125
fax: 404-753-4884

Sisterspace & Books
Faye Williams
1515 U Street, NW
Washington, DC 20009
202-332-3433
fax: 202-986-7092

That Old Black Magic
Store Manager
163 Mamaroneck Avenue
White Plains, NY 10601
914-328-7215

The Black Bookworm
Sonia Williams-Babers
PO Box 3087
Ft. Worth, TX 76113-3087

Vertigo Books
Bridget Warren
1337 Connecticut Avenue, NW
Washington, DC 20036
202-429-9272
fax: 202-429-9505

## THE DISTRIBUTORS

Possibly the most invisible element in the transfer of books from the warehouse to the consumer is the "distributor," who often supplies retailers. In recent years, a number of black-owned distributors have emerged to fill the gap left by an absence of white firms servicing the African American community. They have been a true support to black booksellers, who frequently have account woes with the publishers and traditional distributors and need more lenient credit lines to keep their stores stocked.

Carl Webber, owner of the African American Bookstore in New York City, says these distribution companies will give the black independents (like him) inventory if they have the cash to pay and without the extensive credit probe usually needed. "These black distributors ask that you can pay for the books and nothing more," Webber adds. "White publishers demand a credit application and clearance before any sale. The black distributors will ship COD or for cash. This break means a lot to stores who spend so much on basic rent and overhead."

Such flexibility means a great deal to the struggling black stores and authors with self-published books to sell. Maxwell Taylor, of the A&B Book Distributors in Brooklyn, New York, says he deals mainly with independents and small outlets. He feels pressured by established mainstream publishers who deal with bookstores directly. "They're offering them free shipping and other discounts. We can't beat those terms. To counter this, we have moved to a wider base with more independent black publishers, getting more self-published books. We have decided to be a one-stop shopper for those stores."

Another avenue taken by A&B and other black-owned distributors is to get into the publishing business themselves, printing and marketing books under their own imprint. A&B has been doing this since 1992, publishing reprints and originals, and other companies have followed suit. Many of the black-owned distributors started as street vendors in major cities, selling hard-to-get books to passersby searching for out-of-print or self-published books.

These distributors use a small sales force and sometimes a catalog. They take books, especially privately printed volumes, by consignment, which means they get a percentage of the total sales profits.

Larry Cunningham of Culture Plus, a distributor specializing in African American books, has outlets in New York and Los Angeles. "There is no major competition from the majors because we know the business and the audience," he says. "They often do not invest in books that we take. The African American book market is exploding, and it's grown to the point where the industry can't handle all the business. There is room for everybody because there are more African American readers than ever. We support black books and readers."

### General Book Distributors
American Wholesalers
Anderson News
Baker & Taylor
Book Link Inc.
Book People
Bookazine
Consortium Book Sales & Distribution
Golden Lee Book
Hastings
Ingram Book Co.
Koen Book Distributors
Levy Home Entertainment Distribution
LPC Group
National Book Distributors
New Leaf Distributing Co.
News Group—Atlanta
Publishers Group
Publishers Group West
Scholarly Book Services
Small Press Distribution
Spring Arbor Distributors

## African American Distributors

A & B Book Distributors
1000 Atlantic Avenue
Brooklyn, NY 11238
718-783-7808
fax: 718-783-7267

Africa World Press, Inc.
  & The Red Sea Press, Inc.
11-D Princess Road
Lawrenceville, NJ 08648
609-844-9583
fax: 609-844-0198
*awprsp@africanworld.com*
For ordering only, call
  800-789-1898

African World Book Distributors
2217 Pennsylvania Avenue
Baltimore, MD 21217
410-383-2006
fax: 410-383-0511

Culture Plus Book Distributors
291 Livingston Street
Brooklyn, NY 11217
718-222-9307 and 310-671-9630
fax: 718-222-9311

D & J Book Distributors
229-21B Merrick Boulevard
Laurelton, NY 11413
718-949-6161
fax: 718-949-5400
*djbook@angelfire.com*

Lushena Book Distributors
1804 W. Irving Park Road
Chicago, IL 60613
773-975-9945
fax: 773-975-0045

# WHEN HOLLYWOOD BECKONS

Money, not aesthetics or art, drives the hunger of some writers to sell their work to Hollywood. The lure of large dollars and the allure of fame keeps them hunched over their PCs far into the night, dreaming that theirs will be the goose that lays the golden egg. Following the sale and production of Terry McMillan's bestseller *Waiting to Exhale,* Tinseltown fever worsened as writers saw a growing number of books optioned, although only a scant number actually made it to the big screen.

## WHY SOME BOOKS ARE
## MORE BIG-SCREEN FRIENDLY

Book critics often point out that the novels of Michael Crichton, Stephen King, Robin Cook, and John Grisham seem written expressly for the movies. Often they are dialogue driven, with short, punchy scenes and just enough gaps in the action to fit in much-needed special effects. Hollywood is always on the prowl for fresh stories, and old recycled master plots. Not one of the studio heads wants to admit the tremendous pressure now exerted on the film industry by the rapid emergence of the adventurous cable networks, some of whom finance their own productions rather than bankroll outside projects. If the studios could conjure up a miracle, they would neutralize the competition—HBO, Showtime, USA Network, Turner Studios—that currently eats into their audience market share.

Agents and producers read the newspapers and magazines,

scouring features and gossip columns for the next Big Thing, another twist on the old and familiar, hoping to keep their restless superstars in the stable. The established actors and actresses, understanding that they are only as good as their last box-office success, need properties that will keep them in front of the public in successful vehicles. Sometimes the stars take matters into their own hands, reading the latest popular novels and stories, looking for that special something that can be presented to the studio for backing. They know what is in with fickle moviegoers; modern Westerns, exorcist tales, and tear-jerking morality tales are passé. The market is currently hot for quirky romances, high-tech science fiction, disaster thrillers, and tales of the young and confused.

Any story with obvious box-office appeal will catch Hollywood's eye, especially if it can be used as a star vehicle — something for Wesley, Denzel, or even Arnold, Bruce, or Harrison. Properties featuring a strong, virile male character in action and suspenseful situations are always popular. Actresses generally find the selection of appealing material fairly slim, frequently forcing them to write, produce, and direct their own films. A well-developed story, focused and coherent, rarely misses. The smart novel or short story, with an effective narrative voice, will succeed despite an overreliance by Hollywood on sex, car chases, and explosions. Witty, sharp dialogue has also made a comeback. However, plots and concepts that are wildly original or far-fetched get little consideration from agents or producers.

## THE AGENT WITH HOLLYWOOD CONTACTS

If your goal is to go from word to image, and get the widest audience possible, seek out an agent who knows what Hollywood needs and who possesses the good West Coast contacts. The agent should be someone who understands the whys and wherefores of placing books as film, TV, and direct-to-video properties — a true maker of the deal. Sometimes you can find these people with the big agencies, sometimes not. If you are a newcomer, be prepared to be ignored unless you have a sensational property for sale. Know up front what you want as a writer. Realistic goals and expectations are essential in negotiating your relationship with Hollywood.

As I said in an earlier section, "The Truth about Agents and Writers," check out the agents' track record with film rights, options, and deals. How many of their book deals have made it to the screen? If you cannot locate an agent wise in film negotiations, rights, and contracts, consider retaining an attorney with expertise in entertainment law, a person capable of hammering out a profitable contract. However, there is the drawback that since lawyers do not work for a flat commission, their bills for legal services can be sizable.

## HOW MUCH WILL I GET PAID?

What kind of money are we talking about here? We all know that a book can be optioned and developed, and the final script may not meet the expectations of the studio. So a developmental deal is worked with a producer—for instance, a one-year option on your book. That one-year option is the first installment of a 10 to 15 percent share of the full purchase price for a book property. With this option, the producer retains control of the property until he can finalize a deal with a film studio, TV network, or production company. Then, once the deal is made and work begins on the script, you, as the author, get full payment.

But what happens if it does fit the bill? What happens if everything falls into place with the initial sale? According to premier agents, the top-of-the-line novels sell for between $2 and $3 million, whereas capably wrought works with lower appeal can go for $1 million or less. The big guns, Grisham, King, and Crichton, can command $8 million or more for each work.

Following the sale, many writers choose not to get involved

with the filming; consequently, the final product may bear little resemblance to the one that came from countless nights at
the PC. They deposit the check for the sale and go on to their
next work. Compromises, both artistic and financial, can entirely reshape the feel of the book. Novelists often say they
must divorce themselves from the movie characters rather
than become depressed by witnessing the mutation of the people created on their pages.

Once the sale is made, the writer no longer owns anything
in the novel, even though its cast of characters may feel like
the author's children. The artistry of a film will rarely surpass
that of a masterly novel, despite the presence of even unre-
servedly high abilities in its director and scriptwriters. A film
can restate major scenes, imply the protagonist's mental state,
and bring scenery and setting to life, but the deep connection
between reader and page cannot be displaced. Great literature
seldom translates into great film entertainment. The suspense
and power of the text too often goes limp on the screen.
Nevertheless, a good film can sell books and make its author a
household name.

IN 1944, the poet Owen Dodson was invited to the
home of Orson Welles, a film and theater director, producer, writer, and actor—the creator of the movie *Citizen Kane*. The two men discussed the making of a film
based on the life of Toussaint L'Ouverture and the
founding of Haiti, the first free black republic in the
Western Hemisphere. Welles, a brilliant maverick, was
eager to do the project. He said he would direct the film
for free, adding that he saw the work as a part of a trilogy.
The grand cinematic work, he insisted, would be filmed
in color and could be made for several million dollars.
Dodson was elated, until he heard Welles wryly ask him:
"You can raise that money, can't you?"

## THE DREAM AND THE REALITY

Ultimately, any relationship with Hollywood is a waiting game. Nothing happens at the speed of light. Read what Sheneska Jackson, author of *Caught Up in the Rapture* and *Blessings*, recently told a *Mosaic Literary Magazine* interviewer about her film flirtation: "I was all excited until I heard about all the books that get optioned. Now, even though I have more suitors, I know not to get caught up in Hollywood. Everything takes a really long time."

That cold-eyed view of the film industry was shared by John Ridley, a screenwriter and the author of two noir novels, *Stray Dogs* and *Love Is a Racket*. In a Knopf publicity statement, he cautioned against believing that a film sale would immediately take its author from rags to riches. "When I first came to Los Angeles from New York, I used to sit around and wait for the one Hollywood phone call that would change my life," he explained. "What I discovered is that there's never one specific thing that changes your life. Instead there's a succession of small, incremental changes until you wake up one day and realize things are different."

## BOOKS AND FILMS: OLD FRIENDS AND MUCH HISTORY

Traditionally, Hollywood and the literary community have been partners in a big way, since the start of the film industry at the beginning of the century. Witness D. W. Griffith's infamous *Birth of a Nation*, based on the racist novel *The Clansman*. Witness Margaret Mitchell's Old South potboiler *Gone With the Wind*, which caused a sensation in 1939. Racial issues in a film rarely make for a productive Oscar night—possibly because so few African American writers and directors occupy positions of prestige and bankable clout in Hollywood. Maybe Spike Lee, Bill Duke, Carl Franklin, John Singleton, and Forest Whitaker can get a project through the studio maze after intense wrangling, but even this select group still lacks the influence of Steven Spielberg or Barry Levinson. And Spielberg himself, with his slave rebellion epic, *Amistad*, was largely ignored at Oscar time. Some say the oversight could be laid to the legal battle with the black novelist Barbara Chase-Riboud over rights to the story. Others say it was the subject itself that turned the Academy members off.

Just a highly select few African American writers have ever been welcomed into the film world in the manner that greeted William Faulkner, F. Scott Fitzgerald, Raymond Chandler, Nathanael West, Aldous Huxley, and John Dos Passos during that golden era of the 1930s and 1940s. In contemporary times, the McMillan magic is an exception, with Alice Walker's *The Color Purple* and Walter Mosley's *Devil in a Blue Dress* also entered as winning rarities. Hollywood largely sticks with the comfortable commercial formulas, venturing out into new frontiers only when prodded by the independent film industry. The independents, always on the cutting edge, have traditionally provided black writers and directors the opportunity to work and excel, from Melvin Van Peebles's pioneering *Sweet Sweetback's Baadasssss Song* to the recent offerings of *Daughters of the Dust*, *Eve's Bayou*, and *Soul Food*.

Yes, Hollywood buys several hundred books yearly. But remember that while 60,000 books reach the shelves annually, only slightly more than 450 films are produced yearly. Don't think that your book will never be lensed if it isn't purchased by Hollywood. There is always television, which, historically and presently, betters the record of the film industry in using black talent. Ask Oprah. Dorothy West's *The Wedding* never would have appeared on the big screen; Haley's *Roots* phenomenon never could have occurred at the big studios—too much risk. Can you imagine any of the majors producing Ellison's *Invisible Man*, Walker's *Meridian*, Baldwin's *Another Country*, Jones's *Corregidora*, Schuyler's *Black No More*, Butler's *Kindred*, Wright's *The Outsider*, or Reed's *Flight to Canada*? No way. It's unlikely that any of these works will be premiering at your local movie theater anytime soon.

Still, there has been some progress and, surprisingly, more African American writers are getting projects "green-lighted" by TV studios than ever before. Agents see all kinds of opportunities opening up there. The TV networks believe they can strike gold again with another miniseries à la Haley's *Roots*, so they've used two of his lesser posthumous works, *Queen* and *Mama Flora's Family*, both modest successes by comparison. Television offers respectable dollars for rights to a nonfiction book or a novel, hitting seven figures in exceptional cases, but the customary payment is between $200,000 and $300,000.

Needless to say, the big money remains in a Hollywood sale. There was a time when all the writing in Hollywood was done by a handful of authors—the Ben Hecht types. That is changing. The science of economics, and not affirmative action or Christian charity, is altering the rules of the game. Take a look at the *Hollywood Reporter* and *Daily Variety*, where the slow but steady progress of African American writers and directors can be charted. Keep writing. If your book is good, it can find its way to your local Cineplex.

And with the increasing popularity of black fiction and nonfiction, especially books concerning historical figures and personalities, the potential for transforming African American topics into marketable film material is slowly being realized. And have we failed to mention that more blacks than any other segment of our population are regular moviegoers? We love the big screen, and that translates into money for Hollywood. Where there is a market, there is interest. As with all things black—whether hairstyles, dances, TV sitcoms, or music—economics underlies every decision made about which books are published and which books are adapted for film. Thus, this very lucrative African American market is now getting closer consideration from Hollywood. So, writers, take a chance, be patient, and get your books out there!

# SMALL-PRESS PUBLISHING

## FINDING A PRESS TO PUBLISH YOUR BOOK

When you have explored every avenue of mainstream publishing, another possibility exists for bringing your work of fiction, nonfiction, or poetry to the bookstores. Publishing with a small press may be just what you need to make that breakthrough. Indeed, the role of small presses has grown in recent years, due to the ever-increasing emphasis among the major publishing houses on books that bring in huge profits. That stress on blockbusters and bestsellers has left many writers of serious fiction and poetry out in the cold until they explore other alternatives.

Officials at the Council of Literary Magazines and Presses have served as cheerleaders of the small presses for years, touting them as the choice for the younger writer with talent and no established track record with a major house. Small presses, like most commodities in the marketplace, come in all shapes and sizes, including those with specialties and regional appeal. Unlike many of the book conglomerates, many of the smaller presses will take a chance on the untested author.

## SMALL PRESSES

Dealing with a small press requires patience, for many independent publishers have limited staff and are inadequately funded. Often their profits barely cover their costs of production, distribution, and marketing. Although many small presses receive thousands of manuscripts yearly, they frequently publish only three to six books annually. Your patience may be tested as you wait for a response on your submission, but remember that a response may take time with a small staff. Upon acceptance, your advance may be small or no advance may be offered, and the publisher may ask you to wait for royalties that come only after a substantial number of the print run has actually been sold. Don't expect the first print runs at a small publishing house to run in the thousands. An average print run of a novel, poetry volume, or short-story collection may be fewer than one thousand copies.

To accomplish the task of getting your book some ink in the media, you must assume a greater role in the marketing and promotion of your work. Don't expect the independent publisher with his limited budget and tiny staff to focus all his time, energy, and resources on you. There are things you can do to speed the process along while taking responsibility for the promotion of your book:

· Send out review copies to local and regional newspapers yourself.
· Identify regional and national magazines or Internet sites that can review, excerpt, or promote your book.
· Create press releases and fliers to announce your book's publication and increase your market share.
· Take a marketing or self-promotion seminar and learn how to be hands-on in every area of the marketing campaign for your book.

Most small presses will be delighted to see you take an active role, as long as the emphasis is on your partnership in making your book a success.

# INDEPENDENT AFRICAN AMERICAN PUBLISHERS

▲▲

*"It must be very, very difficult not to write because there's certainly plenty of things to write, but the whole context of the novel seems to have moved into another ballfield, you can do almost anything you want . . . yet you have to remain in contact with the consciousness of your reader at the same time you are seeing things yourself. How much can we feed back, how much should we feed back, and how much does our audience want us to give back?"*

— WILLIAM DEMBY
From *Interviews with Black Writers*

▲▲

The legacy of the small independent press in the African American community is a long one. Historically, the number of small black publishers was a tiny fraction of the larger market before the advent of the growth of nationalist consciousness, which seeded the Black Arts Movement in the 1960s, when an explosion of specialty houses emerged to meet the readership in inner-city neighborhoods.

In 1921, Carter G. Woodson, the noted educator, founded the Associated Publishers, which published many significant trade books by influential African American authors until his death in 1950. Another important midsize black publisher, the Associates in Negro Folk Education, headed by Howard University professor Alain Locke in the 1930s, released several noteworthy titles by such authors as Sterling Brown and Ralph Bunche.

In the 1960s and 1970s, other small presses produced poetry and nonfiction, primarily essays, highlighting the political and social concerns of the African American community.

Among those in the forefront of this Black Arts revolution was Dudley Randall's Detroit-based Broadside Press, which published such poets as Sonia Sanchez, Nikki Giovanni, Haki Madhubuti, and Lance Jeffers. Madhubuti's Third World Press reworked the Black Aesthetic with a long-standing series of volumes on cultural and psychological issues by writers such as Chancellor Williams, Gwendolyn Brooks, Frances Cress Welsing, Useni Eugene Perkins, Delores P. Aldridge, Acklyn Lynch, and Amiri Baraka. Brooks's *Blacks* and Welsing's *The Isis Papers* have been huge sellers for the Chicago-based company. Naomi Long Madgett's Lotus Press was also one of the pioneers of this highly creative period, producing a host of first-rate poetry volumes.

Currently, a number of midsize African American publishers have stepped forward to fill the cultural information gap not satisfied by mainstream publishers. With thousands of small presses in operation, only a modest twenty of that number are run by African Americans, including Black Classic Press, Arabesque/BET, Genesis Press, Urban Ministries Inc., Writers & Readers, African American Images, Third World Press, Pines One Publications, Black Words, Africa World Press, and Just Us Books.

African American Images of Chicago emphasizes a more political bent with provocative authors such as Mary C. Lewis, Pansye Atkinson, Jawanza Kunjufu, and Thomas Parham. Three Continents Press in Colorado Springs, Colorado, has released an ongoing line of Caribbean, African, and Latin American studies. Writers & Readers, under the guidance of Glenn Thompson, has continually released quality books from its eclectic line, including the popular For Beginners series, *Drops of This Story* by Suheir Hammad, and *Seasons of Dust* by Ifeona Fulani. Black Classic Press in Baltimore publishes both reprints and new titles.

## INFORMATION ABOUT INDEPENDENT PUBLISHERS

Anyone seeking to determine what small press may be right for his or her work can purchase a copy of the *International Directory of Little Magazines and Small Presses*, which includes more than a thousand pages of entries for independent publishers. With nearly 30,000 small presses currently in operation, doing a bit of preparation and research will go a long way in preventing a waste of time and energy in your search. Feel free to call or write any prospective publisher with your questions and concerns.

For many writers, finding the appropriate small publisher begins with a trip to the library and browsing the current issue of the *Literary Market Place (LMP)*. Another outlet for small-press publishing owners, would-be publishers, writers, and anyone interested in finding out how this form of publishing works can write to the Small Press Center (20 W. 44th Street, New York, New York 10036, 212-764-7021). The center offers a number of audiotapes on the business of small-press publishing and periodic workshops with successful independent publishers. Other areas covered by the center are editors on editing; legal and business basics for independent publishers; selling your books to chain stores, independent bookstores, distributors, and wholesalers; and book advertising, promotion, and publicity.

One important avenue of information about independent publishers is COSMEP, the International Association of Independent Publishers, with a membership of nearly 1,500. The organization's monthly newsletter is full of facts and figures of great interest to small publishers and self-publishers with topics such as stores and libraries that feature small-press books, lists of expos and conferences, grant news, and new data on innovations in production and marketing.

Many established writers will often attempt to dissuade a young author from publishing with a small press, noting their low budgets and distribution problems. But they fail to mention the fine quality of book production and personal care given to the volumes printed by many of these independent publishers. The market for independent presses has been increasing steadily and many of these houses are on the cutting edge in finding new methods for increasing their visibility in the marketplace. Don't be discouraged by naysayers. If you're considering the small-press option, research the track record of the publishers best suited to your work by requesting a catalog and identifying their particular niche. Query your favorite bookseller about the publisher's reputation. Take a chance. The rewards for your efforts may surprise you.

## PAUL COATES

### PUBLISHER OF BLACK CLASSIC PRESS

For Paul Coates, the publisher of Black Classic Press, the idea for the black-owned independent publishing house grew out of a community political action movement in 1972. The quiet and assured Coates, a former Black Panther member, was determined to find new ways to promote the struggle of African Americans in the communities that most needed the self-affirming messages of his self-determination organization. Black Classic Press, as originally envisioned, would be a bookstore, a printing company, and a publishing firm.

"I wanted to assure that black people had a voice, that we could articulate ourselves," Coates recalled of the 1978 start-up of his Baltimore-based press. "The books we publish must articulate ourselves and serve the needs of our community now and 200 years from now. Someone in our community must maintain our image with integrity. We must be true to ourselves. We must keep an accurate record of ourselves, our mistakes and triumphs, so it can be studied and critiqued."

The Black Classic Press, having passed its twentieth anniversary in 1999, now includes in its catalog more than seventy fiction, nonfiction, and poetry titles by and about people of

African descent, with a specialty of resurrecting nonfiction books currently out of print. In 1996, Coates's resourcefulness embraced the concept of virtual books as part of BCP's Publishing On Demand program, which uses a digital printer to publish one copy of a book or more copies, as ordered. Along with offering this service to small publishers, he has overcome many of his company's production difficulties, such as paper costs, and transferred nearly one-third of his titles into the on-demand process.

"Many of the books we'll publish with this system will not be black books," Coates admits. "We're not limited to publications by African Americans, because, politically speaking, there are some books we wouldn't publish."

As a leading official of the National Association of Black Book Publishers, which was established in 1973, Coates explains that many independent African American publishers are fighting for survival as some financial resources and black-owned book outlets have dwindled. The association, with twenty-three members, has been in the vanguard of the battle to form a coalition to aid the black independent presses in keeping afloat fiscally during rapidly changing times in the publishing world.

"In some respects, publishing is in a financial downturn," the BCP publisher says. "There is currently an adjustment in this high-tech environment, going from the old to the new. The whole industry is changing and so many of the old models of delivering information are no longer effective. As independents, we are not immune to the financial environment. We've got to keep our eyes open for the things people want to read. We've got to see ourselves as publishers, finding money, conducting sound businesses. We've got to keep moving ahead."

In January 1997, Coates's BCP dream got a big boost when it published *Gone Fishin'*, the first book in the highly commercial Easy Rawlins mystery series, written by Walter Mosley. The move earned the publisher plenty of media coverage and praise. Mosley, an ardent supporter of the African American independent press, was hailed for backing the courageous venture at a time when the book could have grabbed a huge fee from his publisher, W. W. Norton.

"The deal worked out fine, since this book allowed us to gain a tremendous amount of experience and exposure," Coates says. "Walter hoped it would start a trend with established writers. On the other hand, I wanted a structure to bring those people into, because a move like this has its demands. If another person of Mosley's stature brought a book to us, we'd have to struggle to publish it. But this was a monumental breakthrough."

Other African American independent publishers point to BCP as one of the houses pushing ahead in publishing to alter the status quo. Coates understands that the future may be rocky economically for many of the black independents, including his company.

"As a publishing company, our future lies in two directions," he explains. "First, there is our ability to raise the money to be a serious publishing company. This money will allow us to maintain, expand, and keep our publishing program intact during times of adversity. Second, we hold open the possibility of working with a larger company, which will permit us to accomplish larger things. The goal is a solid, productive business."

Asked if the African American independent press can survive, Coates is at once very optimistic and cautious. "Some will survive and others will thrive," he concludes. "The question is, just how many of these black companies will survive?"

## GLENN THOMPSON

### WRITERS & READERS PUBLISHING INC.

Glenn Thompson, born in Harlem, started Writers & Readers Publishing Inc. in 1974, publishing over 300 titles to date. He says the company began with a $300 nest egg and a determined effort to publish the type of books for the African

American community that he couldn't find in English book-stores. As an expatriate, he felt there were political and cul-tural topics that were neglected in print and taboo in open discussion.

Thompson's For Beginners series, created for lay readers who "wanted to know everything," became an instant hit and the commercial spine for the rapidly developing publishing house. The highly popular series, known for its witty narrative and hip graphics, covers an incredibly wide range of topics, including Fanon, black women, Che, structuralism and post-structuralism, Zen, Chomsky, erotica, I Ching, Sartre, Mal-colm X, the Jewish Holocaust, Miles Davis, Virginia Woolf, and sex, among others.

The rebellious publisher also published several inter-national authors, translating French, Turkish, Russian, and Greek works. "I wanted my company to have a very global view," Thompson explains. "I wanted to publish controversial books and make them popular. I wanted to be different from other black publishers. I wanted to be global, with no subject being out of bounds. I believed that we as publishers can have breadth and depth outside of our defined role."

To continue that maverick tradition, he founded Harlem River Press in 1990 with the goal of publishing some of the younger, pioneering black voices. Some of the titles featured on the imprint are *In The Tradition: An Anthology of Young Black Writers*, edited by Kevin Powell and Ras Baraka; *Seasons of Dust*, by Ifeona Fulani; *Drops of This Story*, by the Pal-estinian poet Suheir Hammad; *Weather Reports*, by Quincy Troupe; and two classic reprints by the late Black Panther Huey Newton, *Revolutionary Suicide* and *To Die for the People*. The imprint was involved in a lawsuit with the successful author Iyanla Vazant over the rights to her Writers & Readers book, *Interiors: A Black Woman's Healing . . . in Progress*. However, the matter was ultimately settled amicably.

Thompson also founded Black Butterfly Children's Books, top-rated fiction and nonfiction created by such award-winning talent as Eloise Greenfield, Jan Spivey Gilchrist, and Tom Feelings. Recently, he brought in a new publisher, Deborah Dyson, to run both imprints, believing her youth and expertise would energize them. Despite some financial constraints, Thompson sees bigger and brighter days ahead for Writers & Readers and its imprints, continuing to publish new titles each year.

## HAKI R. MADHUBUTI

### THIRD WORLD PRESS

Haki Madhubuti was born Don L. Lee in Little Rock, Arkansas, and relocated with his family to Detroit in 1943. Upon his mother's death when Lee was sixteen, he moved to Chicago, where he worked briefly as a magazine salesman following his graduation from high school. Later, he served three years in the army.

"I started writing in 1960, but one incident awakened me to the power of the word. While in the army, I was reading Paul Robeson's *Here I Stand* when a white army officer snatched the book out of my hands, saying: "What are you doing reading this black communist?" He tore the pages out of the book and gave them to other recruits to use as toilet paper. I understood what the written word could do right then and there." Lee's world was transformed when, as a young poet, he met Dudley Randall, the legendary publisher of Broadside Press. Randall, who became a mentor to the novice writer, published his first book of poems, *Think Black*, in 1967. As Lee commented in his early years, "Poetry is the most liberating form in all literature. It is the foundation for all other things." Six other poetry volumes for Broadside followed, and Lee's reputation as an inventive, politically conscious poet with a lifesaving message grew in black America.

As his work was distributed from coast to coast, Lee became an undisputed leader of the Black Arts Movement of the 1960s. He established the Third World Press with $400 saved from poetry readings as a means of bringing other vital African American voices to the public. The following year, the new publisher pumped more funding into his fledgling press by working as an instructor at a number of local universities. He toured constantly, taking his words of community self-determination and black pride to college campuses and youth and community centers: "The poets opened my creative vision and soul: Langston Hughes, Melvin Tolson, Claude McKay, Jean Toomer, Arna Bontemps, and Gwendolyn Brooks. They touched me with their passion and imagination. Music had the same effect, especially my idols, Satchmo and Miles. Music is the basis of all language, most notably classical black language.

"I never put myself in a situation where anybody outside of my culture would know more about me and my people than I did. Study became my first love. I read a book a day. Being intellectual and thirsty for knowledge opened doors. If you're ignorant, you don't know how the world works and how power operates.

"When I founded Third World Press in 1967, there were five or six black publishers, and that number has risen to seventy-five today. The company is located in a three-story building in Chicago's South Side, a full-service publishing house, with fourteen people on staff. We've had several million-copy sellers, including Chancellor Williams's *Destruction of Black Civilization*, Frances Welsing's *Isis Papers*, and my essays, *Black Men: Obsolete, Single, Dangerous?* We understand that our people read everything and have a wide range of interests. In the future, we want to move to compete with the large New York publishing companies, offering our writers comparable financial packages. We're moving to pursue older, established writers while discovering many of the exciting new voices out there."

A voracious reader, Lee channeled his commitment to African American literature into his 1971 founding of the *Black Books Bulletin*, a quarterly review periodical that he got off to a promising start but which failed after a solid eight-year run, falling victim to the usual economic maladies that destroy new magazines, including distribution woes and a lack of paid subscribers. In 1973, Lee assumed the Swahili name Haki Madhubuti, and he launched a more intense campaign for the promotion and strengthening of black cultural and educational institutions through the late 1970s and 1980s.

Madhubuti's efforts in the 1990s have stressed political action to address the crucial social and political issues confronting the African American community. A global citizen, Madhubuti remains a tireless advocate for African American literature and is currently the director of the Gwendolyn Brooks Center at Chicago State University. He is the proud father of five children, and husband to Safisha Lee, a writer and professor at Northwestern University.

# UNIVERSITY PRESSES

For many authors of scholarly or academic works, a mainstream publisher may not be the place to submit their manuscripts. Most do not acquire that type of book, since the majority of these volumes are not commercial sellers. University presses, where most manuscripts are approved by an editorial board of faculty members and scholars, seek out well-researched manuscripts pertaining to education, literature, art criticism, sociology, anthropology, history, cultural issues, philosophy, and the sciences. Often, these houses use in-house scholars and professors to fill out their publishing roster, but they are known to enlist experts in various fields to produce outstanding books on timely topics and controversial subjects.

Funded through university budgets or grants, these presses do not have the large financial backing to launch a large promotional or marketing effort to help a book find an audience. That is often left to the enterprising author, who will pursue ad space in literary magazines or journals to get the word out to the reader. University presses frequently publish foreign reprints of popular books, out-of-print volumes, or books deemed not profitable by big commercial publishers. In some cases, books come from referrals by faculty, who may have a text worthwhile to their classes or research.

Don't think that university presses only publish books favored by academia, because they have a fine reputation for showcasing some of this country's best, unpublicized poets. These presses print works by established writers as well as promising new talent. In every category published by university presses, every effort is made to attain the highest scholarly and literary standards, even if the book has only a regional emphasis. Although the size of the audience may be small or the print run may be limited, they try not to cut corners on production costs, so the final book from these presses is often quite exceptional in quality and artistry.

As a writer, do not expect to be paid a large advance from a university press. Their funding cannot sustain such huge outlays of cash; many of them operate on a very tight budget. Most of the editorial boards at these presses acquire books with the hope that they will become profitable over the long run, and many of them do, going back for another printing as still another generation of readers seeks out these specialized texts.

Some writers like university presses due to their willingness to consider a manuscript without the presence of an agent. However, their response time for a new work may be longer than a commercial house's, since these presses employ much smaller staffs and their editors are often overworked. It is not unusual for a well-written query letter or proposal to land a contract with one of these presses if the topic is timely or thought-provoking. Also, a writer submitting work to a university press will be greatly helped with the inclusion of a distinctive résumé or curriculum vitae, which indicates a particular expertise in a field of study or profession if the proposed project pertains to that area. Remember that these presses publish only a small number of titles each year.

Finally, the number of university presses with an exceptional catalog of current publications and strong backlists has grown in recent years. For the writer seeking to go this route, the following is a selected list of some of the more successful university presses across the country. Since the addresses of the presses are subject to change, please consult the current edition of *Literary Market Place* for up-to-date information.

Cambridge University Press
Colorado Associated University Press (University of
    Colorado Press)
Columbia University Press

Duke University Press
Georgia University Press
Harvard University Press
Howard University Press
Indiana University Press
The Johns Hopkins University Press
Kent State University Press
Louisiana State University Press
Michigan State University Press
The MIT Press
The New York University Press
Ohio State University Press
Ohio University Press
Oxford University Press
The Pennsylvania State University Press
Princeton University Press
Rutgers University Press
Southern Illinois University Press
Stanford University Press
State University of New York Press
Syracuse University Press
Temple University Press
University of Alabama Press
University of Arizona Press
University of California Press
University of Chicago Press
University of Georgia Press
University of Illinois Press
University of Massachusetts Press
University of Michigan Press
University of Minnesota Press
University of Missouri Press
University of Nebraska Press
University of New Mexico Press
University of Notre Dame Press
University of Oklahoma Press
University of Pittsburgh Press

University of South Carolina Press
University of Tennessee Press
University of Washington Press
University of Wisconsin Press
University Press of Kentucky
University Press of Mississippi
University Press of New England
University Press of Virginia
Wayne State University Press
Wesleyan University Press
Yale University Press

# SELF-PUBLISHING

## A PUBLISHING ALTERNATIVE

Why self-publishing? Unfortunately, there are times when a writer can't find the proper outlet, a willing publisher to produce his work. You send the manuscript out to the houses on your list, and it keeps coming back rejected. However, all of the feedback has been excellent, and you know there's a market out there for what you've written. One viable alternative can be self-publishing, printing your own work. When you truly believe in your manuscript and there are no takers in the publishing industry, self-publishing can be a satisfying, productive option. Still, there is much to learn before you take on a task equivalent to writing, directing, and starring in your own film. Here are some of your options:

## VANITY PUBLISHERS

One possibility is to inquire into the so-called vanity, or subsidy, publishing route, but you must exercise extreme caution to ensure that you get what you pay for. There are about twenty major vanity publishers, who dominate this market by printing over 80 percent of all subsidy books. According to industry figures, nearly 6,500 titles are printed by these companies annually. While some vanity publishers will promise anything to get your money, offering what seems to be an incredible deal to publish your work, it pays to shop around before investing your hard-earned cash with the first such firm you encounter. Don't let inflated dreams of hitting the literary big time cloud your judgment here, because many of these companies do not deliver on their promises.

The truth about vanity presses is that most people in the publishing industry will not take a second look at their books because of their reputation as shoddy outfits. Vanities, if you must consider this avenue of publishing, should be approached with caution and skepticism. Quiz them on their success record and ask to see some of their product. Also, contact the local Better Business Bureau to check on their background as a way of deciding whether they merit your trust.

Think about this. These publishers usually convince the author to sign a contract granting them 40 percent of the retail price and 85 percent of the subsidiary rights. Also, the entire bill for getting your manuscript printed and bound can top $25,000, the cost of a brand-new car. The vanity publishers will tell you that all promotion and distribution will be handled by their company, but the books rarely surface on any book-shelf after the printing.

For the most part, vanities are in business to make money—at your expense. After you submit your finished manuscript to them, they will publish your work in either cloth or paper at a cost that guarantees them a substantial profit. Usually, the vanity publisher will mail you about eighty free copies and send another seventy review copies out to libraries and book-stores. Most major literary publications, including *Publishers Weekly* and *The New York Times Book Review*, will not con-sider a book coming from a vanity publisher for review space in their pages. Also, remember that even if 2,000 to 3,000 copies of your book are printed, only a fraction of that number will actually be bound and completed for sale. Everything is designed to benefit the vanity publisher, not the author.

Suppose your book really starts to sell; this is where the scam begins to show itself. If your book becomes hot, the pub-lisher will pay a reasonable royalty, a percentage of the list price. But the chances of getting a bestseller from a vanity publisher are almost nil, considering the limited publicity and distribution of books published by these companies. Beware of their contracts, with the odd clauses and obscure language. Some of these companies are under investigation by the Federal Trade Commission for bilking would-be authors with their bogus contracts. If you get nervous about the confusing contract they present to you, take it to a lawyer. Also, be aware that the vanity publisher pays a substantially lower royalty on reprints of the book. No matter how much money you may spend on getting your work printed by one of the companies, the final product is often amateurish, with unprofessional covers, weak binding, and cheap paper.

What distributor wants to handle such a product? The independent and chain stores refuse to promote vanity books. Only a few libraries will allow the vanity releases access to their shelves; and most mail-order purchases will go to family and friends, who feel pity and compassion for all the money spent on such a no-win venture. If you think these vanity companies command a lion's share of the market, visit one of the independents or chains and look for their product. You find nothing, right? Overall, any dealings with a vanity publisher can only end badly for you as an aspiring author. Steer clear.

## DOING IT YOURSELF

Self-publishing has many advantages, especially over entrusting your work to a vanity publisher. First, as an author, you retain absolute control over the production, marketing, and distribution of your book. There is no editor, no publicity department or publisher to enrage with your demands. When you publish your own work, you determine the appearance of your book, the release date, and the methods of marketing and promotion. Furthermore, there is no middleman between you and your profits.

The tradition of self-publishing writers is a strong one, and the list of notable names is very long. In world literature, some are very recognizable: James Joyce, D. H. Lawrence, Edgar

Allan Poe, Mark Twain, Walt Whitman, George Bernard Shaw, and Carl Sandburg, among others. In African American literature, the roll call is just as impressive: Paul Lawrence Dunbar, Elijah Muhammad, Ishmael Reed, Nikki Giovanni, David Walker, Harriet E. Wilson, Oscar Micheaux, Frances E. W. Harper, and J. A. Rogers. Sadly, most of these brave souls did not make money on their privately printed books, but their endeavors opened the door for greater visibility and later renown.

The self-publishing option has worked very well for many current bestselling authors. E. Lynn Harris turned the fortunes of black male fiction around when he self-published his first novel, *Invisible Life*, in 1992. With the novel, a candid tale of bisexual love and deception, he traveled cross-country, peddling it to black beauty shops and black bookstores. *Invisible Life* gained so much notice that a major publisher bought the paperback rights and contracted him for a sequel, *Just As I Am*. His second novel sold solidly, followed by his third, *And This Too Shall Pass*, which soared to *The New York Times*'s bestseller list. Another writer, Kimberla Lawson Roby, used the same winning formula with her privately printed novel, *Behind Closed Doors*, which she published after fourteen agents and eight major publishing houses had rejected it. After tireless promoting, the book made the Blackboard African American bestseller list within one month of its publication. Her second book, *Here And Now*, was picked up by Kensington, a mainstream publisher, before achieving bestselling status.

Other authors, such as Omar *(Fly Girl)* Tyree, Van *(Beeperless Remote)* Whitfield, and Anita *(Emily, The Yellow Rose of Texas)* Bunkley have accomplished their dream of getting into print and gaining a contract with a mainstream house by self-publishing and promoting their first novels to success. Each of these writers persisted with hard work and determination, first identifying their audience and then effectively getting their work out into the marketplace.

No one can guarantee you a profit from your self-publishing effort. In order to minimize the chance of a financial loss, carefully plot out your self-publishing campaign. This is not an easy task, there being no publisher to cover all of the major and minor chores needed to make this venture a success. A self-published author must be detail-oriented, totally organized, and cool under fire. As the head of your publishing venture, you assume responsibility for the care and grooming of the manuscript, the editing, proofreading, copyediting, design, typesetting, production, promotion, sales, and distribution of the final product. Those're a lot of hats to wear. But if you expect to get the completed book that you imagined at the start of the project, wear them you must.

Or maybe not.

Here's a list of pointers that will make your job somewhat easier:

· Don't trick yourself into thinking that you can do everything by yourself. Bring on other people to handle those areas that you can't manage or that you lack the skills necessary to do effectively.

· Give special attention to the editing of your text. If you're not skilled enough to tackle that task, hire a freelance editor and/or copyeditor.

· Don't be cheap if you want a finished book that reflects the best of your talent. Your cover must be aesthetically intriguing, informative, and evocative of the book's contents. Readers often buy books just on the power of the cover, so do not ignore its importance.

· If you scale back financially during the production of the book, that action will undercut the attractiveness and allure of the product. You do not want something that resembles a cheaply manufactured vanity release.

You must set your goals for this effort. Know why you're doing this. You want to make a profit. You want to get your book to the marketplace so your work can be read. You know how you want your book to look. You want the recognition and respect given to a published writer.

To make this dream a reality, you must manage your time and energy well.

· Research your target audience, whether the book is fiction, nonfiction, or poetry. If the book is nonfiction, research your topic carefully and thoroughly. If it is prose or poetry, make sure it's the best effort you can do at the time. Put your all into it.

· Decide on the most economical method of bringing your book to print. One of the most cost-effective ways of publishing is to submit the manuscript on a disk to a printer. This cuts typesetting costs and assures that your project will meet your release date.

· To save money, you might consider printing and binding only half of your first run, holding the remaining number on sheets to print as the demand increases. Your printer may have other ways to save you both money and time on your printing project.

· Now, with a personal computer and publishing software, you can exercise even greater control of the cost, quality, and manufacture of your book. Computer software such as Page-Maker and Quark have revolutionized the task of creating a book.

There are many books and courses available on the art of desk-top publishing, which can enable you to take advantage of all of the options offered by your computer. Invest in yourself and your book by taking the available training.

## PROMOTING YOUR BOOK

Possibly the most challenging part of self-publishing comes in the promotion, marketing, and distribution of your book. An extensive tour, with strategically scheduled signings and readings, can go a long way in getting your book to the public. Visit the chain and independent stores with copies of your book. This is where your sales abilities come into play. Despite some customary resistance to stocking privately printed volumes, more chain outlets are accepting works by African American authors in all categories.

· Explore alternative distribution outlets such as Ingram, Baker & Taylor, Small Press Distribution, and Consortium. While the first two book wholesalers are the most widely used in the industry, the last two options can be very effective in getting your book into the smaller specialty stores and independents.

· Contact every significant African American bookstore, since many of them will promote your book in a more direct, personalized manner that can generate sales. These bookstores are a valuable resource that cannot be ignored, especially if you have dreams of making it onto the Blackboard list. Amazon.com should be another stop in your marketing campaign.

· Create an attractive, informative, professional-quality press kit to mail to local and national African American newspapers, publications, and television and radio stations. Don't forget to send press releases and fliers to national organizations and associations, because some of them will invite you to sign or speak at their expos, conferences, and conventions.

· Retain the services of a professional publicist to assist you in reaching the widest audience.

· Lastly, create a website to capture the on-line market, which offers up an endless supply of highly literate and enthusiastic book buyers. Word-of-mouth support from this readership can often boost sales and gain the attention of a major book publisher.

So don't let rejection and disappointment keep you from accomplishing your goal of becoming published. If you do not believe in your work, no one else will. Self-publishing may be just the spark to get your career going. Prepare, plan, research, then take a chance!

## SELF-PUBLISHING RESOURCES

The following books can help you produce, distribute, and market your book more effectively by allowing you to master every area of the self-publishing process:

*The Complete Guide to Self-*
  *Publishing*
Tom and Marilyn Ross
c/o Writer's Digest Books
1507 Dana Avenue
Cincinnati, OH 45207

*The Publish-It-Yourself Handbook:*
  *Literary Tradition and How-To*
Edited by Bill Henderson
Pushcart Press
P. O. Box 380
Wainscott, NY 11975

*Personal Publishing*
P. O. Box 3019
Wheaton, IL 60109

*The Self-Publishing Manual: How*
  *to Write, Print & Sell Your Own*
  *Book*
Dan Poynter
Para Publishing
P.O. Box 4232
Santa Barbara, CA 93140-4232

*Selling Your Book: The Writer's*
  *Guide to Publishing and*
  *Marketing*
Dorothy Kavka
Evanston Publishing Inc.
1216 Hinman Avenue
Evanston, IL 60202

# ESSENTIAL TAX TIPS

1. Every writer, whether novice or established, has to contend with the demands of the Internal Revenue Service (IRS). Stay informed of any changes in the federal and state tax laws regarding professional writers. Remember that your goal is to control your tax burden.

2. If you feel ill-equipped to handle the financial end of your writing business, feel free to acquire the services of an accountant.

3. Keep orderly records, with all of your original stubs and receipts, in a neat, organized fashion. It is not uncommon for full-time writers working from their home to be audited by the IRS. Be prepared.

4. To stay in the IRS's good graces, maintain your records so that you can support any deductions claimed in your tax filings. Any claimed deduction must be backed by the proper documentation.

5. All writing income and expenses should be kept in separate folders and stored apart from the tax records of your family and yourself. A special marked folder for them, clearly labeled, should also contain all records of items purchased with credit cards, checks, or money orders.

6. As a fail-safe measure, record every bit of income and expense in a ledger, which will make any reference a very easy task. Don't forget to note money spent on supplies such as pens, paper, staples, and resource materials such as books and magazines.

7. Note that the ledger should contain the dates of all income and purchases, sources of income, explanations of items

bought or writing sold, along with the type and amount of payment made, such as by credit card, cash, or money order.

8. If you work from home, keep check stubs, receipts, and other transaction documentation for office expenses available in your records for your self-employment tax and home-office claims. For instance, you would keep the receipts of the purchase of a new computer or software used in your work.

9. Since tax laws on personal deductions change rapidly, see further details about deduction requirements from any local or regional IRS branch. At the office, tax personnel can supply you with basic IRS publications for your review, or consult with your accountant. A home-office deduction can get tricky if you do not know all of the guidelines.

10. For more information, log on to the IRS website (http://www.irs.ustreas.gov), if your schedule doesn't permit a visit to the branch office.

# PART II

# THE AFRICAN AMERICAN
# LITERARY HALL OF FAME

*"There is material among us for the broadest comedies and the deepest tragedies, but, besides money and leisure, it needs patience, perseverance, courage, and the hands of an artist to weave it into the literature of the country."*

—FRANCES E. W. HARPER

From her novel, *Iola Leroy* (1892)

# AFRICAN AMERICAN BOOK TIMELINE

1773 — *Poems on Various Subjects, Religious and Moral*: Phillis Wheatley's volume of verse becomes the first book of poetry published by an African American.

1789 — Olaudah Equino, an African slave, writes *The Life of Olaudah Equino or Gustavus Vassa, the African, Written by Himself*, a popular account of slavery, which made its author an international celebrity.

1791 — Benjamin Banneker, an inventor and astronomer, publishes the first scientific book written by a black author, *Banneker's Almanac*, distributed for ten years to an ever-widening readership.

1831 — Mary Prince acquires some notoriety as the first black woman in America to pen a slave narrative, *The History of Mary Prince, A West Indian Slave, Related by Herself, with the Supplement by the Editor, to Which Is Added the Narrative of Asa-Asa, a Captured African*.

1852 — Martin Delany, a physician and cofounder with Frederick Douglass of *The North Star*, stirs up controversy with his book, *The Condition, Elevation, Emancipation, and Destiny of the Colored People of the United States, Politically Considered*, which indicts abolitionists for their efforts to integrate blacks into a segregated nation.

1853 — William Wells Brown publishes the first novel by an African American writer, *Clotel: or, The President's Daughter*, the story of a mulatto in Thomas Jefferson's household.

1854 — Frances E. W. Harper, born of free blacks, promotes her book of verse, *Poems on Miscellaneous Subjects*, which sold 10,000 copies in five years.

▲▲

*"Words are now useful only as they stimulate us to blows. The office of speech is now only to point out when, where, and how to strike to the best advantage."*

— FREDERICK DOUGLASS
From *Life and Times of Frederick Douglass* (1882)

▲▲

1855 — Frederick Douglass is lionized after the release of his autobiography, *My Bondage and My Freedom*, which elevates him to national status as an African American leader and spokesman.

1859 — Harriet Wilson publishes *Our Nig*, the first novel written by an African American woman in the United States.

1862 — Alexander Crummell, an educator and minister-activist, supervises the publication of his first book, *Future of Africa*, criticizing white bigotry while celebrating the black ancestral link to Africa.

1884 — T. Thomas Fortune, often called "The Dean of Negro Newspapermen," authors *Black and White: Land, Labor and Politics in the United States*, a scathing analysis of the American political system.

1893 — Paul Lawrence Dunbar tours to support his first book of poems, *Oak and Ivy*, a volume published from his salary earned as an elevator operator.

1899 — Charles W. Chesnutt publishes his best-known work, *The Conjure Woman*, a short-fiction collection with the theme of slavery. He would later receive the Spingarn Medal for his writings.

SOMETIMES QUALITY comes with quantity. John O. Killens, a highly prolific novelist and essayist, wrote that his
understanding of what defines a long productive career
widened after a visit to W. E. B. Du Bois, author of *The
Souls of Black Folks* and numerous other works. "I vividly
recall the first time I was in Dr. Du Bois' home and
stared in respectful awe at a veritable library of books, an
institution of black erudition, and underneath the title of
almost every book was the name W. E. B. Du Bois, some
of which were published in the nineteenth century. It
was an inspiring, though chastening experience. Here is
what I mean by long-distance running."

1903—W. E. B. Du Bois, the first African American to earn a
    Ph.D., intensifies his ongoing debate with accommoda-
    tionist Booker T. Washington with the release of his clas-
    sic book, *The Souls of Black Folk*.

1912—James Weldon Johnson, poet and civil rights activist,
    shows he's a true renaissance man by publishing his in-
    fluential novel, *The Autobiography of an Ex-Colored Man*.

1922—Claude McKay, poet, achieves a major position
    among the writers and artists of the Harlem Renaissance
    with the publication of his book *Harlem Shadows*.

1923—Jean Toomer produces a classic work of the New Ne-
    gro movement, *Cane*, an imaginative blend of poetry,
    fiction, and dramatic sketches.

1926—Langston Hughes, poet and novelist, establishes his ca-
    reer in New York literary circles after the publication of
    his first verse collection, *The Weary Blues*.

1927—Countee Cullen, poet and novelist, releases one of his
    most important poetry collections, *Copper Sun*, a beauti-
    fully crafted work full of skillfully written observations.
    He was awarded more important literary prizes than any
    other African American writer of his time.

1929—Wallace Thurman tackles the problem of color preju-
    dice among African Americans in his satirical novel *The*

*Blacker the Berry*, now considered one of the essential works of the Harlem Renaissance.

**1932**—Sterling Brown, educator and poet, redefines the traditional ideas about black speech with his unique blend of message and metaphor in his book, *Southern Road*.

F REQUENTLY, A spirit of independence and individuality can inform a writer's entire body of work. Such was the case of Zora Neale Hurston, whose writings stood out from many of her peers in the Harlem Renaissance on account of the author's lack of rage, racial angst, or self-pity. "But I am not tragically colored," Hurston wrote in the 1928 essay "How It Feels to Be Colored Me": "There is no great sorrow dammed up in my soul, nor lurking behind my eyes. I do not mind at all. I do not belong to the sobbing school of Negrohood who hold that nature somehow has given them a lowdown dirty deal and whose feelings are all hurt about it. Even in the helter-skelter skirmish that is my life, I have seen that the world is to the strong regardless of a little pigmentation more or less."

**1937**—Zora Neale Hurston's most accomplished work of fiction, *Their Eyes Were Watching God*, arrives in bookstores with its unforgettable female protagonist, Janie Crawford.

**1939**—J. Saunders Redding, educator and literary critic, reaches a personal best with his definitive study of black literature, *To Make a Poet Black*.

**1940**—Richard Wright astounds the publishing world with his *New York Times* bestselling novel, *Native Son*, the first Book-of-the-Month Club Main Selection by a black author.

**1941**—William Attaway, a graduate of the Federal Writers' Project, publishes *Blood on the Forge*, often described as one of the most perceptive novels of the Great Mitigation.

**1947**—John Hope Franklin, noted historian and educator, presents an alternative view of the history of African Americans in his well-documented book, *From Slavery to Freedom*.

**1950**—A Pulitizer Prize is awarded to Gwendolyn Brooks for her brilliant poetry book, *Annie Allen*, a first for a black woman.

**1952**—Ralph Ellison earns a National Book Award with his landmark novel, *Invisible Man*.

**1953**—James Baldwin, a youth minister in Harlem, launches a distinguished literary career with his novel *Go Tell It on the Mountain*, a work that immediately establishes him as a major American writer.

**1962**—Lerone Bennett, historian and *Ebony* magazine editor, produces his monumental historical survey, *Before the Mayflower: A History of the Negro in America*.

**1965**—*The Autobiography of Malcolm X*, as told to Alex Haley, is published shortly after the political leader's assassination.

**1966**—Amiri Baraka (Leroi Jones) achieves greater stature as a cultural spokesman in the black community upon the release of *Home: Social Essays*.

**1967**—The last prophetic, full-length book from civil rights leader and Nobel laureate Martin Luther King, *Where Do We Go from Here: Chaos or Community?* adds militarism to his former targets of racism and poverty.

**1968**—Black Panther spokesman Eldridge Cleaver ignites a national debate about crime and punishment with his inflammatory book, *Soul on Ice*.

**1969**—Poet Maya Angelou brings a new candor and wisdom to American readers with her unforgettable memoir *I Know Why the Caged Bird Sings*.

**1970**—Nikki Giovanni captures the emotional fury of the Black Arts Movement with her breakthrough collection, *Black Feeling, Black Talk, Black Judgement*, published by Dudley Randall's Broadside Press, prompting her recognition as a role model for the young poets of her day.

**1971**—Ernest Gaines seizes the imagination of the nation

with his critically acclaimed novel, *The Autobiography of Miss Jane Pittman*, which chronicled the eventful life of a 108-year-old former slave.

1972 — Ishmael Reed's fictional masterpiece, *Mumbo Jumbo*, catches critics by surprise with its ingenious use of occult elements, American history, slapstick humor, collage, wit, and spontaneity.

1973 — Ai, a Guggenheim winner, stuns the poetry world with her powerful first volume, *Cruelty*.

1974 — Henry Dumas's mythic collection of posthumously published short fiction, *Ark of Bones and Other Stories*, earns critical praise after his tragic shooting death by New York City police in 1968.

1975 — Gayl Jones explores the sexual victimization of black women in her absorbing debut work, *Corregidora*, a novel that garnered glowing endorsements from literary icons James Baldwin and John Updike.

1977 — Alex Haley creates an American cultural phenomenon with his novel of African American generations, *Roots*, an international bestseller.

1978 — James Alan McPherson wins the Pulitzer Prize for his book of meticulously crafted short fiction, *Elbow Room*.

1979 — The role of African American women in their communities takes on a new meaning after the release of Michele Wallace's perceptive work, *Black Macho and the Myth of the Superwoman*.

1980 — The cultural essays of Houston A. Baker, *The Journey Back: Issues in Black Literature and Criticism*, brings new insights to the examination of the Black Aesthetic.

1981 — David Bradley's novel, *The Chaneysville Incident*, wins the hearts of reviewers and critics across the nation.

▲▲

*"Creativity cannot exist without the feminine principle, and I am sure that God is not merely male or female but He—She—Our Father—Mother God. All nature reflects this rhythmic and creative principle of feminism and femininity: the sea, the earth, the air, fire, and all life whether plant or animal. Even as they die, are born, grow, reproduce, and grow old in their cyclic time, so do we in lunar, solar, planetary cycles of meaning and change."*

— MARGARET WALKER
From *The Writer on Her Work,*
edited by Janet Sternburg

▲▲

1982—Alice Walker soars to literary heights upon the publication of her provocative novel *The Color Purple*, winner of the Pulitzer Prize and the National Book Award.

1983—Gloria Naylor's first novel, *The Women of Brewster Place*, is awarded the American Book Award for Best Novel.

1984—Samuel R. Delany, one of the legends of American science fiction, produces one of his most complex works, *Stars in My Pocket Like Grains of Sand,* a pioneering futuristic look at the issues of gender, sexuality, race, and power.

1985—The publication of James Baldwin's collected nonfiction, *The Price of the Ticket*, is eagerly anticipated, reaffirming that few writers could match his skill with the essay.

1988—Toni Morrison's fifth novel, *Beloved*, the critically acclaimed account of a black woman's battling spirit during slavery, is awarded the Pulitzer Prize.

1989—Tina McElroy Ansa's sensitive novel, *Baby of the Family*, heralds a major new talent in African American letters.

**1990**—Walter Mosley elevates the private-eye genre with the introduction of his character Easy Rawlins in his first novel, *Devil in a Blue Dress*.

**1991**—Educator Charles V. Hamilton constructs a superb political biography of the most effective black lawmaker, *Adam Clayton Powell, Jr.: The Political Biography of an American Dilemma*.

▲▲

"I find that I am activated by a strong sense of race consciousness. This grows upon me as I grow older, and though I struggle against it, it colors my writing in spite of everything I can do. There may have been many things in my life that have hurt me and I find the surest relief from these hurts is in writing."

— COUNTEE CULLEN
From "A Study of Countee Cullen" in *Crisis* (March 1926)

▲▲

**1992**—Terry McMillan redefines the terrain of African American fiction with her blockbuster novel *Waiting to Exhale*, ultimately selling 3 million copies and inspiring a film.

**1992**—bell hooks, cultural critic, publishes her passionate observations of gender and color prejudice in her book *Black Looks: Race and Representation*.

**1993**—Octavia Butler's tenth novel, *Parable of the Sower*, confirms the Hugo and Nebula award-winning writer's status as one of the most original minds in the science-fiction genre.

**1994**—Rita Dove selected as first African American U.S. poet laureate.

**1994**—E. Ethelbert Miller edits landmark poetry anthology

*In Search of Color Everywhere: A Collection of African American Poetry.*

1995 — Colin J. Powell, former chief of staff, releases his autobiography, *An American Journey,* amid speculation of his possible run for the presidency.

1995 — Editors Herb Boyd and Robert Allen's *Brotherman: The Odyssey of Black Men in America — An Anthology,* finds solid acceptance among black book buyers.

1996 — Nell Irvin Painter's exceptional biography, *Sojourner Truth: A Life, a Symbol,* is published to critical acclaim.

1996 — Poet Paul Beatty is lauded for his witty, raucous debut novel, *The White Boy Shuffle.*

1997 — Former *Miami Herald* columnist Tananarive Due explores the supernatural in her novel *My Soul to Keep.*

1998 — Reginald McKnight, award-winning author, returns to the literary scene with a haunting collection of short fiction, *White Boys.*

1998 — The enduring myth of civil rights leader Rev. Martin Luther King is explored fictionally with the publication of Charles Johnson's brilliantly written novel, *Dreamer.*

1998 — *The Autobiography of Martin Luther King,* a collection of the civil right's leader's personal writings, edited by Clayborne Carson, is published thirty years after his death.

1998 — Gayl Jones's first novel in almost two decades, *The Healing,* hails the comeback of a unique literary voice with a tale of transcendence and redemption.

1999 — Ralph Ellison's long-awaited novel *Juneteenth* is published posthumously.

1999 — Harvard University professors Kwame Anthony Appiah and Henry Louis Gates Jr. fulfill a dream of the late black scholar W. E. B. Du Bois with their landmark reference volume, *Africana: The Encyclopedia of African and African-American Experience.*

1999 — Novelist Randall Kenan's chronicle of his six-year American odyssey, *Walking on Water,* gives readers a fascinating view of black life in the last decade of the twentieth century.

**1999**—The works of philosopher/social critic Cornel West, a Harvard University professor, are assembled in an eclectic sampler of his articles, essays and interviews, *The Cornel West Reader*.

**2000**—New York University professor of journalism David J. Dent attacks racial myths and stereotypes with his candid portrait of the black community, *In Search of Black America: Discovering the African American Dream*.

**2000**—Editor Sheree R. Thomas, founding editor of the literary journal *Amansi*, presents *Dark Matters*, a pioneering anthology of African American science fiction, fantasy, and speculative fiction.

▲▲

*"Words are to be taken seriously. I try to take seriously acts of language. Words set things in motion. I've seen them doing it. Words set up atmospheres, electrical fields, charges. Words conjure. I try not to be careless about what I utter, write, sing. I'm careful about what I give voice to."*

—Toni Cade Bambara
From *The Writer on Her Work*,
edited by Janet Sternburg

▲▲

# CLASSIC AFRICAN AMERICAN FICTION

▲▲

*In literature, fiction is prized for many reasons. Pauline E. Hopkins, a leading writer of the early twentieth century, explained its role in her 1900 work,* Contending Voices: *"Fiction is of great value to any people as a preserver of manners and customs—religious, political, and social. It is a record of growth and development from generation to generation. No one will do this for us; we must ourselves."*

—PAULINE E. HOPKINS
From *Contending Voices* (1900)

▲▲

*And Then We Heard the Thunder,* John O. Killens (1962)
*The Autobiography of an Ex-Coloured Man,* James Weldon Johnson (1912)
*Autobiography of Miss Jane Pittman,* Ernest Gaines (1971)
*Black Thunder,* Arna Bontemps (1936)
*The Blacker the Berry,* Wallace Thurman (1929)
*Beloved,* Toni Morrison (1987)
*Brown Girls, Brownstones,* Paule Marshall (1959)
*Cane,* Jean Toomer (1923)
*The Catacombs,* William Demby (1965)
*Corregidora,* Gayl Jones (1975)

*The Color Purple*, Alice Walker (1982)
*The Flagellants*, Carlene Hatcher Polite (1967)
*Invisible Man*, Ralph Ellison (1952)
*Kindred*, Octavia Butler (1979)
*The Landlord*, Kristin Hunter (1966)
*The Learning Is Easy*, Dorothy West (1996)
*The Learning Tree*, Gordon Parks (1963)
*Lonely Crusade*, Chester Himes (1947)
*Manchild in the Promised Land*, Claude Brown (1965)
*Middle Passage*, Charles Johnson (1990)
*Mumbo Jumbo*, Ishmael Reed (1972)
*Native Son*, Richard Wright (1940)
*Passing*, Nella Larsen (1929)
*Roots*, Alex Haley (1976)
*Sally Hemings*, Barbara Chase-Riboud (1979)
*The Salt Eaters*, Toni Cade Bambara (1980)
*The Street*, Ann Petry (1946)
*Their Eyes Were Watching God*, Zora Neale Hurston (1937)
*There Is a Tree More Ancient Than Eden*, Leon Forrest (1973)
*The Women of Brewster Place*, Gloria Naylor (1982)

JEAN TOOMER'S classic fictional montage, *Cane*, has its roots in the author's two-month stay in 1921 as an interim principal at the Sparta Agricultural and Industrial Institute, in the Georgia town of Sparta. The book, with its magical blend of poetry and prose, made Toomer a literary star, although it sold fewer than five hundred copies. However, he abandoned the New Negro cause, denying any role as a black writer, and instructed his publisher, Boni and Liveright, never again to use the word "Negro" in connection with him. The writer declined all offers to appear in future black anthologies and did not publish again with a major house. In 1980, Howard University published a collection of Toomer's writings, *The Wayward and the Seeking*, edited by Darwin T. Turner.

# CLASSIC AFRICAN AMERICAN NONFICTION

FRIENDS AND family became greatly worried when Arna Bontemps, one of the pioneers of the Harlem Renaissance, decided to remain in the Deep South even as the civil rights campaigns became bloodier and more violent. Trying to quell their fears, he wrote in 1965: "For my own part, I am staying on in the South to write something about the changes I have seen in my lifetime, and about the Negro's awakening and regeneration. That is my theme, and this is where the main action is. . . . Having stayed this long, it would be absurd not to wait for the third act—and possibly the most dramatic."

*Ain't I a Woman: Black Women and Feminism,* bell hooks (1981)

*Before the Mayflower: A History of Black America,* Lerone Bennett Jr. (1962)

*Black Man's Burden,* John O. Killens (1965)

*Black Men: Single, Obsolete, Dangerous?,* Haki Madhubuti (1990)

*The Black Anglo-Saxons,* Nathan Hare (1965)

*The Black Book,* Middleton A. Harris (1974)

*The Black Bourgeoisie,* E. Franklin Frazier (1957)

*Black Power: The Politics of Liberation in America,* Kwame Ture and Charles V. Hamilton (1967)

*Black Rage,* William H. Grier and Price M. Cobbs (1968)

*The Cancer Journals,* Audre Lorde (1980)

*The Choice: The Issue of Black Survival in America,* Samuel Yette (1971)

*Climbing Jacob's Ladder: The Enduring Legacy of African-American Families*, Andrew Billingsley (1992)

*The Crisis of the Negro Intellectual: A Historical Analysis of the Failure of Black Leadership*, Harold Cruse (1967)

*The Destruction of Black Civilization: Great Issues of a Race from 4500 B.C. to 2000 A.D.*, Chancellor Williams (1971)

*Families in Peril: An Agenda for Social Change*, Marian Wright Edelman (1987)

*The Fire Next Time*, James Baldwin (1963)

*From Slavery to Freedom: A History of Black Americans*, John Hope Franklin (1947)

*Malcolm X: The Man and His Times*, John Henrik Clarke (1969)

*Message to the Blackman in America*, Elijah Muhammad (1965)

*The Mis-Education of the Negro*, Carter G. Woodson (1933)

*On Being Negro in America*, Saunders Redding (1951)

*Seize the Time: The Story of the Black Panther Party and Huey P. Newton*, Bobby Seale (1970)

*Sex and Racism in America*, Calvin Hernton (1965)

*Shadow and Act*, Ralph Ellison (1964)

*The Shadow That Scares Me*, Dick Gregory (1968)

*Soul on Ice*, Eldridge Cleaver (1968)

*The Souls of Black Folk*, W. E. B. Du Bois (1903)

*Strategies for Freedom: The Changing Patterns of Black Protest*, Bayard Rustin (1976)

*12 Million Black Voices*, Richard Wright (1941)

*To Be Equal*, Whitney M. Young (1964)

*Where and When I Enter: The Impact of Black Women on Race and Sex in America*, Paula Giddings (1984)

*Where Do We Go from Here: Chaos or Community?*, Martin Luther King Jr. (1967)

# CLASSIC AFRICAN AMERICAN ANTHOLOGIES AND COLLECTIONS

*Amistad,* edited by John A. Williams (1970)

*The Best Short Stories by Negro Writers: An Anthology from 1899 to the Present,* edited by Langston Hughes (1967)

*Black Fire: An Anthology of Afro-American Writing,* edited by Larry Neal and Leroi Jones (1968)

*Black Literature in America,* edited by Houston A. Baker Jr. (1972)

*Black Short Story Anthology,* edited by Woodie King (1972)

*The Black Woman: An Anthology,* edited by Toni Cade [Bambara] (1970)

*Breaking Ice: An Anthology of Contemporary African American Fiction,* edited by Terry McMillan (1994)

*Brotherman: The Odyssey of Black Men in America,* edited by Herb Boyd and Robert Allen (1995)

*Cavalcade: Negro American Writing from 1760 to the Present,* Arthur P. Davis and Saunders Redding (1971)

*A Century of the Best Black American Short Stories,* edited by John Hendrik Clarke (1993)

*Dark Symphony: Negro Literature in America,* edited by James Emmanuel and Theodore L. Gross (1968)

*Daughters of Africa: An International Anthology of Words and Writing by Women of African Descent,* edited by Margaret Busby (1994)

*Giant Talk: An Anthology of Third World Writings,* edited by Quincy Troupe and Rainer Schulte (1975)

*Midnight Birds: Stories of Contemporary Black Women Writers,* edited by Mary Helen Washington (1980)

*The Negro Caravan,* Sterling Brown (1941)

*New Black Voices,* edited by Abraham Chapman (1972)
*The New Negro,* edited by Alain Locke (1925)
*Soon, One Morning: New Writing by American Negroes,
    1940–1962,* Herbert Hill (1963)
*We Be Word Sorcerers,* edited by Sonia Sanchez (1973)

## CLASSIC AFRICAN AMERICAN MEMOIRS AND AUTOBIOGRAPHIES

THE ROLE of a collaborator or a ghostwriter requires discipline, compromise, and patience. Alex Haley, of *Roots* fame, learned this lesson while working with Malcolm X on the leader's autobiography. The former Black Muslim, under pressure from angry Nation of Islam members and snooping FBI agents, trusted few people outside his family and longtime friends in the final, most turbulent, years of his life. He once called Haley in the dead of night and said: "I trust you seventy percent." Then he hung up before the writer could say anything. In time, the suspicions passed and the two men became close friends, completing the work necessary for the book that *Time* magazine praised as one of the ten most important nonfiction books of the twentieth century.

*A Lonely Rage, The Autobiography of Bobby Seale*, Bobby Seale (1978)

*A Long Way from Home*, Claude McKay (1937)

*A Man Called White: The Autobiography of Walter White*, Walter White (1948)

*A Taste of Power: A Black Woman's Story*, Elaine Brown (1992)

*Alone with Me: A New Autobiography*, Eartha Kitt (1976)

*Along This Way: The Autobiography of James Weldon Johnson*, James Weldon Johnson (1933)

*Angela Davis: An Autobiography*, Angela Davis (1974)

*The Autobiography of Leroi Jones*, Amiri Baraka (1984)

*The Autobiography of Louis Armstrong*, Louis Armstrong (1979)

*The Autobiography of Malcolm X*, Malcolm X (with Alex
   Haley) (1965)
*Barbara Jordan: A Self-Portrait*, Barbara Jordan (1970)
*The Big Sea: An Autobiography*, Langston Hughes (1940)
*Black and Conservative: George S. Schuyler*, George S.
   Schuyler (1966)
*The Black Notebooks: An Interior Journey*, Toi Derricotte (1998)
*Bone Black: Memories of Girlhood*, bell hooks (1996)
*Breaking Barriers: A Memoir*, Carl Rowan (1991)
*The Color of Water: A Black Man's Tribute to His White
   Mother*, James McBride (1996)
*Colored People: A Memoir*, Henry Louis Gates Jr. (1994)
*A Colored Woman in a White World*, Mary Church Terrell
   (1940)
*Coming of Age in Mississippi*, Anne Moody (1969)
*Die! Nigger, Die!*, H. Rap Brown (1969)
*Dust Tracks on a Road*, Zora Neale Hurston (1942)
*Here I Stand*, Paul Robeson (1958)
*I Know Why the Caged Bird Sings*, Maya Angelou (1970)
*In My Place*, Charlayne Hunter-Gault (1992)
*Josephine*, Josephine Baker and Jo Bouillon (1976)
*Journey to Justice*, Johnnie L. Cochran Jr. (1996)
*Laughing in the Dark: From Colored Girl to Woman of Color*,
   Patrice Gaines (1994)
*Lena*, Lena Horne with Richard Schickel (1966)
*Life Notes: Personal Writings by Contemporary Black Women*,
   edited by Patricia Bell-Scott (1994)
*Makes Me Wanna Holler: A Young Black Man in America*,
   Nathan McCall (1994)
*Mama's Girl*, Veronica Chambers (1996)
*Manchild in the Promised Land*, Claude Brown (1965)
*Migrations of the Heart*, Marita Golden (1987)
*Miles: The Autobiography*, Miles Davis with Quincy Troupe
   (1989)
*The Motion of Light in Water: Sex and Science Fiction
   Writing in the East Village, 1960–1965*, Samuel R. Delany
   (1988)

*Music Is My Mistress*, Duke Ellington (1973)

*Narrative of the Life of Frederick Douglass*, Frederick Douglass (1845)

*The Narrative of Sojourner Truth*, Sojourner Truth (1850)

*Nigger: An Autobiography*, Dick Gregory (1964)

*Parallel Time: Growing Up in Black and White*, Brent Staples (1994)

*The Prisoner's Wife*, Asha Bandele (1999)

*The Quality of Hurt: The Autobiography of Chester Himes*, Chester Himes (1971)

*Report from Part One: An Autobiography*, Gwendolyn Brooks (1972)

*Revolutionary Suicide*, Huey P. Newton (1973)

*Standing Fast: The Autobiography of Roy Wilkins*, Roy Wilkins (1982)

*Unafraid of the Dark: A Memoir*, Rosemary Bray (1998)

*Up from Slavery*, Booker T. Washington (1901)

*Voluntary Slavery: My Authentic Negro Experience*, Jill Nelson (1993)

*Wayward Child: A Personal Odyssey*, Addison Gayle Jr. (1977)

THE JAZZ trumpeter Dizzy Gillespie once recalled how the popularity of the author-entertainer-activist Paul Robeson thrived in African American communities despite an eight-year federal government ban on the man's performing or traveling. Privately printed collections of Robeson's speeches circulated in black neighborhoods long before the controversial publication of the great man's popular 1958 autobiography, *Here I Stand.*

"A well-known baseball player was sitting in a Harlem restaurant and somebody passed out a petition for Robeson," Dizzy recalled. "The athlete said he didn't want to sign anything for a traitor and the entire restaurant gathered around him until he took back his statement."

# BIRTHS OF NOTABLE AFRICAN AMERICAN AUTHORS

| | |
|---|---|
| 1711 | Jupiter Hammons |
| 1753 | Phillis Wheatley |
| 1812 | Martin Delany |
| 1813 | William Wells Brown |
| 1815 | Henry Highland Garnet |
| 1817 | Frederick Douglass |
| 1825 | Frances E. W. Harper |
| 1837 | Charlotte L. Forten |
| 1849 | Archibald H. Grimke |
| 1856 | T. Thomas Fortune |
| | Booker T. Washington |
| 1858 | Charles W. Chesnutt |
| 1859 | Pauline E. Hopkins |
| 1862 | Ida B. Wells |
| 1863 | Mary Church Terrell |
| 1869 | W. E. B. Du Bois |
| 1871 | James Weldon Johnson |
| 1872 | Paul Lawrence Dunbar |
| 1875 | Carter G. Woodson |
| | Alice Moore Dunbar Nelson |
| 1881 | William Pickens |
| 1886 | Alain Locke |
| | Georgia Douglas Johnson |
| 1887 | Marcus Garvey |
| | Rudolph Fisher |
| 1889 | Claude McKay |
| 1891 | Nella Larsen |
| 1893 | Walter White |
| 1894 | Jean Toomer |

| 1895 | Jessie Redmon Fauset |
| | George S. Schuyler |
| 1898 | Melvin B. Tolson |
| 1900 | Howard Thurman |
| 1901 | Zora Neale Hurston |
| 1902 | Arna Bontemps |
| | Langston Hughes |
| | Gwendolyn Bennett |
| | Wallace Thurman |
| 1903 | Countee Cullen |
| 1907 | Dorothy West |
| 1908 | Ann Petry |
| | Richard Wright |
| 1909 | Chester Himes |
| 1910 | Pauli Murray |
| | Cyrus Colter |
| 1911 | Augusta Baker |
| | William Attaway |
| 1912 | Gordon Parks |
| 1913 | Robert Hayden |
| 1914 | Ralph Ellison |
| | Owen Dodson |
| | Dudley Randall |
| 1915 | John Hendrik Clarke |
| | John Hope Franklin |
| 1916 | John O. Killens |
| | Albert Murray |
| | Frank Yerby |
| 1917 | Gwendolyn Brooks |
| | Margaret Taylor-Burroughs |
| 1921 | Alex Haley |
| 1922 | Louis Lomax |
| | William Demby |
| | Mari Evans |
| 1924 | James Baldwin |
| 1925 | Carl Rowan |
| 1927 | Hoyt Fuller |
| 1928 | Julian Mayfield |

Maya Angelou
Ted Joans
1929   Paule Marshall
1930   Lorraine Hansberry
1931   Toni Morrison
Etheridge Knight
1933   Ernest Gaines
1934   Leroi Jones (Amiri Baraka)
Audre Lorde
Henry Dumas
Sonia Sanchez
1935   Ed Bullins
Eldridge Cleaver
1936   Lucille Clifton
June Jordan
Clarence Major
1937   William Melvin Kelley
Larry Neal
Claude Brown
Walter Dean Myers
1938   Michael S. Harper
Ishmael Reed
1939   Toni Cade Bambara
Barbara Chase-Riboud
Charles Fuller
Julius Lester
1941   Stokely Carmichael (Kwame Ture)
Arnold Rampersad
John Edgar Wideman
1942   Haki R. Madhubuti
Samuel R. Delany
1943   Nikki Giovanni
James Alan McPherson
Elaine Brown
Houston A. Baker Jr.
Cecil Brown
1944   Alice Walker
Angela Davis

1945    August Wilson
        Carolyn M. Rodgers
        Stanley Crouch
1947    Octavia Butler
        Nathaniel Mackey
        Ai
1948    Ntozake Shange
        Pearl Cleage
        Paula Giddins
1949    Gayl Jones
        Thulani Davis
1950    Bebe Moore Campbell
        Henry Louis Gates Jr.
        Gloria Naylor
        E. Ethelbert Miller
1951    Terry McMillan
1952    Rita Dove
1954    K. Anthony Appiah
        Opal Palmer Adisa
        Thylias Moss
1955    Patricia Smith
1957    Cyrus Cassell
1962    Elizabeth Alexander
        Paul Beatty
1963    Reginald Shepard
1969    Colson Whitehead

W.E.B. DU BOIS, the great writer and activist, was the guest of honor at a bash celebrating his ninety-second birthday. A troupe of whirling African spear dancers performed their number exceptionally close to the legendary sage's chair. Dorothy Parker, then queen of the barbed tongue and a celebrated Algonquin Round Table member, chuckled when several spear movements barely missed Du Bois's head. "Watch it, mate," she said from a nearby seat, "or you'll never see ninety-three."

# LITERARY AWARDS

Most writers try to imagine how it would feel to have their work recognized by their peers or some esteemed organization; how the prestige and adulation would boost their career and bring their writing to a wider audience. Sales of their books would be increased as the public sought out everything with their name on the cover, even the backlisted items.

Awards and prizes do tend to confer a certain power, sometimes even completely revitalizing a sagging career or jump-starting a fledgling one. Some question whether the most honored prizes are awarded with a nod to political concerns or in deference to public tastes, rather than in celebration of quality or craftsmanship; but few will deny the clout of the prize in advancing a writer's work, lending luster to that author's earlier books that were formerly considered "minor" or were ignored altogether.

In the awarding of these prizes, often mistakes are made and oversights are committed because of the egos and campaigning of the various committee members making the selections. Also, the individual tastes and diversities among the members come into play during the process. Although that process may be called democratic, with all entries having an equal chance at the glory, judges may have a grudge against a particular writer or a definite bias for the work of another, so awards and prizes may not always honor the finest work or the highest standards of literary excellence. Still, it is generally conceded that most of the top prizes in literature are awarded without consideration for what sells best or generates the most controversy.

The most important awards and prizes are the following:

the Nobel Prize, the Pulitzer Prize, the National Book Awards, the PEN/Faulkner Award, the National Book Critics Circle Awards, the Newbery Medal, and the Caldecott Medal.

The Nobel Prize for Literature, established by Alfred B. Nobel, the Swedish inventor of dynamite, rates highest among literary awards. Since 1901, this most prestigious of awards has been presented annually to prose and poetry writers who have produced an exceptional body of work. Selected by the members of the Swedish Academy of Literature, Nobel laureates get a gold medal, a cash award of $1 million, and an international audience. The Nobel Prize presentation occurs annually in December, when recipients are feted.

Next in order of importance of literary awards, the Pulitzer Prizes, named in honor of Joseph Pulitzer, an American newspaper publisher born in Hungary, have been presented yearly since 1917 at Columbia University. The prizes for achievement are granted in the fields of history, fiction, drama, biography or autobiography, poetry, and general nonfiction. Sometimes the board does not see fit to award a prize in a given category. Awardees get a certificate and $5,000 at the ceremony each spring.

In 1950, the National Book Award was created by the Book Manufacturers Institute, the American Book Council, and the American Booksellers Association to celebrate notable works of fiction, nonfiction, and poetry by American writers. Supervised by the National Book Foundation, the prizes now also include the category of literature for youth. Winners receive a $10,000 honorarium at the annual November ceremony.

In honor of William Faulkner, who endowed an award for young novelists with his Nobel Prize winnings, the PEN/Faulkner Award was founded in 1980 by writers who wanted to recognize the works of their fellow authors. Annually, a panel of writers selects five books from a field of more than 250 novels and short-fiction collections. The top prize is $15,000. Runners-up receive $5,000 each. Winners are honored every May in a presentation at the Folger Shakespeare Library in Washington, D.C.

The Newbery Medal, named for John Newbery, the first American publisher of children's books, is presented yearly by the American Library Association for the most accomplished and innovative book written for children. Established in 1921, it is the oldest of the children's book awards.

Hailed as one of the highest literary honors, the National Book Critics Circle Award has been given by book critics and book review editors to established writers in the categories of fiction, general nonfiction, autobiography/biography, poetry, and criticism since 1975. Winners get a scroll and citation at an annual ceremony.

The Coretta Scott King Award was first presented to African American authors and illustrators in 1970 for books that "promote an understanding and appreciation of the culture and contributions of all people to the realization of the American dream." The award program was finally adopted as a part of the presentation ceremony of the American Library Association in 1982.

Since 1980, the Before Columbus Foundation has sponsored the American Book Awards, which celebrate the nation's diversity in multicultural, multiethnic, and multiracial letters. The organization was founded by the multitalented Ishmael Reed, author of several cutting-edge novels, nonfiction collections, plays, and poetry books.

The Black Caucus of the American Library Association presents two prizes annually in fiction and nonfiction to black writers, along with a recognition of a first novelist. The top prizes are $500 each.

## African American Awardees by Year

1950   Pulitzer Prize (Poetry), Gwendolyn Brooks for *Annie Allen*
1953   National Book Award, (Fiction), Ralph Ellison for *Invisible Man*
1970   Coretta Scott King Award, Lillie Patterson for *Dr. Martin Luther King, Jr: Man of Peace*
1971   Coretta Scott King Award, Langston Hughes and Charlemae Rollins for *Black Troubadour*

1972    Coretta Scott King Award, Elton C. Fax for *Seventeen Black Artists*

1973    Coretta Scott King Award, Jackie Robinson as told to Alfred Duckett for *I Never Had It Made: The Autobiography of Jackie Robinson*

1974    Coretta Scott King Award, Sharon Bell Mathis for *Ray Charles*

1975    Coretta Scott King Award, Dorothy Robinson for *The Legend of Africania*

1975    The Newbery Medal, Virginia Hamilton for *M. C. Higgins, The Great*

1975    The National Book Award (Children's Books), Virginia Hamilton for *M. C. Higgins, The Great*

1976    Coretta Scott King Award, Pearl Bailey for *Duey's Tale*

1977    The Newbery Medal, Mildred D. Taylor for *Roll of Thunder, Hear My Cry*

1977    The National Book Critics Circle Award (Fiction), Toni Morrison for *Song of Solomon*

1977    Coretta Scott King Award, James Haskins for *The Story of Stevie Wonder*

1978    Pulitzer Prize (Fiction), James Alan McPherson for *Elbow Room*

1978    Coretta Scott King Award, Eloise Greenfield for *Africa Dream*

1979    Coretta Scott King Award, Ossie Davis for *Escape to Freedom: A Play About Young Frederick Douglass*

1980    Coretta Scott King Award, Walter Dean Myers for *The Young Landlords*

1981    Coretta Scott King Award, Sidney Poitier for *This Life*

1982    Coretta Scott King Award, Mildred D. Taylor for *Let the Circle Be Unbroken*

1982    PEN/Faulkner Award, David Bradley for *The Chaneysville Incident*

1983    Pulitzer Prize (Fiction), Alice Walker for *The Color Purple*

1983    National Book Award (Fiction), Alice Walker for *The Color Purple*

1983   Coretta Scott King Award, Virginia Hamilton for
       *Sweet Whispers, Brother Rush*

1983   National Book Award (First Novel), Gloria Naylor for
       *The Women of Brewster Place*

1984   Coretta Scott King Award, Lucille Clifton for *Everett
       Anderson's Goodbye*

1984   PEN/Faulkner Award, John Edgar Wideman for *Sent
       for You Yesterday*

1985   Coretta Scott King Award, Walter Dean Myers for
       *Motown and Didi: A Love Story*

1986   Coretta Scott King Award, Virginia Hamilton for *The
       People Could Fly: American Black Folktales*

1987   Coretta Scott King Award, Mildred Pitts Walter for
       *Justin and the Best Biscuits in the World*

1987   Pulitzer Prize (Poetry), Rita Dove for *Thomas and
       Beulah*

1988   Pulitzer Prize (Fiction), Toni Morrison for *Beloved*

1988   Coretta Scott King Award, Mildred D. Taylor for *The
       Friendship*

1989   Coretta Scott King Award, Walter Dean Myers for
       *Fallen Angels*

1990   Coretta Scott King Award, Patricia C. McKissack and
       Frederick McKissack for *A Long Hard Journey: The
       Story of the Pullman Porter*

1990   National Book Award (Fiction), Charles Johnson for
       *Middle Passage*

1990   National Book Critics Circle Award (Nonfiction),
       Shelby Steele for *The Content of Our Character: A
       New Vision of Race in America*

1991   Coretta Scott King Award, Mildred D. Taylor for *The
       Road to Memphis*

1991   PEN/Faulkner Award, John Edgar Wideman for
       *Philadelphia Fire*

1992   Coretta Scott King Award, Walter Dean Myers for *Now
       Is Your Time! The African American Struggle for Freedom*

1993   The Alfred B. Nobel Prize for Literature, Toni
       Morrison

1993    Coretta Scott King Award, Patricia C. McKissack for
        *The Dark Thirty: Southern Tales of the Supernatural*

1993    National Book Critics Circle Award (Fiction), Ernest
        J. Gaines for *A Lesson Before Dying*

1994    National Book Critics Circle Award (Criticism),
        Gerald Early for *The Culture of Bruising: Essays on
        Prizefighting, Literature, and Modern American
        Culture*

1994    Pulitzer Prize (Biography), David Levering Lewis for
        *W. E. B. Du Bois: Biography of a Race 1868–1919*

1994    Pulitzer Prize (Poetry), Yusef Komunyakaa for *Neon
        Vernacular*

1994    Black Caucus of American Library Association
        (Fiction), Ernest Gaines for *A Lesson Before Dying*

1994    Black Caucus of American Library Association
        (Nonfiction), David Levering Lewis for *W. E. B.
        Du Bois: Biography of a Race 1868–1919*

1994    Coretta Scott King Award, Angela Johnson for *Toning
        the Sweep*

1995    Black Caucus of American Library Association
        (Fiction), Maxine Clair for *Rattlebone*

1995    Black Caucus of American Library Association
        (Nonfiction), Sara Lawrence-Lightfoot for *I've Known
        Rivers: Lives of Loss and Liberation*

1995    Black Caucus of American Library Association (First
        Novel), Helen Elaine Lee for *The Serpent's Gift*

1995    Coretta Scott King Award, Patricia C. McKissack and
        Frederick McKissack for *Christmas in the Big House,
        Christmas in the Quarters*

1996    Black Caucus of American Library Association
        (Fiction), Walter Mosley for *R. L.'s Dream*

1996    Black Caucus of American Library Association
        (Nonfiction), Herb Boyd and Robert L. Allen (editors)
        for *Brotherman: The Odyssey of Black Men in America*

1996    Black Caucus of American Library Association (First
        Novel), devorah major for *An Open Weave*

1996    Coretta Scott King Award, Virginia Hamilton for *Her*

*Stories: African American Folktales, Fairy Tales and True Tales*

1997　Black Caucus of American Library Association (Fiction), Florence Ladd for *Sarah's Psalm*

1997　Black Caucus of American Library Association (Nonfiction), Nell Irvin Painter for *Sojourner Truth: A Life, a Symbol*

1997　Black Caucus of American Library Association (First Novelist), Sapphire for *Push*

1997　Coretta Scott King Award, Walter Dean Myers for *Slam!*

1998　Black Caucus of American Library Association (Fiction), Sandra Jackson-Opoku for *The River Where Blood Is Born*

1998　Black Caucus of American Library Association (Nonfiction), Toi Derricotte for *The Black Notebooks: An Interior Journey*

1998　Black Caucus of American Library Association (First Novel), Brian Keith Jackson for *The View from Here*

1998　Coretta Scott King Award, Sharon M. Draper for *Forged by Fire*

1999　Black Caucus of American Library Association (Fiction), Gayl Jones for *The Healing*

1999　Black Caucus of American Library Association (Nonfiction), Carolyn Mazloomi for *Spirits of the Cloth: Contemporary African American Quilts*

1999　Coretta Scott King Award, Angela Johnson for *Heaven: A Novel*

# WHAT DID YOU DO BEFORE
# YOU GOT YOUR BIG BREAK?

Very few writers come out of the starting blocks with a best-seller or even a modest success. For many African American writers, the literary life was earned with sacrifice, persistence, and long nights of hard labor with a pencil and blank sheets of paper or an empty computer screen. These writers staved off monthly assaults from creditors and landlords with a host of odd jobs and low-paying positions, some of which were as far away from the writing world as a Hyundai is from a Rolls-Royce. These were the occupations that allowed them to preserve their "writing time."

Here is just a sampling of the labors that determined African American scribes used to support themselves en route to publication:

Ai—janitorial assistant
Maya Angelou—cabaret singer
Tina McElroy Ansa—journalist
William Attaway—seaman
James Baldwin—child preacher
Toni Cade Bambara—welfare investigator
Gwendolyn Brooks—maid, secretary
Frank London Brown—machinist, government employee,
    bartender, jazz singer
Octavia Butler—factory worker
Colin Channer—copywriter
Alice Childress—actress
Maxine Clair—medical technologist
Eric Jerome Dickey—computer programmer, teacher, comic

Percival Everett—jazz musician, ranch hand

E. Lynn Harris—computer salesman

Calvin C. Hernton—welfare counselor

Chester Himes—hotel bellhop, bartender

Langston Hughes—waiter

Sandra Jackson-Opoku—travel writer, airlines reservationist,
  teacher

C. O. R. James—professional cricketer

Charles Johnson—cartoonist

Kristin Lattany—screenwriter, information officer for city of
  Philadelphia

Helen Elaine Lee—lawyer

Haki Madhubuti—post office clerk

Diane McKinney-Whetstone—publicist

Toni Morrison—teacher

Walter Mosley—computer programmer

Willard Motley—farm worker, waiter, cook, clerk

Gloria Naylor—telephone operator

Sonia Sanchez—teacher

Joyce Carol Thomas—telephone operator

Alice Walker—welfare department employee

Margaret Walker—social worker

John A. Williams—welfare case worker

Carter G. Woodson—railroad construction laborer, coal miner

Richard Wright—street cleaner, porter, post office clerk

Frank Yerby—defense plant worker

Shay Youngblood—Peace Corps worker, Parisian au pair,
  model

PART III

▼▼▼▼▼▼▼

# LITERARY PATHFINDERS:
# THE OLD SCHOOL PROFILES

▼▼▼▼▼▼▼▼▼▼

▲▲

"I always want to do something different from what I have done before; I don't want to repeat myself. If I belong to a certain tradition, I don't want to belong, because my writing would be very boring if I always wrote in a particular style."

—ANN PETRY
From *Interviews with Black Writers*, edited by Janet Sternburg

▲▲

# AFRICAN AMERICAN AUTHOR PROFILES

In high school and college studies, classes on African American literature often include the usual cast of authors such as James Baldwin, Toni Morrison, Ralph Ellison, Alice Walker, Richard Wright, and Langston Hughes, among others. While this is not a bad thing, considering that only a few short years ago even these stellar writers were not given a brief mention, triggering a storm of student protests calling for more relevant curriculums, there are many black authors who have made valuable contributions to the American literary canon and who have been neglected or forgotten. Some are living, others are dead, but all are worthy of our attention.

African Americans have so much to celebrate in the area of fiction because our novelists have continually pressed forward in the most dire of circumstances, creating a body of work that any ethnic group or race would be proud to claim as its own. In compiling this brief list of talents, some names have been left out after a grueling selection process, but they are not forgotten. Each of the following profiles showcases an author who has challenged the status quo, taken artistic risks, followed a particular vision, often to the detriment of a career or financial gain or community support. Not all of them walked in step with the political or cultural beliefs of their day. Still, we salute them and all the hours of reading wonder they gave to us!

# GEORGE S. SCHUYLER
## NOVELIST, JOURNALIST, ESSAYIST

Born: February 25, 1895. Died: August 31, 1977. George S. Schuyler escaped the worst forms of Jim Crow racism as the son of middle-class parents in Providence, Rhode Island. His parents relocated to a racially integrated neighborhood in Syracuse, New York, where he studied at public schools. Choosing to pursue a life of uncertainty, he quit high school and joined the army at age seventeen. The seven years spent in the military concluded in 1918 with Schuyler holding the rank of first lieutenant and a passion for writing. Hard times struck and a period of homelessness followed, with Schuyler taking his place among the downtrodden on New York's Bowery. In 1921, he became a member of the Socialist Party of America, a decision he would later disavow.

Schuyler was hired as a columnist with the *Pittsburgh Courier* in 1924, which permitted him to write as a correspondent from Africa, the Caribbean, and South America. However, association with the Socialists led to a meeting with activist A. Philip Randolph, who employed him as an editor with the *Messenger*, where he worked until 1928. In 1934, he penned his most notable work, *Black No More*, the first black satire on the national race dilemma, using the fantastic premise of a machine that transformed blacks into whites. That same year, he served as an investigative reporter in Liberia, producing a series of articles on the country's slave trade. The information gathered from the trip was later used in his novel, *Slaves Today: A Story of Liberia* (1931). As a journalist, he worked for several publications, covering a wide range of topics, both cultural and political. The tone of his work took on a more con-

AFRICAN AMERICAN AUTHOR PROFILES     205

servative edge as time passed, causing many blacks to view him as a race traitor and an iconoclast. Going against the social mores of the times, he shocked both communities by marrying a white woman, a union that lasted until her death in 1969. The marriage yielded one child, Philippa, a musical prodigy, who later earned some celebrity as an author and journalist.

In his later years, his writings as a columnist and critic drew fire from his African American counterparts for their fiercely right-wing and anti-Communist views. A work of nonfiction, *The Communist Conspiracy Against the Negro* (1947), was one of the earliest condemnations of the Soviet Union in the postwar era. He staunchly backed Senator McCarthy's "witch hunts" in the 1950s. His departure from the *Pittsburgh Courier* in 1966 stemmed from the paper's refusal to print his damning criticisms of the civil rights movement. Only recently has his work as a novelist come to light, with the publication of two volumes containing four of his serialized fiction stories from the 1930s. During that time, he published more than fifty short stories and twenty novels under a pen name. He completed his autobiography, *Black and Conservative*, in 1966, a book that thrust him once more into the literary limelight.

Toward the end of his life, Schuyler was dogged by tragedy as his daughter, Philippa, was killed in a helicopter crash in 1967 while covering the Vietnam War. He felt the sting of grief again two years later when his beloved wife died. Alone and embittered, he spent his remaining years working for the conservative *Manchester* [New Hampshire] *Union-Leader* until his death in a New York hospital in 1977.

Posthumously, four of Schuyler's novels have been reprinted by Northeastern University Press in two volumes: *Black Empire* (1991) and *Ethiopian Stories* (1995).

## IN HIS OWN WORDS

*On the importance of individualism:* "People are not the same. You have immense differences between individuals, regardless of color. They both love and hate, sometimes at the same time. These things were apparent to me very early. There's really no validity to the generalization that white people or black people per se think a certain way. They don't at all. They think as individuals, unless they are childish, and then they rush to concede the generally accepted thing. But I find so many exceptions to the rule."[1]

*On the national view of black creativity:* "White men who claim to be intelligent and reasonable beings persist in registering surprise whenever they hear of or meet a Negro who has written a novel, a history, or a poem, or who can work a problem in calculus. Because of this naïveté, many mediocre Negroes are praised to the high heavens as geniuses of the first flight, and grow sleek and fat. Such fellows are frequently seized upon by gullible whites and labeled as leaders of the Negro race, without the Negroes being consulted on the matter."[2]

*On intelligence, the foundation of creativity:* "Certainly if the best measure of intelligence is the ability to survive in a changing or hostile environment, and if one considers that the Negro is not only surviving but improving all the time in health, wealth, and culture, one must agree that he possesses a high degree of intelligence. In their efforts to fight off the ravages of color prejudice, the blacks have welded themselves into a homogeneity and developed a morale whose potentialities are not yet fully appreciated."[3]

1. From Ishmael Reed, *Shrovetide in Old New Orleans* (Garden City, N.Y.: Doubleday, 1978), 196.
2. George Schuyler, "Our White Folks," in *Speech and Power*, vol. 2, ed. Gerald Early (Hopewell, N.J.: Ecco Press, 1993), 295.
3. Ibid., 297.

# WILLARD FRANCIS MOTLEY
## NOVELIST

Born: July 14, 1909. Died: March 4, 1965. Willard Francis
Motley was born the second son of a Pullman porter in a
largely white neighborhood on Chicago's South Side. His
older brother, Archibald Motley, later became a leading African American painter, whose works are in museum collections around the world.

Motley decided to become a writer at an early age, and
earned some notoriety as a thirteen-year-old when, in 1922, a
short story sent to the *Chicago Defender* was published in
three installments. Later that year, he took over a children's
column for the same paper and held that post for two years.
The Great Depression halted Motley's plans to attend college
after graduation from high school, but he moved into a slum
apartment in one of the city's roughest neighborhoods to
understand the evils of poverty. Restless, he traveled across the
country, gaining new experiences, some of them quite harsh —
this seasoning by life later served as the fuel for the work he
would produce. Penniless, he ate at soup kitchens or did odd
jobs, and spent a month in a Wyoming jail for stealing gas.

In 1940, Motley joined the WPA Federal Writers Project
and cofounded a literary journal, which introduced him to the
inner circle of Chicago's leading writers and artists. Soon his
short fiction, featuring his trademark naturalistic style, which
entered the minds of his characters so convincingly, appeared
in several national publications. When his first novel, *Knock
on Any Door*, was published in 1947, it was overwhelmingly
popular, selling nearly 48,000 copies in its first three weeks on
the shelves. The book, with its unflinchingly honest story of

the moral corruption of an Italian American choir boy into a brutal cop-killer slated for the electric chair, made Motley an instant celebrity and sold more than 350,000 copies in two years. *Look* magazine ran a large story on the author and the tough neighborhood depicted in the book. In 1949, Humphrey Bogart starred in a hit movie based on Motley's work.

Key critics such as Walter Rideout labeled Motley's debut as one of the ten major novels of the forties, and others compared him to literary realists Richard Wright, Theodore Dreiser, and Sinclair Lewis. Some black intellectuals blasted Motley for refusing to play up his race or to permit his photo to be used on his book. Motley countered that blacks are just like other groups, with the same problems, and no writer should be forced to speak for a racial group. He wanted to address what he considered the underlying social and political issues confronting postwar America, of which he saw race as just one of many crucial national challenges.

Toward this aim, Motley returned to his dissection of American life with his second novel, *We Fished All Night* (1951), a more complex work than his commercially successful debut novel. Critics were not so kind to this ambitious follow-up, slamming its rambling story of three homecoming vets, and its accompanying themes of urban politics, organized labor, ethnic racism, and rampant capitalism. Later, Motley entered an ongoing feud with the three leading black writers of the time: Richard Wright, Chester Himes, and James Baldwin, whom he criticized especially as "writers who peddled their race for dollars."

Hoping to regain his winning streak, Motley returned to the social themes of his most popular work, writing a sequel to the tragic Nick Romano tale in *Let No Man Write My Epitaph*, in 1958. The novel offered a detailed look at Nick Romano Jr., the illegitimate son of the executed lead character in his first book, and Louie Romano, Nick's youngest brother from the original novel. The sequel proved to be a solid success, but it fell far short of expectations. Hollywood cranked out a weak version of the second novel in 1960, featuring

James Darren, Shelley Winters, Ricardo Montalban, and Ella Fitzgerald.

Disappointed and increasingly disillusioned, Motley spent more time in Mexico, where he had purchased a house in 1951, a retreat from the demands of his profession and the pressures of living in America. During the last years of his life, he wrote two final novels about his adopted country: *My House Is Your House*, an unpublished book, and *Let Noon Be Fair*, which was published in 1966, the year after his death. Critics observed that Motley's literary swan song was completed just two weeks before his death and left largely unedited. His Mexican hosts were incensed that Motley's work attacked the Catholic Church, the Mexican political and social elite, and land developers for abusing the poor. His literary acclaim, so potent in the 1940s, had diminished in the years before his death largely because Motley refused to write solely about black American life. In recent years, his reputation has been resurrected somewhat as scholars examine the importance of the "raceless" novels authored by Wright, Hurston, Petry, Baldwin, and Yerby as the antidote to the Jim Crow era's barriers in American publishing.

## IN HIS OWN WORDS

*On his writing habits:* "I like writing late at night and when the story is coming good I generally work from twelve to fourteen hours a day until I hit a cold spot. Then there are several days when I loaf and wait for the story to take hold of me again. I think that I most enjoy sitting in bars, restaurants, etc., watching people, listening in on their conversations and wondering about them, who they are, what their lives are."[1]

*On his apprenticeship:* "As far as writing is concerned, I went through several periods starting with trying to write short stories for pulp magazines. I even tried writing 'confessions.'

1. Interview, *The New York Tribune Book Review*, 7 October 1951.

Finally I moved to the slums of Chicago after being bored with the middle-class neighborhood in which I was reared and there I discovered 'myself' and the sort of thing I wanted to put on paper."[2]

*On the work of writing:* "I feel that the writer is the lay figure in the hands of his characters and material rather than the other way around and that they—the characters and materials—dictate his style. I want to be a writer speaking not for but 'with' my characters; that chameleon who can wear the coloration of the environment he deals with. . . . Don't make me too respectable and polished."[3]

2. Ibid.
3. From Jerome Klinkowitz, ed., *The Diaries of Willard Motley* (Ames, Iowa: Iowa State University Press, 1979), xviii.

# FRANK GARVIN YERBY
## NOVELIST

Born: September 3, 1916. Died: November 29, 1991. Frank Garvin Yerby was born in Augusta, Georgia, and raised, along with his three siblings, mostly by his mother. His father worked as a hotel doorman in Miami and Detroit. A stellar student, he attended Haines Institute in his hometown before going on to earn a B.A. degree in English from Paine College in 1937 and an M.A. in English from Fisk University the following year. Money woes forced Yerby to halt his bid for a Ph.D. at the University of Chicago.

While working at the Federal Writers Project in Chicago, Yerby met several notable black writers such as Arna Bontemps, Richard Wright, and Margaret Walker. He taught at two black universities, Florida A&M and Southern University, in the Jim Crow South between 1939 and 1941 before returning north to Dearborn, Michigan, for a job at a defense plant. His wartime writing failed to make an impression until the publication of his short story "Health Card," which was featured in *Harper's* in 1944. The story, an examination of racial stereotypes, also won the O'Henry Memorial Award. Yerby's early stories examined racial bigotry, but his later work largely steered clear of social issues and centered on the moral and social failures of whites.

In 1946, Yerby published *The Foxes of Harrow*, an Old South historical romance that sold millions of copies. It was adapted as a film in 1951. An astute observer of American tastes, he used the key events of American and European history as the topics for his fiction. An early attempt to write a protest novel in the gritty tradition of Richard Wright failed, so he returned to the popular fiction techniques to build a faithful audience. Despite their criticism of his adherence to a specific stylistic formula, reviewers admired his ability to tell a story. His peers blasted him for not using black characters and plots in his stories, exerting increasing pressure on the novelist to write about Jim Crow, lynching, and bias in the military. He refused their demands, following his debut book with *The Vixens* (1948), *The Golden Hawk* (1949), and *Pride's Castle* (1949).

In the 1950s, Yerby created several commercial bestsellers with titles like *A Woman Called Fancy, Captain Rebel, Fair Oaks, The Serpent and the Staff,* and *Jarrett's Jade.* Something happened to Yerby during the civil rights movement of the late 1950s. Like many black writers of that time, he expatriated to Europe, settling in Spain, where he watched the situation at home with great interest. His anger at the harsh treatment of black protestors against segregation by southern police altered his fictional lexicon and more emphasis was placed on racial prejudice and antebellum politics in such books as *The Garfield Honor* (1961), *Griffin's Way* (1962), and *An Odor of Sanctity* (1965). His first fully realized black character appeared in *Speak Now* (1969), a story of a black expatriate in France during the turmoil of the late 1960s. He continued that trend with blacks in *The Dahomean* (1971) and *A Darkness at Ingraham's Crest,* two of his best works.

Bucking the trend of protest fiction popular in the late 1940s and early 1950s, Yerby sought to succeed in the commercial fiction arena, to string together a series of bestsellers. No other African American writer ever succeeded so well for so long. He attacked the myth of the Old South aggressively and continuously, writing a book a year from 1947 to 1986. Thirty-three novels carried his name, with more than 55 million copies sold.

Yerby spent his last years quietly, shunning the celebrity of his glory days. He died of heart failure in Madrid, Spain, on November 29, 1991.

## IN HIS OWN WORDS

*On writing on the issue of race:* "I said that novels which touch on racial problems put a terrible burden on the writer to avoid slipping into propaganda. My point is that for the young beginning writer, they are almost too difficult to write. . . . That isn't to say he shouldn't write them, that he shouldn't try them. But it's so hard when you enter things with your heart and soul and the last millimeter of your innermost guts, to avoid maybe exaggerating or losing your artistic objectivity."[1]

*On writing love and romance in his bestselling costume novels:* "The action of the costume novel's plot is carried forward by our hero's failure to realize that in any movie of life there are literally dozens, if not hundreds, of women who will do just as well if he doesn't win fair Susan's dainty hand; and that very probably he will catch a most interesting variety of hell if he does win it. Which, come to think of it, is not unrealistic: emotional maturity is one of the rarest qualities in life."[2]

*On his change in later years to a more serious message:* "I'm going to get into a tremendous fight with [publishers] because, after all, they have a vested interest in my continuing to write the kind of novels I've been writing. I find myself standing in the slave market. . . . I'm going to try to convince them that, if they will gamble on this, the sale will be great. . . . I am not going to sign any contract which does not permit me to do any kind of book I choose."[3]

1. Hoyt W. Fuller, "Famous Writers Face a Challenge," *Ebony*, June 1966, 190.
2. Frank Yerby, "How and Why I Wrote the Costume Novel," *Harper's*, October 1959, 149.
3. Fuller, 194.

# ANN PETRY
## JOURNALIST, NOVELIST

Born: October 12, 1908. Died: April 28, 1997. Ann Petry was
born Ann Lane, the youngest of three children in a set of
cramped rooms above her father's drugstore in Old Saybrook,
Connecticut, a member of the only black family in the small
white town. She endured very little racial conflict in this isolated hamlet, and later, after finishing her studies at the local
public schools, attended the University of Connecticut School
of Pharmacy until her graduation in 1931. Following her departure from academia, she worked for seven years in her family's drugstore as a pharmacist.

In 1938, she married her hometown sweetheart, George
Petry, and made plans to move to New York City to make a
writing career, which she pursued with all of her New England determination. She was seduced early on by Harlem.
Petry worked as a reporter for *The Amsterdam News* from 1938
to 1941, followed by a productive period at *The People's Voice*,
a local weekly, as a reporter and editor of the woman's page. As
a columnist for the publication, she churned out a weekly piece
about Harlem's upper middle class called "The Lighter Side."
It was as a journalist that she developed her trademark eye
for detail and sharp ear for dialogue that would enrich all of
her later work. According to Marjorie Greene of *Opportunity*
magazine, Petry covered all manner of stories during her time
on the Harlem streets with a pad and pencil, approaching
each one with an impressive and energetic professionalism.

Ever eager to strengthen her skills, Petry enrolled in creative writing courses at Columbia University in the evenings
while offering her days as a teacher at a Harlem experimental

school for poor children. Much of her early fiction, which was published in *Crisis* magazine, was based on stories covered as a reporter, and one of them, "Like a Winding Sheet," the tale of a day in the life of a black factory worker, gained her national attention when it was printed in the anthology *The Best American Stories of 1946*. Petry was riding a wave of popularity when her first novel, *The Street*, won the Houghton Mifflin Literary Fellowship that same year and established her as a notable talent. The book, a story of an enterprising black woman battling poverty and inner challenges, was written by Petry during ten grueling months in almost total seclusion.

If *The Street* startled critics with its narrative power, emotional revelations, and social honesty, then her second novel, *Country Place*, published in 1947, stunned them when Petry turned her attention to the lives of New England whites. The black woman narrator chronicles the bitter truths of the intimate lives of whites, without any sentimentality or protest, much like a member of the family matter-of-factly discussing the shortcomings of the clan. Petry's basic premise in the novel was that no one, regardless of race or economic privilege, can escape the influence of change. Critics were again forced to acknowledge her naturalistic skill with dialogue, texture, and characterization.

While Petry's reputation as a premier short-story writer soared through her submissions to leading magazines, she became concerned with the lack of accomplished African American fiction and nonfiction for black youngsters. Her first children's book, *The Drugstore Cat*, appeared in 1948, and led to a well-received essay on Harlem for the popular *Holiday* magazine the following year. The literary world got a chance to see her analytical side when she wrote an informative essay on the novel as social criticism, bashing the concept of art for art's sake and endorsing the use of prose as a tool for societal change.

With her next novel, *The Narrows*, published in 1953, Petry explored the psychology of interracial love with the story of Link Williams, a black man, and his ill-fated romance with

Camillo Treadway Sheffield, an heiress to industrial wealth. The critics and her fans were very pleased with the results, and her reputation as a capable writer continued to build. Not content to abandon her quest for suitable books for black youth, she wrote three more juvenile titles, all of which brought her more acclaim: *Harriet Tubman, Conductor on the Underground Railroad* (1955), *Tituba of Salem Village* (1964), and *Legends of the Saints* (1970). Throughout the 1950s and 1960s, Petry became a regular contributor to the pages of the prestigious *New Yorker* magazine with perceptive short fiction, including "Has Anybody Seen Miss Dora Dean" (1958) and "The New Mirror" (1965). These works were published in the excellent short-story collection *Miss Muriel and Other Stories*, which secured her position as one of the most significant African American writers of this century. Petry's private papers are collected at the Mugar Memorial Library at Boston University, at Yale University, and at Atlanta University. In later years, she served as a lecturer at Miami University of Ohio and a visiting professor at the University of Hawaii. She died in 1997.

## IN HER OWN WORDS

*On writing her landmark novel,* **The Street:** "I tried to write a story that moves swiftly so that it would hold the attention of people who might ordinarily shy away from a so-called problem novel. And I hope that I have created characters who are real, believable, alive. For I am of the opinion that most Americans regard Negroes as types—not quite human—who fit into a special category and I wanted to show them as people with the same capacity for love and hate, for tears and laughter, and the same instincts for survival possessed by all men."[1]

1. From James W. Ivy, "Ann Petry Talks About First Novel," in *Sturdy Black Bridges: Visions of Black Women in Literature*, ed. Roseann P. Bell, Bettye J. Parker, and Beverly Guy-Sheftall (New York: Doubleday, 1979), 199.

*On creating characters:* "I don't think that a character appears in its entirety. Characterization is part of a process whereby you have probably surprised yourself several times by the time you have finished, because the character changes or grows or does things that you did not expect. It comes to you as you write."[2]

*On the process of writing:* "When I'm writing I work in the morning from 8:00 A.M. to about noon. If I'm going to do any revising I do it in the afternoon. The first draft is in longhand. The planning and the writing go hand in hand for the most part. I revise endlessly. . . . I do not work at night if I can avoid it."[3]

---

2. From John O'Brien, ed., *Interviews with Black Americans* (New York: Liveright Publishing, 1974), 155.
3. Ibid. 160.

# WILLIAM GARDNER SMITH
## NOVELIST, JOURNALIST

Born: February 6, 1927. Died: November 5, 1974. Smith was one of four children born to Edith Smith, who remarried and lived in the grim South Philadelphia ghetto in the 1940s. The youngster read everything in the small neighborhood library, leading his class in most of his studies. His early favorite novels before the age of eleven were the works of Hemingway and Maugham, which he devoured nightly following his after-school job at the grocery store. Throughout high school, he earned the praise of his teachers for his superior achievements in a wide range of activities: photography, editor of the school paper, captain of the fencing team, and judge of the student court. One of his English teachers suggested he consider a career in writing, and soon Smith was working part-time at the *Pittsburgh Courier* before graduating from high school at age sixteen.

Following his graduation, Smith took a full-time post at the newspaper, but his new occupation didn't have a chance to jell before he was drafted in 1946 by the army. He was assigned to a base in occupied Berlin after completing basic training. His arduous military experience compelled Smith to write his first novel, *Last of the Conquerors*, in 1948, which he finished after his tour of duty while a student at Temple University. The novel, which stirred the ongoing national debate about America's segregated armed services, provided the country with a controversial fictional look at its troops in devastated Germany. It detailed the exploits of Hayes Dawkins, a young black soldier, and his interactions with Germans, who accepted the African Americans more readily than did their fellow white Americans. Critics admired the twenty-one-year-old Smith's courage in depicting the rampant racism in the military so boldly in the novel, which sold very well, causing several reviewers to compare the young author to Richard Wright. Some of the unblinking candor about prejudice in Smith's book came from a pivotal incident in which the writer, in his army uniform, was viciously beaten by a group of white sailors while walking with a light-skinned black woman they had mistaken for white. Smith never forgot the racial attack or the chants of onlooking whites for the men to kill him.

Harrison Smith, noted critic at the *Saturday Review of Literature*, wrote in an August 28, 1948, review that the book "will be attacked with considerable venom. It will be entertaining to read what a few southern critics have to say about it, since it violates certain principles held to be true and indivisible, that white and black are not equal, and so should not have the same opportunities, either in life, or in love, or in hope for the future."

While white critics were stumped by *South Street*, one of the first black militant novels, African American reviewers applauded the scope and ambition of Smith's classic tale of the three Bower brothers striving to resume their lives in South Philadelphia after the racial murder of their father. Following the publication of the book, Smith became news editor of English language services for Agence France-Presse, a strategic move on his part to find new topics for his fiction.

Two of his subsequent manuscripts, nonprotest novels, were rejected before he started *The Stone Face* (1963), his last published fiction. The novel, published at the bloody height of the civil rights campaigns in America, reveals the Parisian world of American and African expatriates as seen by Simeon Brown, a black painter. Brown, a fixture in the city's café society, gets his political reawakening when he sees the French treatment of Algerian residents during their colonial war. He reviews his life in exile after some enlightening talks with the Africans and decides to return home to join in the struggle for equality there. Again the reviews were mixed along racial and ideological lines, but the acclaim for the highly political novel was spectacular. Nick Aaron Ford, writing in a 1964 issue of *Phylon*, said it was the best novel by a Negro writer since Ellison's *Invisible Man*. Critic Joseph Friedman in the November 17, 1963, issue of *The New York Times Book Review* lauded the novel's achievement, adding that Smith should be considered "among the most worthy young writers, Negro or white."

In 1964, Smith relocated to Accra, Ghana, to assume the post of assistant editor-in-chief of Ghana Television, upon an invitation of Shirley Graham Du Bois, the widow of the great writer and activist. He began a new life with his second wife and infant son, but that was interrupted when a military coup overthrew the government. He was deported and returned to Paris. A book proposal on his Ghanaian experiences was roundly rejected, so he took an assignment in 1967 to cover the increasing wave of deadly race riots in America. Smith came home for the first time in sixteen years and immediately became a celebrity during his journey to the country's major cities. His fifth book, *Return to Black America* (1970), analyzed the Black Power movement and its significance in the civil rights battle, its strengths and faults, and white resistance to promoting true equality and opportunity for all.

Smith divorced his second wife and remarried in 1970. A daughter was born to the couple the following year. In 1973, a medical exam uncovered cancer. William Gardner Smith died on November 5, 1974, in Thiais, France, unsure of his place in African American letters.

## IN HIS OWN WORDS

*On the writer and success:* "To grasp social and individual truth, it is my opinion that the novelist must maintain emotional contact with the basic people of his society. At first glance, this appears a simple thing; but in reality, it is difficult. Consider the material circumstances of the 'successful' writer. He becomes a celebrity. He makes money. Usually, he begins to move in the sphere of people like himself—authors, artists, critics, etc. . . . In a word, he moves, to some degree, into an ivory tower; he becomes, in a fashion, detached from the mainstream of American life."[1]

*On writing and publishers:* "As my books shifted from 'communication' to the unaggressive affirmation of our own worth, I think they became less accessible to white readers (or at least to white publishers). 'Remember that you are writing for the white middle class, which can afford to pay six dollars for a book,' a publisher once told me."[2]

*On the gifts of the African American writer:* "The Negro writer, if he does not make the tragic error of trying to imitate his white counterparts, has in his possession the priceless 'gift' of thematic intuition. Provided he permits his writing to swell truthfully from his deepest emotional reaches, he will treat problems of real significance, which can strike a chord in the heart of basic humanity. He will be able to convey suffering without romanticizing; he will be able to describe happiness which is not merely on the surface; he will be able to search out and concretize the hopes and ambitions which are the basic stuff of human existence."[3]

1. From Robert Hemenway, ed., *The Black Novelist* (Columbus, Ohio: Charles E. Merrill, 1970), 200.

2. From LeRoy S. Hodges Jr., *Portrait of an Expatriate: William Gardner Smith* (Westport, Conn.: Greenwood Publishing, 1985), 95.

3. From Hemenway, *The Black Novelist*, 202.

# JOHN O. KILLENS
## NOVELIST, SCREENWRITER, PLAYWRIGHT

Born: January 14, 1916. Died: October 27, 1987. Killens was born in Macon, Georgia, to parents who encouraged him to read African American literature. His father, Charles, a fan of poet Langston Hughes, pushed his son to read the writer's weekly pieces in the popular newspaper, the *Chicago Defender*, while his mother, Willie Lee, often recited poetry to the young boy. The exploits of Killens's southern childhood would later appear in his novels and plays, adding a rich authenticity not frequently seen in many of the early protest novels by black writers of the 1950s and 1960s.

Killens departed Macon in 1936, moving to Washington, D.C., where he secured a position with the National Labor Relations Board. During World War II, he served with the U.S. Army in the South Pacific from 1942 to 1945. Many of his wartime experiences were later used as background for his noted second novel, *And Then We Heard the Thunder*. It was during this period that he abandoned his early dreams of becoming a doctor or lawyer to focus his attentions on a writing career. By 1946, Killens was living in Brooklyn with a family, working as a union organizer, which led to major disillusionment when he realized that racism was alive in the labor movement as well. His first novel, *Youngblood*, was published to positive reviews, chronicling the struggles of a poor black family in the bigoted American South. His second novel, *And Then We Heard the Thunder*, was published in 1962, and attacked the military's Jim Crow policies, a move that brought him mixed notices from the critics.

Seeking to widen his base of knowledge, Killens attended several universities during his formative years, including Edward Waters College, Morris Brown College, Atlanta University, Howard University, Columbia University, and New York University. His thirst for education and new experiences never waned. In the 1940s, he teamed with Rosa Guy, John Hendrik Clarke, and Walter Christmas to establish the legendary Harlem Writers Guild, which later produced such talents as Julian Mayfield, Paule Marshall, Maya Angelou, Piri Thomas, Douglas Turner Ward, Loften Mitchell, Arthur Flowers, and Terry McMillan. From the 1960s through the 1980s, he taught and lectured at a number of colleges throughout the country, teaching creative writing to aspiring novelists.

The spirit of protest for racial equality that emerged after World War II was not a passing fancy for Killens, who devoted much of his time from 1954 through 1970 to the civil rights movement. He joined with King in the pivotal Montgomery bus boycott in 1955 and later continued his work in the North. After hearing the fiery Malcolm X speak in the early 1960s, Killens's views of the struggle for equal opportunity changed to a more militant stance as he embraced black nationalism. Both of his important works of that period, *Black Man's Burden* (1965), a volume of political essays, and *'Sippi* (1967), a novel, yielded a deeper perspective of the man's political growth and more aggressive stance on the battle against white racism. His essays warned of the possible failure of nonviolent resistance against the stubborn institutional brand of racism, while the novel detailed the bombings, shooting, and terror of the black college-student movement in the heat of the protests in Mississippi in the 1960s.

In the following decade, Killens turned his attention to the quality of life within the black community, producing a classic satire of middle-class blacks and their assimilation of white culture, *Cotillion; or, One Good Bull Is Half the Herd* (1971). He uses the annual ball organized by a group of black society matrons in Brooklyn as the point of departure for a cutting session of "the dozens," which strips the attendees of their veneer of pretense and false civility. This raucous literary work caught critics by surprise, earning Killens enthusiastic reviews and a Pulitzer Prize nomination.

Killens's writings brought him an international audience and prompted him to travel widely abroad. He journeyed to Africa in 1961 and later to the Soviet Union with a group of artists and teachers in 1968 and 1970. In 1973, he visited China, where he was warmly received as one of the more popular writers of the region. He continued writing through the 1970s and 1980s, producing two young-adult books, *Great Gittin' Up Morning: A Biography of Denmark Vesey* (1972) and *A Man Ain't Nothin' but a Man: The Adventures of John Henry* (1975), along with a novel, *The Great Black Russian: A Novel on the Life and Times of Alexander Pushkin*, which was published after his death in 1989 by Wayne State University Press. He also wrote two notable screenplays, *Odds Against Tomorrow* (1959) and *Slaves* (1969). Killens died in 1987 of cancer.

## IN HIS OWN WORDS

*On writing:* "By the end of the war, I knew that writing was the thing for me. It would be my raison d'être, and nothing else would matter. . . . I found out, of course, that writing was the damnedest, hardest, and loneliest buck a man could make, especially if that man was black."[1]

*On black and white editors:* "We need black editors. White editors are not competent to edit the black experience. One, they have no frame of reference for the black experience. Two, they come to a black manuscript with all kinds of preconceived notions of what it should be, and with a guilty conscience and a kind of subjectivity that makes them identity with the white characters and be overly protective and defensive of them. We had problems like this with every one of my books except *And Then We Heard the Thunder*."[2]

1. Obituary, *The Washington Post*, 3 November 1987, D6.
2. John O. Killens, "Rapping with Myself," from *Amistad 2: Writings on Black History and Culture*, ed. John A. Williams and Charles Harris (Washington, D.C.: Howard University Press, 1971), 109.

*On finding young black writers seeking topics for their work:*
"Don't write about the Negro, write about Americans. But surely the American Negro is the most uniquely American of all Americans, because he was created here, in this place, physically, psychologically, sociologically, culturally, economically. He is an American product. The Negro, in his black presence, is the barometer of this nation's Constitution, and all its democratic traditions yet unrealized. Still deferred."[3]

3. John O. Killens, "The Black Writer vis-a-vis His Country," from *The Black Aesthetic*, ed. Addison Gayle (Garden City, N.Y.: Anchor Books, 1971), 372.

# JOHN A. WILLIAMS
## NOVELIST, JOURNALIST, ESSAYIST, EDITOR

Born: December 5, 1925. John A. Williams was born in Jackson, Mississippi, but grew up in Syracuse, New York. He later completed high school after a tour of duty in the U.S. Navy during World War II. He then attended Syracuse University and graduated in 1950. He briefly enrolled in graduate school but was forced to leave due to financial concerns. For two years, he worked as a caseworker for the county welfare department and as a public relations associate. Once he decided to become a writer, Williams took a series of temporary jobs in New York City, including consultant in television, publicity director for a publishing house, editor for a newsletter, and employee at an insurance company.

During this time, Williams learned his craft as a European correspondent for *Ebony* and *Jet* magazines. He was also a correspondent for *Newsweek* in the mid-1960s. During the latter part of the decade he served as a writing lecturer at two universities, CUNY in New York and the College of the British Virgin Islands. A disciplined writer, he started his career as a novelist with *The Angry Ones* (a.k.a. *One for New York*) in 1960, followed by *Night Song* (1961), *Sissie* (1963), *The Man Who Cried I Am* (1967), *Sons of Darkness, Sons of Light: A Novel of Some Probability* (1969), and *Clifford's Blues* (1999).

Williams centered his literary work around the themes of African American life, exploring racial and cultural inequities and possible political solutions. His no-nonsense writing style was lean and powerful, with a penetrating sense of analysis and insight. Some critics, while lauding his craft, simultaneously labeled him as "an angry writer" due to his unwillingness to compromise his view that racial discrimination could not be tolerated. His emphasis on social conditions also informed his nonfiction work in such books as *Africa: Her History, Lands and People* (1962), *This Is My Country Too* (1965), *The Most Native of Sons: A Biography of Richard Wright* (1970), *The King God Didn't Save: Reflections on the Life of Martin Luther King, Jr.* (1970), *Flashbacks: A Twenty-Year Diary of Article Writing* (1973), *Minorities in the City* (1975), and *If I Stop I'll Die: The Comedy and Tragedy of Richard Pryor* (with his son Dennis A. Williams) (1991).

The 1970s and 1980s found Williams still at a creative peak with a surprising output of novels: *Captain Blackman* (1972), *Mothersill and the Foxes* (1975), *The Junior Bachelor Society* (1976), *!Click Song* (1982), *The Berhama Account* (1985), and *Jacob's Ladder* (1987). Although he has been relatively quiet in the 1990s, Williams's *Clifford's Blues*, recently published by Coffee House Press, is the story of a gay black musician in a concentration camp writing a diary that is smuggled out; it is one of his most ambitious works.

Through his long career, Williams has contributed articles, essays, and fiction to many anthologies. Respected for his fine craftsmanship as a writer, he built on his reputation with several assignments as an editor for various projects, including *The Angry Black* (1962), *Amistad I* (1970), and *Amistad II* (1971), coedited with Charles Harris, along with several others. He has taught at a host of universities, written for television, and been the subject of several articles. With two landmark novels, *The Man Who Cried I Am* and *Captain Blackman*, Williams has been acknowledged as "the finest writer of his generation." He continues to work on several projects and to lecture while maintaining a residence in New Jersey.

## IN HIS OWN WORDS

*On the discipline of writing:* "I work every day so people say I'm disciplined. I write as long as it comes and if it's not, I switch to some other project or correspondence. Doing some manual task keeps me from getting writer's block, freeing up my mind. Poetry is always good to keep the juices flowing. Poetry is the training for any writer. For fiction writers, I'd have them write poetry for a year. It gives you a sense of voice, rhythm, economical use of words for power and mood. It teaches you to be brief. You don't want to bore your reader."[1]

*On revision:* "If you don't revise, you're dead. I don't think first thoughts have that much gold in them. There isn't a computer program that can do the revisions for you. It involves concentration, imagination, and determination. Work until you get it right, with each word meaning what you want it to say. Be sharp."[2]

**On the lack of political issues in today's black fiction:** "Editors get tired of politics and politics is dangerous. I think the relationship genre is easier to handle, rather than the big, thorny issues. We've jettisoned the issues we should be concerned with examining. We're still dealing with race, racism and skin color, and not how we relate to the rest of the world. We must take a more global look at our world and our place in it."[3]

1. Personal interview with writer.
2. Ibid.
3. Ibid.

# KRISTIN (HUNTER) LATTANY
## NOVELIST, SCREENWRITER, TELEVISION WRITER

Born: September 12, 1931. Kristin Lattany was born in Philadelphia, Pennsylvania, to a principal father and a schoolteacher mother, George and Mabel Eggleston. She started reading at age four and later wrote poetry and articles for her school paper. At age fourteen, she founded a teenage social column for the local edition of the *Pittsburgh Courier* and continued working for the publication as a writer until 1952. Kristin graduated with a B.S. in education from the University of Pennsylvania in 1951 and worked for less than a year as a third-grade teacher. The following year, she quit her teaching job and took a copywriting job with a local ad agency.

In 1955, writing as Kristin Hunter, she gained notice for her television script, *Minority of One*, in a national contest sponsored by CBS; it was a work based on the reintegration of an all-black school in Camden, New Jersey. This was the start of her devotion to the themes of poverty, black middle-class complacency, and materialism. She published her first novel, *God Bless the Child*, in 1964, showcasing the bitter aftermath of color bias on three generations of women in a black family. While writing this novel, she left her job with the ad firm and worked as a research assistant at the University of Pennsylvania School of Social Work, which was followed by two assignments as an information officer for the city of Philadelphia.

Her next novel, *The Landlord* (1966), was a popular bestseller, which caught the attention of a Hollywood producer; a film by the same name was released four years later. The book centers around the actions of a confused white man who purchases a tenement in a poor black neighborhood and becomes involved in the lives of its tenants. Both the film and the book were controversial because of the interracial relationship between the owner, Elgar Enders, and the black wife of one of his tenants.

Lattany's editors at Scribner were very surprised at the tremendous reception of her next book, *The Soul Brothers and Sister Lou* (1968), a young-adult novel that stressed the more positive aspects of family life in the black community. Other young adult and juvenile novels followed: *The Boss Cat* (1971), *The Pool Table War* (1972), *Uncle Daniel and the Raccoon* (1972), *Lou in the Limelight* (1981), and a collection of short fiction for children, *Guests in the Promised Land* (1973).

Lattany, however, did not forsake the world of adult fiction, producing another intricate novel, *The Survivors* (1975), which portrayed the gentrification of an inner-city neighborhood by whites and the use of class as a unifying force for racial reconciliation. She followed this effort with *The Laketown Rebellion* (1978), a profound study of black identity and political turmoil. The author's continued examination of the urban African American experience and strong black women in crisis emerged again in her recent novel, *Kinfolks* (1996). Lattany's current novel, *Do Unto Others* (2000), takes political correctness and Afrocentricity and turns them upside down.

## IN HER OWN WORDS

*On her love of the novel:* "The novel gives me space to explore issues fully. Still, it's not up to me to impose political points of view on anybody. Novels tend to move under their own agenda and weight. Short stories are good but read too fast. I like to read novels, something that will occupy my mind for more than twenty minutes. With the influence of television, most people don't want that long, absorbing experience, but I love it. My novels may not be as ambitious as they used to be. My last couple of novels were shorter than before, though. I had to get back into the regime of writing after spending twenty-three years teaching in the English department at the University of Pennsylvania."[1]

*On the role of fantasy in current literature:* "There is a great deal of fantasy in current fiction—money, status, and glamorous objects. I was reading one such book, and said to myself 'I don't know such people.' I don't think it's positive to write this way. To put our hopes and dreams on things and symbols is a mistake. I understand the need to fantasize, but I wish their fantasies were more constructive. We should not become totally caught up in the values of the majority culture. If we do, we'll lose something of ourselves."[2]

*On her writing habits:* "I don't write according to a schedule. I regret that because I'd get more done. I tend to get distracted. Still, I require myself to produce a certain number of pages a day. Every day. That's how a book gets done."[3]

1. Personal interview with writer.
2. Ibid.
3. Ibid.

# WILLIAM MELVIN KELLEY
## NOVELIST, SHORT-STORY WRITER, EDUCATOR

Born: November 1, 1937. William Melvin Kelley was born in
New York City in a home where education and writing were
commonplace. For many years his father, William Melvin
Kelley Sr., was an editor at the *Amsterdam News*, a leading
national African American newspaper, where he was credited
with modernizing the publication. The younger Kelley attended the Fieldston School and Harvard University, and became aware of the value and importance of black literature
very early in his life.

In his developing years, Kelley dreamed of becoming an actor or a painter, but writing won out as his passion after he
took a course during his time at Harvard with the noted novelist John Hawkes. Soon his work began gaining notice as he
earned the Dana Reed Prize from Harvard University in 1960
and became a Bread Loaf scholar two years later. His first
novel, *A Different Drummer* (1962), explores the reaction of
Tucker Caliban, a black man, to slavery with a flight to the
North as the only effective manner to deal with deeply in-
grained racism. Innovative and stylistically remarkable, Kelley's novel won both the John Hay Whitney Foundation Award
and the Rosenthal Foundation Award in 1963. The following
year, he won the *Transatlantic Review* Award for his next effort, *Dancers on the Shore* (1964), a collection of stories using
some of the characters from his previous book and introducing new ones, who would appear in his later works.

Kelley used the New York jazz scene as the backdrop for
his second novel, *A Drop of Patience* (1965), the tale of jazz
saxophonist Ludlow Washington, whose life is subverted by

drugs, late hours, and a push-pull romance with a white woman. But nothing prepared critics and peers for the surrealistic gem that followed, *dem* (1967), a novel that attacks the complexity of skin-color prejudice and the gender wars with a vengeance in a story about a white couple who become the parents of twin boys, one white and the other black.

In 1970, Kelley produced his most experimental work, *Dunford's Travels Everywheres*, using Irish writer James Joyce's work as an inspiration for his creation of a new language to describe the inner conflicts of Chig Dunford, a Harvard-educated African American. The language, according to the writer, was a mix of Pidgin English, Bantu, and Harlem jive blended with standard English. While the critics were baffled by this daring work, Kelley's literary challenge was rewarded with a fiction award from the Black Academy of Arts and Letters that year. Despite a lengthy literary silence, Kelley has continued writing for several publications including *The New Yorker, Esquire, The* (London) *Times Literary Supplement, Newsweek,* and *Harper's.* He is currently working on several projects while teaching creative writing at Sarah Lawrence College in New York.

## IN HIS OWN WORDS

*On his purpose for writing and politics:* "I simply want to write good books. It isn't that I'm naïve, that I'm trying to divorce myself from the racial struggle, but I don't think it should enter into my art in such a way that my writing becomes propagandistic. If my novels are so strongly tied to the times, the book would have no reason to live once the present struggles are over—if indeed they ever will be over. I want my books to have reason to exist."[1]

1. From interview with Kelley as appears in Roy Newquist, ed., *Conversations* (Chicago: Rand McNally, 1967), 198.

*On authors who influenced his work:* "First, Conrad's *Heart of Darkness*, most of Faulkner, and Langston Hughes's Simple series which ran in the *New York Post*. I loved how Langston loved us as a people. Faulkner influenced me to abandon the book by book approach in favor of an ongoing literature that possessed interconnected characters. I loved the poetry of Melvin B. Tolson and Robert Hayden, as well as the essays of James Baldwin. But it was a reading of James Joyce's *Finnegan's Wake* that inspired me to try to remake the language, constantly taking standard words and remolding them in an African style."[2]

*On current American and African American fiction:* "African American literature today, for the most part, is very conservative, with the exception of Octavia Butler and Samuel Delany. In the past, there were writers willing to challenge the status quo, to experiment, to be surreal. I think we're conservative because we don't own our own presses. The big publishers define our culture, and they're very comfortable with us only writing books about the race problem or romance. Or the singular image of black pathology. Anything challenging or innovative is considered difficult. The publishers want us to write about black people; they do not want us to write about America."[3]

2. Personal interview with writer.
3. Ibid.

# CARLENE HATCHER POLITE
## NOVELIST, ACTIVIST, EDUCATOR, DANCER

Born: August 28, 1932. Carlene Hatcher Polite was born in Detroit to John and Lillian Hatcher, a pair of international union representatives. After attending Detroit public schools, she studied at Sarah Lawrence College in New York for a short time before going on to enter the Martha Graham School of Contemporary Dance. An accomplished dancer, she performed with the Concert Dance Theatre of New York City, the Detroit Equity Theatre, and the Vanguard Playhouse from 1955 to 1963.

Living in New York City's Greenwich Village in the early 1960s, Polite became a part of an activist group of writers and artists deeply involved in the civil rights movement. In 1962, she was elected to the Michigan State Central Committee of the Democratic Party, where she worked for greater participation of blacks in electoral politics, and later served on the Detroit Council for Human Rights. Polite joined many key marches and protests against racist shootings and bombings. She founded the Northern Negro Leadership Conference in 1963 and served as an active member of the NAACP during the most turbulent days of the civil rights struggle.

Following the 1964 closing of the Detroit Council for Human Rights, Polite emigrated to Paris, where a French editor recognized her promise as a writer and supported her efforts as a novelist. Her experimental novel of black love and oppression, *The Flagellants*, was published in 1966 by a French publishing house to strong reviews and reprinted in the United States by Farrar, Straus and Giroux in 1967 to similar acclaim. She continued working in Paris as a writer until her departure for America in 1971.

Returning to her native land during the Black Student Movement, Polite immediately assumed a post as associate professor of English at the State University of New York in Buffalo. She rekindled her old ties with the NAACP and established close ties with several prominent black student groups. Her second novel, *Sister X and the Victims of Foul Play* (1975), took her literary experiments of her pioneering first book to a new, more mature level. Her sophomore effort details the story of a dead exotic dancer who performed in Paris as told through the jazzy street chatter of her two confidants, a costume designer and a former lover. While some critics found her adventurous prose somewhat daunting, others praised her courageous, demanding vision.

Since the publication of *Sister X*, Polite has not published another novel and has resisted efforts to bring another of her challenging works to print. She says her current project is a memoir of her early days in New York City during the politically alive 1960s, her life as an expatriate in Paris, and her work in the civil rights movement. Presently, she is a member of the faculty in the English Department at the State University of New York in Buffalo.

## IN HER OWN WORDS

*On reading and writing:* "I've always been a bookworm in anti-intellectual America. I always wanted to write. I was raised around books, my parents' books, and loved words. Words are all and everything to me. For a long time, my experience was to be socially and politically engaged, and I found a way to bring that element of my life to my work. It was Paris that offered me the moment to reflect, to sit down quietly and work without distraction. I became a writer there."[1]

1. Personal interview with writer.

*On the jazz influences in her work:* "I'm a be-bopper. When we first got to New York City, we lived near Fifty-second Street, the heart of bop, and went as often as we could to the jazz clubs. From back home, I knew Yusef Lateef, Kenny Burrell, Tommy Flanagan, and all the cats. We all wanted to come to the big city. You can hear the bop rhythms in my work. I've done readings with Jayne Cortez; that's my spiritual sister. My readings were usually with jazz musicians. Rhythm is rhythm, whether it's words or music. Read Rumi and you'll see what I mean. Or listen to rap or world music, all of it. It's there."[2]

*On criticism:* "I don't usually trust critics or reviewers. It's your words, your writing. That's your blood, sweat you're putting out there. People try to tell you what you meant when that is not what was written. I tell them to read the work closely. Let the words speak to you. Let the words speak for themselves."[3]

2. Ibid.
3. Ibid.

## ALICE CHILDRESS
### NOVELIST, COLUMNIST, PLAYWRIGHT, ACTRESS, DIRECTOR

Born: October 20, 1920. Died: August 14, 1994. Alice Childress was born in Charleston, South Carolina, and raised in Harlem by a grandmother who loved the arts and cultural events. She dropped out of high school after the deaths of her mother and grandmother in the late 1930s. As a young woman she worked several odd jobs during World War II to support her daughter after a failed first marriage. She started her writing career in the early 1940s and later pursued her dreams of being an actress. Disillusioned at the lack of acting opportunities for blacks in New York City, Childress became a founding member of the American Negro Theater in Harlem, where she remained for eleven years as an actress, teacher, and director. The innovative theater was a breeding ground for such notables as Ossie Davis, Ruby Dee, Frank Silvera, and Sidney Poitier.

It was as a playwright that Childress made her mark in New York with her first play, *Florence* (1949), which was an extended dialogue between a white and a black woman at a train station. This acclaimed production was followed by several others including *Gold Through the Trees* (1952), *Trouble in Mind* (1955), *Wedding Band: A Love/Hate Story in Black and White* (1966), *String* (1969), *Mojo: A Black Love Story* (1970), *When the Rattlesnake Sounds* (1975), *Let's Hear It for the Queen* (1976), *Sea Island Song* (1977), and *Moms* (1986). Childress also wrote and directed many other Off-Broadway productions, while performing and writing for films and television. She received many honors and citations for her stage work, including the coveted Obie Award for *Trouble in Mind* in 1955—making her the first African American woman to be so honored—a Rockefeller grant, an award from the John Golden Fund for Playwrights, and a Harvard appointment to the Radcliffe Institute for Independent Study.

Despite her many successes in professional American theater, Childress was constantly pressured to make compromises in the presentation of scathing racial themes in her work, but she refused to yield. For example, she would not bend to demands to alter the antilynching theme of *Trouble in Mind* to gain more financial backing and a longer theater run. She was unafraid of controversy, tackling in her work such topics as interracial romance, racial violence, heroin addiction among schoolchildren, and institutional racism.

Ever the cultural critic, the social and political concerns of African Americans informed her novels and commentary as well. She published her first novel, *Like One of the Family: Conversations from a Domestic's Life*, in 1966, followed by several others: *A Hero Ain't Nothin' but a Sandwich* (1971); *A Short Walk* (1979); *Rainbow Jordan* (1981); and her last novel, *Those Other People* (1989). The African American characters in her writings, whether male or female, were always resilient, bold, multidimensional, and courageous under pressure. Childress, a prolific writer, also wrote for many leading publications such as *The New York Times*, *The Washington Post*, *Newsweek*, *The New Yorker*, *Nation*, *Ms.*, and countless black periodicals such as *The Crisis*, *Freedomways*, and the *Negro Digest*. She died August 14, 1994, on Long Island, while working on her sixth novel.

## IN HER OWN WORDS

*On her ability to create in many literary disciplines:* "Books, plays, teleplays, motion picture scenarios, etc. . . . an idea comes to me in a certain form and, if it stays with me, must be written out or put in outline form before I can move on to the next event. I sometimes wonder about writing in different forms; could it be that women are used to dealing with the bits and pieces of life and do not feel as compelled to specialize? The play form is the one most familiar to me and so influences all of my writing—I think in scenes."[1]

**On the role of African American women in literature:** "The Negro woman will attain her rightful place in American literature when those of us who care about truth, justice and a better life tell her story, with the full knowledge and appreciation of her constant, unrelenting struggle against racism and for human rights."[2]

**On the Black Writer:** "I've heard some of us say, 'I am not a *Black* writer, I'm a person, an artist.' I've never heard any whites decry being *white* for fear that being *white* and a *person* might cancel one or the other. . . . A Black writer *is a person* and there should be no room for contradiction. The twisted circumstances under which we live are grist for the writing mill, the living, hating and discovering, finding new handles for old pitchers, and realizing there is no such thing as the Black experience; the pain and pleasure are many faceted. . . . Of course the greatest challenge is to write well. With all of its trials, for me there is no creative process more fulfilling than that of writing."[3]

**On censorship:** "Without censors we may have more rather than fewer confrontations. Every well written book is not necessarily a very good one. Some books will naturally draw forth a negative response. We could request equal time for other views. It is necessary to examine and refute ideas printed not only in books, but the mass media as well."[4]

1. Sharon Malinowski, ed., *Black Writers*, 1st ed. (Detroit, Mich.: Gale Research, 1994), 190.

2. Alice Childress, "The Negro Woman in Literature," *Freedomways*, vol. 6, no. 1, (winter 1966), 19.

3. From Mari Evans, ed., *Black Women Writers (1950–1990): A Critical Review* (Garden City, N.Y.: Anchor Books, 1984), 115.

4. Alice Childress, "On Censorship," *Schomberg Center Journal*, vol. 3, no. 3, (summer 1984), 2.

*On Becoming a Writer:* "I continue to create because writing is a labor of love and also an Act of defiance, a way to light a candle in a gale of wind: In the beginning was the Word, and the Word was with God, and the Word was God. . . . I never planned to become a writer, I never finished high school. . . . Time, events, and Grandmother Eliza's brilliance taught me to rearrange circumstances into plays, stories, novels, and scenarios and teleplays. I recall teachers urging me to write composition papers about Blacks who were 'accomplishers'—those who win prizes and honors by overcoming cruel odds; the victory might be won over racial, physical, economic or other handicaps but the end result had to be to inspire the reader/audience to become winners. . . . I turned against the tide and to this day I continue to write about those who come in second, or not at all . . . and the intricate pattern of a loser's life. . . . I concentrate on portraying have-nots in a *have* society. . . ."[5]

5. From Evans, *Black Women Writers,* 115.

# HENRY VAN DYKE

## NOVELIST, EDITOR, JOURNALIST

Born: October 3, 1928. A Michigan native, Henry Van Dyke lived in Montgomery, Alabama, during his childhood while his father taught black students at Alabama State Teachers College. Van Dyke remembers that both of his parents possessed Ph.D.s, were very middle class, and worked to maintain "an isolated, insulated world." They sent him to Michigan for his high school years, and he later earned an M.A. degree in journalism from the University of Michigan in 1955. A career in journalism meant young Van Dyke was forced to follow the limited job opportunities for African Americans wherever they appeared; this led to a series of moves to Pennsylvania and New York. While working on the editorial staff at Basic Books in New York, he completed his first novel, *Ladies of the Rachmaninoff Eyes* (1965), which enthralled critics with its sardonic analysis of the American race question, especially the relationship between blacks and Jews.

Postive notices greeted the 1969 release of his second work, *Blood of Strawberries*, another Van Dyke fictional outing written with great style and sophistication. The writer, who had been called "talented, witty, and brave," was not prepared for the chilly reception for his next, and probably most biting, novel, *Dead Piano*, in 1971. Slender but loaded with shrewd observations, the book puts the topics of race and class under an unforgiving spotlight as he weaves the story of a successful black bourgeois family who endure a home invasion by a militant group. Their comfortable life unravels right before the reader's eyes during the tense twelve-day siege. Sixteen years passed before the publication of *Lunacy and Caprice* (1987), a Bohemian novel of interracial fun and frolic in Greenwich

Village. Currently, the author is retired from his former post as writer-in-residence at Kent State University and finishing a new novel, a satire of the art world, his first in several years.

## IN HIS OWN WORDS

*On the art of fiction:* "I'm very involved with the texture of the prose. If one is going to write fiction, you must get inside the character. When one doesn't, I close the book because how a novel is written is as important as what it says. The art of fiction, for me, is how. There are only a few plots that are new. It's all a matter of ear; it's a matter of the rhythm and color of the words. The absolute how, the tonality and color, cannot be learned. It's natural, and singular like a fingerprint or one's individual smell."[1]

*On revision and discipline:* "There are very few people who can write well without revision. So many things must be juggled when you write fiction. It rarely comes out complete the first time. Rewriting is absolutely necessary. I work every morning, every day. I don't think in terms of pages but in terms of hours. I spend a lot of time at the library. I don't wait for inspiration because it might occur twice a year. It's painful to sit in front of that blank page."[2]

*On difficulty in getting published:* "I'm having a hard time getting published because I refuse to compromise. Even if that was my wish, I wouldn't know how to do it. You, as a person, are your style. As you develop, your writing is a reflection of what you have lived. In the publishing world, there is a collective view of blacks, a singular view of our creative potential. I resent whites seeing us as a monolith. We come in many varieties. And yes, not getting published is very disappointing, but I knew very early that I wouldn't be a commercial writer. It's my cross to bear."[3]

1. Personal interview with writer.
2. Ibid.
3. Ibid.

# TONI CADE BAMBARA
## WRITER, ESSAYIST, SCREENWRITER

Born: March 25, 1939. Died: December 9, 1995. The writer was born Toni Cade in New York City and later added Bambara in 1970 from a name she found in a sketchbook in her great-grandmother's trunk. During their formative years Toni and Walter, her brother, lived in a variety of settings in New York, New Jersey, and the South. However, it was Harlem that made an indelible mark on the young woman's artistic and cultural consciousness. Bambara published her first short story, "Sweet Town," in 1959 while she completed a theater arts degree at Queens College. After graduation, she worked as a caseworker for two years with the New York Department of Welfare, beginning work on an M.A. degree in American literature from City College of New York.

In 1961, Bambara served as a director of recreation in the psychiatric division at Metropolitan Hospital in New York City, a job that lasted a year before the red tape and bureaucratic games made her restless. She returned to her love of community work and acted as a program director from 1962 to 1965 at the Colony Settlement House while finishing up her M.A. degree. In 1970, she compiled and edited *The Black Woman*, a groundbreaking anthology that defined the African American woman's role in both the civil rights movement and the women's movement through nonfiction, fiction, and poetry from such names as Alice Walker, Nikki Giovanni, Audre Lorde, Verta Mae Grosvenor, Jean Carey Bond, and Paule Marshall. The following year, she published another anthology, *Tales and Stories for Black Folks*, which mixed the work of some students with that of more established names, such as Ernest Gaines, Langston Hughes, and Alice Walker.

Bambara's literary reputation was secured with the 1972 publication of *Gorilla, My Love,* a collection of fifteen short stories filled with unforgettable vignettes of black love and portraits of African American women that defied the usual cultural stereotypes. Reviews for the book were exceptionally positive, and Bambara's audience grew, but it was not until 1977 that another fiction collection appeared, *The Sea Birds Are Still Alive.* Critical reaction to this book was not as favorable as the first, with some pundits reprimanding her for its mix of foreign locales and social activism.

Her first novel, *The Salt Eaters,* published in 1980, caught reviewers by surprise because of its experimental form, lengthy roster of characters, and exquisite control of language and theme. A tale of a black woman's quest for mental and spiritual health, the book won the American Book Award and the Langston Hughes Society Award. Bambara received a National Endowment for the Arts Literature Grant the following year as her essays and fiction were translated into German, French, Spanish, Japanese, Swedish, and Dutch. In the 1980s, Bambara devoted much of her time to lecturing, working with various community and women's groups, and filmmaking. In 1986, she served as writer and narrator for Louis Massiah's riveting film, *The Bombing of Osage Avenue,* earning the Best Documentary Academy Award and several other citations. Numerous other films benefited from her excellent skills as a writer and editor before her death due to cancer in 1995.

Toni Morrison, her close friend and mentor, who edited her posthumously published 1996 collection of fiction and essays, *Deep Sightings and Rescue Missions,* wrote in its preface: "Bambara is a writer's writer, an editor's editor, a reader's writer." Bambara's final novel, *Those Bones Are Not My Children,* based on the Atlanta child murders of the early eighties, was published in October 1999.

## IN HER OWN WORDS

*On her origins as a writer:* "I was writing stories long before I learned to spell. My father used to get the *Daily Mirror*, and there were very fat margins, so I would scribble in the margins. When I had someone captive, like my mother in the bathtub, I would read this scribble-scrabble to her and she would listen. Essentially, it was my mother's respect for the life of the mind. She gave us permission to be artists."[1]

*On the importance of writing:* "Stories are important. They keep us alive. In the ships, in the camps, in the quarters, fields, on the road, on the run, underground, under siege, in the throes, on the verge—the storyteller snatches us back from the edge to hear the next chapter. In which we are the subjects. We, the hero of the tales. Our lives preserved. How it was, how it be. Passing it along in the relay. That is what I work to do: to produce stories that save our lives."[2]

*On seeking the joy in her work:* "If I'm not laughing while I work, I conclude that I am not communicating nourishment, since laughter is the most sure-fire healant I know. I don't know all my readers, but I know well for whom I write. And I want for them no less than I want for myself—wholesomeness."[3]

1. From Toni Morrison, ed., *Deep Sightings and Rescue Missions: Fiction, Essays, and Conversations* (New York, Pantheon Books, 1996), 212.

2. From Mary Evans, ed., *Black Women Writers (1950–1990): A Critical Review* (Garden City, N.Y.: Anchor Books, 1984), 41.

3. From Janet Sternburg, *The Writer on Her Work* (New York: Norton, 1992), 157.

# AL YOUNG
## POET, NOVELIST, ESSAYIST,
## SCREENWRITER, EDUCATOR

Born May 31, 1939. Albert James Young, the son of a musician, was born in Ocean Springs, Mississippi, and his family later relocated to Detroit, Michigan. Upon graduation from high school, he attended the University of Michigan, while earning a living as a freelance musician performing on flute and guitar. His uncanny ability with language was rewarded with a Wallace E. Stegner Fellowship in creative writing at Stanford University from 1966 to 1967, which was followed by Bachelor of Arts studies at the University of California at Berkeley in 1969. To support himself, he worked as a disc jockey and writing instructor, and in the 1970s became a screenwriter for First Artists and Universal Studios. His efforts in Hollywood were well received as several of his writing collaborations made it to the big screen, including *Sparkle* (1972) and *Bustin' Loose* (1986).

Committed to quality literature, Young cofounded and edited numerous multicultural literary publications with writer Ishmael Reed, including *Quilt*, *The Yardbird Reader*, and *Califia: The California Poetry*. He began his post as director of the Associated Writing Programs in 1979 and served as writer-in-residence at the University of Washington, Seattle, in 1981 and 1982. His work in poetry and fiction has garnered several awards and honors including National Endowment for the Arts fellowships (1968, 1969, 1975), a Guggenheim fellowship (1974), the *New York Times* Outstanding Book of the Year citation (1980), and the Before Columbus Foundation Award (1982).

A gifted stylist and storyteller, Young's mastery of poetry and brilliant lyricism are also reflected in the subtle yet naturalistic nuances of form, theme, and characterization that appear in his prose. His poetry collections include *Dancing* (1969), *The Song Turning Back into Itself* (1971), *Geography of the Near Past* (1976), *Heaven: Collected Poems 1958–1988* (1989), *Straight No Chaser* (1994), and *Conjugal Visits* (1995). His imaginative novels, *Snakes* (1970), *Who Is Angelina?* (1975), *Sitting Pretty* (1976), *Ask Me Now* (1980), and *Seduction by Light* (1988), with their wise philosophical view of life, have been greeted with enthusiastic reviews.

Throughout his literary career, Young's writing has bene-fited from a rhythmic musical sense reminiscent of jazz, grow-ing from his deep appreciation of the spontaneous art form. That love is evident in his essay collections about musicians and their craft: *Bodies & Soul: Musical Memoirs* (1981), *Kinds of Blue* (1984), *Things Ain't What They Used to Be* (1987), and *Mingus/Mingus* (1991), a collaboration with Janet Coleman. Currently, Young serves as a visiting lecturer for several Ameri-can universities and European learning centers, while work-ing on a prequel to his novel *Sitting Pretty*.

## IN HIS OWN WORDS

*On the role of the writer in society:* "The role of the writer in society is that of the truth teller and the reflector of that society. In the last one hundred years, we've seen the artist transformed into a solo performer, a product, strictly for enter-tainment, for commerce. Now, art is so commercially driven that we let others choose our artists, our writers for us. That choice, for the most part, has been taken out of our hands."[1]

*On current fiction:* "Fiction is constantly changing. I remem-ber a student telling me that he found Dickens's novel, *Great Expectations* too boring, adding that it had 'too much data' and pages where nothing was happening. I replied that Dick-

1. Personal interview with writer.

ens, with his rich characterizations, was out to both entertain and inform the readers of his day. Things have changed. Novelists cannot compete with television and film today, with their emphasis on action, explosions, and special effects. But novels can do things that neither of them can do, for it can explore feelings and other mind states. Novelists, like all writers, have to keep their chops strong. They must develop and deepen, and be open to all influences."[2]

*On the ongoing black book boom:* "I don't think it will ever go away because you have an increasingly literate audience out there. Black women are going into stores and buying three and four books at a time. Black women writers now are reading and writing their anger and disappointment with men, and other nonblack females are reading them. Back in the 1960s and 1970s, it was acceptable for black men to read books, especially those with a political message. That changed for a while, but black male writers are beginning to find an audience for their work once more. A black man who writes now, who has something to say, can be heard."[3]

2. Ibid.
3. Ibid.

# PART IV

# GENRE FICTION, POETRY, AND CHILDREN'S BOOKS

# AFRICAN AMERICAN MYSTERIES

For many years, there were no African American talents working in the genre of mystery writing. Rudolph Fisher produced possibly one of the earliest works of this type, *The Conjure Man Dies: A Mystery Tale of Dark Harlem,* in 1937. Critics have often wondered, Where are *our* Sherlock Holmeses, our Lord Peter Wimseys? Where are our writers such as John D. MacDonald or Ruth Rendell or Georges Simenon? Today we can proudly answer: They're here!

Since African American writers are fairly new in the field, there has not been the time to produce our version of Chandler, Hammett, Cain, or Highsmith. Instead, African American mystery writers are gearing up, growing an audience, perfecting their craft so they too can experience a Golden Age or a realist New Wave or a hard-boiled school. There is still the search for the bad guy amid the maze of confusing clues, lies, deceit, and general mayhem until the crime is solved.

The modern-day father of the contemporary African American mystery, Chester Himes, originator of the noted series featuring Harlem detectives Grave Digger Jones and Coffin Ed Johnson, would be pleased with his heirs currently writing in the genre: Walter Mosley, Gar Anthony Haywood, Gary Hardwick, among others. Himes set the standard for the black urban mystery in his *For Love of Imabelle* (1957), *The Real Cool Killers* (1959), *Cotton Comes to Harlem* (1965), and *Blind Man with a Pistol* (1969). Reviewers also pointed out that there was an ample sprinkling of social commentary in Himes's work, as the writer believed that the novelist had a responsibility to inform as well as entertain.

MEETINGS BETWEEN exceptional artists can produce great results, but not all of the time. Chester Himes, known for his gritty Harlem detective novels, describes a much anticipated tête-à-tête with the painter Picasso in his 1976 memoir, *My Life of Absurdity*. Long an American expatriate living in France, Himes and friends drove from Paris to Cannes, where the writer was informed that, the master of Cubism was considering drawing a comic strip based on one of the writer's books. Instead, Picasso spent time explaining to Himes the virtues of washing a dog when it has been swimming in salt water, while he bathed the animal with water from the tap. After that, the artist ate his dinner, showed some paintings to a few buyers, and said very little to the man who had come so far to see him. The comic-strip project was not discussed, then or ever.

That legacy of political awareness has not been lost, as Walter Mosley's Easy Rawlins novels reveal, with their subtle but strong observations of racism, class, and gender. Throughout his Rawlins series, Mosley has sharpened his skills as a master weaver of suspense, action, and crisp dialogue in his books, *Devil in a Blue Dress* (1990), *A Red Death* (1991), *White Butterfly* (1992), *Black Betty* (1994), and *A Little Yellow Dog* (1996). Also, a growing legion of fans have welcomed Haywood's chilling sleuthers, including his *Fear of the Dark* (1988) and *Going Nowhere Fast* (1994).

What is the appeal of the new African American mystery? "I'm writing crime novels, about people committing crime and trying to elude getting caught," says Mosley, whose novels have captured the essence of Jim Crow America. "However, I try not to write simplistic characters who will become boring as soon as you read them. There was a strong bond among blacks during the days of Jim Crow. They realized there was no chance of help coming from outside the community. They knew they were only a hairsbreadth from misfortune happening to any one of them if they didn't help each other. I'm very interested in this quality. A lot of my readers understand this element in my work. They know this is a hard life. They understand what Easy and his community are going through in their effort to survive. They understand that you have to get back up after you've been knocked down. They understand you have to take chances to move forward."

While the traditional mystery writers' establishment formerly showed reluctance about accepting the possibility that there might be an audience for black novels in the genre, they now feel compelled to promote the current wave of African American suspense writers, due to the increased readership they have brought into bookstores. Black mystery readers, like romance novel fans, are loyal and spend sizable sums to satisfy their hunger.

In recent years, a number of African American women have prospered in detective fiction, a subgenre of the mystery realm with a flood of exceptional female sleuths: Valerie Wilson Wesley's Tamara Hayle, Eleanor Taylor Bland's Marti MacAlister, Barbara Neely's Blanche White, Grace F. Edwards's Mali Anderson, and Pamela Thomas-Graham's Nikki Chase.

While still employing the device of the detective in a serial role, these series take the concept of the specific genre to another level through their exploration of the African American community, with its folklore, myths, and troubling social issues. Each of the women writers mentioned has brought something special to this form of literature, which has frequently been dismissed as formula writing or low-grade entertainment. In their hands, these important works in the genre become vital, compelling fiction. Each writer's tone and style is unique—accomplished yet powerful.

One example of such bestselling work is Wesley's popular Tamara Hayle series, which sells solidly not only in the United States but also in France, England, and Germany. She knows the awesome responsibility of the mystery writer and takes it very seriously.

"People ask me why do I write about crime," Wesley says.

"Crime stories are basically morality plays, good versus evil. Murder is the worst thing that can happen. Mysteries are puzzles. If they're created well, the reader will think the solution is right at his fingertips but suddenly all of the pieces change. And he's stumped. It's the journey to the answer, to the solution, that keeps the readers coming back. That's probably why there will always be an audience for the mystery, no matter who writes it."

For the aspiring mystery writer, this genre offers endless possibilities, since the old formula of the suspense tale is being altered by the new black voices in much the same way that Ailey changed ballet or Woods revived golf. The African American artistic sensibility, with its unique vantage point, is now accomplishing a similar metamorphosis in this genre, as evidenced in these wise words from Eleanor Taylor Bland in a recent interview with Paula L. Woods, another mystery writer with an excellent debut work, *Inner City Blues*: "Mystery fiction isn't glib, superficial, or just another quick read. We write about people you know, issues you are involved in, neighborhoods you live in. . . . We get down, use motherwit and street smarts. We care about what we say and how we say it."

## Notable African American Mystery and Suspense Fiction
*Cotton Comes to Harlem* (1965), Chester Himes
*Fear of the Dark* (1988), Gar Anthony Haywood
*Devil in a Blue Dress* (1990), Walter Mosley
*Blanche Among the Talented Tenth* (1994), Barbara Neely
*Keep Still* (1996), Eleanor Taylor Bland
*Devil's Gonna Get Him* (1995), Valerie Wilson Wesley
*Sunrise* (1994), Chassie West
*Double Dead* (1997), Gary Hardwick
*A Toast Before Dying* (1998), Grace F. Edwards
*Inner City Blues* (1999), Paula L. Woods

# AFRICAN AMERICAN ROMANCE NOVELS

One of the most popular ways to break into the publishing ranks is to write a romance novel; to combine your love for the genre with your desire to get into print. Most people are surprised to learn that many mass-market authors have entered the more lucrative hardcover field through a commercial career built on a series of romance paperback originals. Many of these women—and, overwhelmingly, romances are created by women—were not originally writers and never attended writing workshops or seminars. While this pattern has held true for white authors, it has not been the case with many veteran black writers who have attempted to make the transition from romance novels into mainstream fiction. Some editors have shown a reluctance to permit romance writers to publish other types of fiction in areas where they lack a large readership base.

However, black writers of romance fiction persist, and their audience is growing steadily across the country. As longtime fans of the romance novel, they insist that the books are truly addictive, with each new title temporarily satisfying an inner emotional need for intimacy while affirming the long-honored conventions of love, commitment, and marriage. Mainstream publishers have watched the popularity of the African American romance novel increase in recent years; but they have exercised caution in entering the field in a significant manner, despite the steadfast loyalty of its fans.

## AFRICAN AMERICAN ROMANCE FICTION AND ITS HISTORY

The first contemporary black romance novel, *Entwined Destinies*, by Rosalind Wells (a.k.a. Elsie B. Washington), was published in 1980 by Dell. Before the 1980s, the African American romance novel was nonexistent, with aficionados of the genre forced to read chiefly "bodice-rippers" with white damsels in distress, knights in shining armor, and swarthy villains lurking in the dark corridors of a castle. None of the faces were black, nor were the situations reflective of the African American experience. Followers of the genre found little in mainstream romances that spoke to their modern lives.

That changed in 1984, when Vivian Stephens, a black editor at Harlequin, bought the African American romance novel *Adam and Eva*, by Sandra Kitt, for a mainstream romance house. In 1990, Leticia Peoples's Maryland-based Odyssey Books opened the door for African American authors, becoming the first African American publisher to reach out to an eager, untapped romance audience. Another imprint, Arabesque, now owned by BET, appeared in 1994, building on that rapidly growing readership. With romances (including black romances) comprising 48 percent of paperback sales, a host of new writers emerged as excellent storytellers of contemporary African American romantic fables, names such as Donna Hill, Francis Ray, Felicia Mason, Rochelle Alers, Anita Bunkley, Patricia Vaughn, Maggie Ferguson, and Brenda Jackson.

"When we started our magazine in 1979, black romances didn't exist," says Louise Snead, publisher of the influential *Affaire de Coeur*, the only black-owned magazine chronicling the romance industry. "We were there at the very beginning. Some editors resisted black writers moving into this field. However, the publishing industry has been surprised at the great reception given to the black women who write romances. All of these women are very intelligent and highly accomplished in their chosen profession."

Currently, romances account for nearly $90 million in revenue, of which the black entries comprise a healthy share of the market. An estimated 20 million readers buy romances annually in the United States, according to industry data. Katherine Falk, founder and publisher of the powerful industry publication *Romantic Times*, believes the audience for black romances will continue to grow as the steady development of writers for that market provides an even more sophisticated, satisfying product for the readers.

"There are some very good African American romances out there now," Falk says. "They are coming into their own because of the accomplished writers now publishing in the genre. There's a strong market for them, and the mainstream publishers are now actively pursuing it. If an author writes a good book, it doesn't go undiscovered."

## ROMANCE WRITERS

One of the pioneering writers in black romances, Sandra Kitt, a library collection specialist with the American Museum of Natural History in New York City, has authored several classics in the category, *Significant Others* and *The Color of Love* among them. "I was the first black writer to publish with the leading romance house, Harlequin, with my novel, *Adam and Eva*, in 1984," Kitt remembers. "My books are mainstream novels with love interests rather than the usual romances. They were very layered, with depth, and complex characters. I wanted to give readers something to think about. My current books are much more character-driven than my earlier ones, with emphasis on psychological and social issues. They all possess a strong, central romance."

Another writer who captured a large following in those early days of African American romances, Donna Hill, continues to juggle romance writing and her job as a publicist for the Queens Borough Library System in New York City, with her passion for creating realistic urban love stories for her many fans. Hill started writing short stories for black romance magazines in 1987, with her first novel, *Rooms of the Heart*, appearing in 1990 from Odyssey Books. Tireless, she has turned out at least twenty-one titles to date.

"Some writers in the genre say my work is edgy, with many subplots and a lot of texture," says Hill, author of the groundbreaking *A Private Affair*. "They're not the usual guy-gets-girl stories. My characters have grown over the years as I have matured. In fact, my first book dealt with adultery, which was then a real taboo in romances, but I changed that. I've taken risks with my fiction, but I've always managed to show the total range of our experience. African American romances allow us to see ourselves positively. We rarely see that in television, film, or other genres. In fiction, we're usually depicted negatively, even from our most acclaimed writers."

As more black authors enter the romance genre, the type of female heroine in the books has become more independent, able to have it all—love, family, and a career. Contemporary romances are more reflective of the current societal changes and cultural trends. In many ways, glitz, glamour, and fantasy are not as fashionable as they have been, while realism and social relevance are now popular with African American romance readers.

For the reader who devours several of these novels a week, nothing beats an engrossing story replete with the heated dynamics of contemporary relationships. Although some critics still consider romances nonliterary and downmarket, fans of the genre crave these tales, which feature a happy ending with love ever triumphant. Negative mainstream reviews of books in this genre are not a purchasing factor to their faithful supporters, as they stand firm in their belief that love can survive any and all challenges.

"Contemporary romances, on the whole, provide the reader with men we feel are desirable," says Gwynne Forster, a former United Nations demographer and author of *Ecstasy* and *Obsession*. "The men are educated, dependable, reliable, generous, and good family men. The man treasures his woman.

He cherishes her. She gives him, in return, his manhood. He's there for her. Our men are loving, upstanding, and take care of their families. If they didn't, our race wouldn't survive. Our romances reinforce that view."

Gay G. Gunn, a social worker, shares this positive opinion of the black community as seen in her novels, *Everlastin' Love* and *Nowhere to Run*. "Whenever we are shown, we're shown with physical abuse and violence but never with love," she says. "We must have morals and true love to maintain our families, which are resources for renewal. My women follow the three S's—sense, sanity, and self-esteem. Good black men exist. My message to black women is to stop settling for less, use patience, and find these men."

Many of the new generation of black romance writers are venturing into areas formerly dominated by their white counterparts, such as historicals and romantic suspense. Maggie Ferguson, author of *Looks Are Deceiving* and *Crime of Passion*, adds an ethnic feel to the romantic suspense subgenre. "Romantic suspense has elements of romance and mystery in equal parts," she says. "Mystery readers love the murder aspect, the thrill of the chase, and the detection of the crime. There are others doing this hybrid, but we call ourselves romance writers. It's good versus evil. The mystery is there, with the romance, woven into the fabric of the plot. In a sense, you're writing two stories at the same time."

## FROM THE EDITOR'S VIEW

Change is apparent not only in the writing of the romance genre but also in its promotion and marketing. Shortly after Kensington started its romance line, Arabesque, it recruited Monica Harris from Dell, where she had edited romances and genre fiction, to head up the Kensington effort. She quickly altered how the publishing world viewed black romances: with a new attitude, a knack for innovation, and superb editorial skills.

"These romances opened up publishing as a whole," says

Harris, now editor-in-chief of the Doubleday-sponsored Black Expressions Book Club. "In the past, there was not enough stress on the commercial end. These books are a fast read, very entertaining. The publishers have matured and now see the black audience is not a monolith. Blacks are interested in a number of things, as you can see in the variety of writers working in the genre. Some critics write romances off as fluff, but their readers take them quite seriously. And the publishers of the genre now do as well, with more money going for packaging, promotion, and marketing."

Harris also notes that the writers are very serious about their books, researching locales and professions to add authenticity to their novels. Regardless of the category, the writers understand the need to remain true to the formula of the genre, although they know that very few of their efforts will cross over into the mainstream market.

"The romances serve as a guide to relationships for the audience," Harris explains. "Sometimes people discover the parameters of their relationships in these books, even if the male point of view is womanized and idealized. The new romances show the maturity of the readers and writers. Women are in the world in a different way. They demand different things from these books. White audiences are often afraid of differences because of the premium placed on skin color and morality. So they do not read black romances, whereas black women will read white romances. The white readers forget that there are more similarities between women than differences."

The popularity of the contemporary African American romance is linked to its emphasis on reality, according to Karen Thomas, who came to BET's Arabesque line after a five-year editorial stint at Berkley. "The appeal for Arabesque is that you have a couple dealing with challenges we all face," Thomas says. "They could be two people you might know. These are everyday situations handled with a romantic feel. These stories must end well. For an African American woman, the books can be inspirational in showing how a heroine overcomes obstacles. No male bashing, no stereotypes. These stories show how we live, face our problems, and learn how to love again."

Indeed, the rise of the contemporary African American romance novels does indicate that there is a market for more positive, affirming stories. Stories with realism, timely topics, and emphasis on family and community will be around for a long time, despite those who frown on the very genre. There will always be those readers who feel that graphic sex leaves nothing to the imagination, that the thrill of that first kiss is worth remembering, that real sensuality and intimacy still matter in relationships. The African American romance novel remains uncharted territory, with new writers and readers falling under its spell every day, so any proclamations that the genre has peaked must be dismissed as false. It remains complex, spirited, and very much alive.

**Memorable African American Romance Novels**
*Adam and Eva*, Sandra Kitt (Harlequin)
*Entwined Destinies*, Rosalind Wells (Dell Candlelight)
*Careless Whispers*, Rochelle Alers (Dell Candlelight)
*Rooms of the Heart*, Donna Hill (Odyssey)
*Yamilla*, Mildred D. Riley (Odyssey)
*Looks Are Deceiving*, Maggie Ferguson (Harlequin Intrigue)
*Forever Yours*, Francis Ray (Arabesque)
*Emily, the Yellow Rose*, Anita Bunkley (Rinard)
*Murmur of Rain*, Patricia Vaughn (Pocket)
*Vivid*, Beverly Jenkins (Avon)
*The Passion Ruby*, Eboni Snoe (Arabesque)
*Breeze*, Robin Lynette Hampton (Genesis)
*Conspiracy*, Margie Walker (Arabesque)
*Midnight Blue*, Monica Jackson (Arabesque)
*Body and Soul*, Felicia Mason (Arabesque)
*Obsession*, Gwynne Forster (Arabesque)
*The Grass Ain't Greener*, Monique Gilmore (Arabesque)
*Shades of Desire*, Monica White (Genesis)
*Everlasting Love*, Gay G. Gunn (Genesis)
*Silver Love*, Layle Giusto (Arabesque)

# AFRICAN AMERICAN SCIENCE FICTION

Most black readers shun science fiction out of a wariness and a belief that it is a genre that has little to say about their lives, largely due to a notion that the fanciful projections of the future rarely capture the pressures and tensions of our daily existence. Science fiction, in the past, was the domain of white men, writers who honed their craft in the pulps and magazines from the glory days of the genre. Writers such as Isaac Asimov, Robert Heinlein, Philip K. Dick, Poul Anderson, Theodore Sturgeon, Arthur C. Clarke, Damon Knight, James Blish, Fritz Leiber, Roger Zelazny, John Brunner, and Clifford D. Simak—all fashioned the language of this field with speculative themes, wild plots and subplots, with a glimpse of a time to come. These men talked of scientific advances, black holes, quasars, and galaxies, using aliens, androids, robots, cyborgs, and interactive computers as the characters of their imagined worlds.

Very rarely were black characters introduced or even made mention of in this future, but that is not to say that African American writers have not historically tried to find their own utopia or to create their own world in this form of fiction. One of the early efforts by a black writer, *Imperium in Imperio*, an 1899 novel written by Sutton E. Griggs, was a fantasy that envisioned a secret society of black men plotting to conquer Texas to form a black state. While there may have been small elements of speculative fiction in some other works by African American writers in the past, none of them were as astonishing as George S. Schuyler's classic 1931 novel, *Black No More*, the futuristic tale of a black man, Max Disher, who is magically transformed by a scientific process into Matthew Fisher, a white man who plots vengefully to marry a white woman who spurned him as a "Colored," while seizing control of a Klan-like group, the Knights of Nordica. Schuyler also wrote two other imaginative novels, *The Black Internationale* and *The Black Empire*, between 1936 and 1938, under a pseudonym. The latter novel featured the use of a weapon of mass destruction that employed deadly proton rays.

SAMUEL R. DELANY, the author of several Nebula and Hugo award-winning science-fiction novels, was particularly inspired by the writings of Robert Heinlein, Clifford Simak, Isaac Asimov, James Baldwin, Richard Wright, and Chester Himes. "To be black in America today," Delany told a reporter, "makes you either analytical—in whatever vocabulary you choose—or bitter; and you are analytical to keep from being bitter. Science fiction can evoke the kind of imaginative mental exercise that can be used to deal with the real world in terms of how we are going to change it. But first, we must have an image of that future. We must begin to think, What are we going to do with our tomorrows?"

No black writer joined the ranks of this exclusive club until the arrival of pioneers such as Samuel Delany and Octavia E. Butler, who placed African American people in the picture. After Delany wrote his first novel, *The Jewels of Aptor*, in 1962 at age nineteen, it was quite obvious that this genre would never be the same. He took the science-fiction world by storm, producing a series of groundbreaking novels of space epics such as *The Fall of the Towers* trilogy (1963–1965), *The Ballad of Beta-2* (1965), *Babel 17* (1966), and *The Einstein Intersection* (1967). Delany examined complex issues in his work, notably among them race, gender, sexuality, liberty, choice, oppression, and power. Critics took notice of his literary prowess, his ability to synthesize scientific concerns with sociological themes in an imaginative, intricate mix of dense wordplay. His novels, *Equinox (The Tides of Lust)* (1973), *Dhalgren* (1975), *Triton* (1976), the four-volume *The Return to Neveryon* (1979–1987), and *Stars in My Pocket Like Grains of Sand* (1984) revealed Delany at the top of his creative powers, offering a lush tapestry of eroticism, moral ambiguity, social commentary, and speculative wonder. In all, Delany has penned twenty novels including the recent *Hogg* and *Mad Man*, three short-story collections, two memoirs, and two collections of nonfiction work.

OCTAVIA BUTLER, one of the reigning queens of science fiction, says that a short-story teacher recognized her gifts very early. The teacher, at Pasadena City College, asked her: "Can't you write anything normal?" Butler later explained to a reporter: "Everything I wrote had something strange in it. . . . The people next door are boring. I write about those who do extraordinary things. It just turned out that it was called science fiction."

Octavia Butler, the first African American woman to make an impact in science fiction, is recognized as one of the most gifted, original writers in the genre. She has written eleven novels, including *Patternmaster* (1976), *Mind of My Mind* (1977), *Kindred* (1979), *Wild Seed* (1980), *Clay's Ark* (1984), and the much acclaimed Xenogenesis trilogy (1987–1989). Her work has won both of science fiction's highest awards, the Hugo Award twice and the Nebula Award once. In her writing, she explores both feminist and racial themes, as well as the limits of scientific progress being exploited for commercial gain at the expense of humankind. Her prose is lean, knowing, loaded with spiritual and philosophical insight. In 1995, Butler was awarded the MacArthur "Genius" Award for her amazing body of work and overall contribution to the world of ideas.

With more black readers finding their way to science fiction after the highly publicized success of the *Star Trek* and *Star Wars* series, African American writers are increasingly venturing into that realm, bringing a new sensibility to the formerly sterile environs of space, myth, and fantasy. Walter Mosley, known for his popular Easy Rawlins books, recently published his science-fiction debut, *Blue Light,* to favorable reviews. The novel, rendered with the customary Mosley flair for style and literary surprise, tells of a cosmic blue light whose fall to earth transforms a few humans into superior beings with great powers of intellect and emotion. This unusual gift makes them a target for the Gray Man, a heartless killer sworn to eradicate all of the blue lighters, the breed capable of moving the earth into a more humane phase of existence.

Like Butler, Steven Barnes, another African American trailblazer in science fiction, hails from California. A novelist and a writer for both television and the screen, he tried to forge a career in the genre after encouragement from science-fiction legend Ray Bradbury, later apprenticing with the talented Larry Niven from the 1980s through the mid-1990s. The pair teamed up to produce the remarkable action-packed Dream Park trilogy, which consisted of *Dream Park* (1981), *The Barsoom Project* (1989), and *The California Voodoo Game* (1991). A collaboration with Niven and SF notable Jerry Pournelle led to two other novels, *The Legacy of Heorot* (1987) and *Beowulf's Children* (1995).

Deciding to establish himself as a solo writer, Barnes quickly earned a sizable following with his series featuring space martial arts hero Aubry Knight, a creation that grew from his love of the sport. The Knight series, with its ever-evolving seeker of Truth, secured Barnes's reputation as a writer of fantasy with *Streetlethal* (1983), *Gorgon Child* (1989), and *Firedance* (1993). His recent novel, *Blood Brothers,* features an odd couple of a black computer-game programmer and a white supremacist, who must confront their prejudices to battle evil.

Possibly no black writer in this field has caused such a stir as Tananarive Due, a journalist who was highly praised by horror maven Stephen King and fellow visionary Octavia Butler for her two unnerving mind twisters, *The Between* (1995) and *My Soul to Keep* (1997). Due's debut novel followed the hauntings of a dark force that stalked a judge's life and dreams in a unique blend of fantasy, horror, and the surreal. To sum up her literary magic and style, imagine Anne Rice, Kafka, H. P. Lovecraft, Shirley Jackson, with a dash of James Baldwin and Toni Morrison tossed in to this tasty, smooth word gumbo. In her second novel, *My Soul to Keep*, a wife discovers that her mate is an ageless killer who bartered his soul for immortality. Due is currently working on another novel.

The potential of the next generation of African American speculative-fiction writers is limitless, as the latest project edited by Sheree R. Thomas, *Dark Matter*, an anthology of black writings of fantasy, myth, magic, and all things scientific, indicates. In the hallowed footsteps of Schuyler, Delany, and Butler, these young creative minds will add new dimensions to the genre, transforming it into a wholly different literary form. Wait and see.

# AFRICAN AMERICAN POETRY

Among African Americans, the need for poetry, as a form of expressing their inner world, surfaced shortly after their arrival on these shores. It was used by slaves to express the anguish and despair born of their experiences in bondage. The early colonial efforts of Lucy Terry, Jupiter Hammons, and Phillis Wheatley tried in various ways to comprehend their times through verse. That impulse alone startled their owners, who never expected to hear such dialogue of the soul from a thing, a tool, an object they owned.

In the period leading to the Civil War, several black poets, most of them not exceptional, wrote poetry mainly touting the glory of God and making very little mention of slavery. One exception, George Moses Horton of North Carolina, went after its many evils in his pre–Civil War work. In a myriad of ways, he provided the foundation for the wave of fervent social protest to come from such voices as Paul Lawrence Dunbar and, later, from early-twentieth-century voices like Waring Cuney, James Weldon Johnson, William Stanley Braithwaite, Georgia Douglas Johnson, Angelina Grimke, and James Edwin Campbell. The force of their outrage toward segregation and inequality was not fully expressed in their poetry, but came forth in a muted, controlled manner that sought not to offend.

Not long after the appointment of the famed abolitionist writer Frederick Douglass to the post of Minister to Haiti, the black statesman met the poet Paul
Lawrence Dunbar and offered him a job as an assistant.
Dunbar gave Douglass a copy of his book of verse, *Oak
and Ivy*, but the leonine-maned leader asked to pay him
for the volume. The poet refused any money, saying the
book was a gift. Finally, Douglass yielded to the young
man's insistence and accepted the present. "If you give
me this," Douglass said, "I shall buy others." Both men
laughed at the brief battle of wills, and a deep friendship
was born.

All that changed with the Harlem Renaissance of the
1920s, when a group of young, fiery poets hailed the New Negro and considered poetry a means of examining the essential
questions of black life. Poetry, to them, was more than just
symbol, metaphor, image, or language. They saw it as an instrument for celebrating black pride, black sound, and black
style. The names of the poets—talents such as Langston
Hughes, Claude McKay, Countee Cullen, Jean Toomer, and
Arna Bontemps—soon became well known for their skill in
verse and dialect.

After the Renaissance declined—through a number of
factors, not least among them the startling force of Wright's
debut in the 1940s—through the early Cold War years, until
President Kennedy's Camelot era of the early 1960s, African
American novelists took center stage. Fiction remained ascen-
dent. Remarkable poets went largely unnoticed in the interim.
There were some exceptions. One poet, Gwendolyn Brooks,
emerged in the 1950s with a strong, lyrical approach that
uniquely used sound, image, and words. She won a Pulitzer
Prize for her 1950 collection, *Annie Allen*. Three other bards,
given some due but not enough, were Sterling Brown, Robert
Hayden, and Margaret Walker, all three of them versatile and
exceptional in their poetic craftsmanship. Some others from
this period were also talented but did not receive acclaim—

people like Melvin B. Tolson, Pinkie Gordon Lane, Conyus, and Russell Atkins.

"Much of the black poetry you read today is Going Some-where," Brooks once wrote. "Where? The poets are not always sure of their destination. Well, that's exciting. We don't know, and they don't know what's to happen next."

K NOWN FOR her no-nonsense manner with the media and her love of privacy, the Pulitzer Prize–winning poet Gwendolyn Brooks addressed her authorial inclination concisely in her book *Report from Part One*: "I am a writer because I am not a talker."

Russell Atkins, another pioneering poet and the editor of the first African American avant-garde literary magazine, *Free Lance*, put it all in perspective. "We have such a long way to go. Look at the amount of work we've actually produced. We don't have enough backlog. There are areas where we've not even explored. Look at the work that survived from the creative period from the Harlem Renaissance to the sixties. It's very small. So much remains to be done."

With the 1960s militancy and the pressing quest for social equality, there came the most forceful transformation in black arts, a renewed effort to build on the poetic legacy of the past while creating a new aesthetic. In poetry, the folk tradition was respected, along with the need to speak to the mood and anxieties of a race seeking full citizenship. In the late 1960s, a group of writers and artists, influenced by the teachings of Malcolm X, created the Black Arts Movement, which stressed race pride, cultural nationalism, self-determinism, and the theory of functional art for the collective. Amiri Baraka (Leroi Jones) was a leading force in this movement, with others including Askia M. Toure, Haki Madhubuti, Ed Spriggs, Marvin X, Sonia Sanchez, Nikki Giovanni, Carolyn Rodgers, Mari Evans, and Audre Lorde. The movement was an unqualified success in so many ways, setting an artistic standard that still influences younger writers and artists.

"I'm concerned with reaching my community, producing work whether for entertainment or political purposes," says Kalamu Ya Salaam, the longtime editor of *Black Collegian*, whose poetry and other writings were molded by the Black Arts Movement. "I would never change my message to get published. Poems can play a major role in liberating our people. However, we're living in a period where many of our writers, especially poets, have not done anything significant."

The spirit of the Black Arts Movement also molded the musicians, writers, and poets of the 1970s through the early 1990s by serving as a means of introspection at a time when selfishness, hedonism, and greed ruled the mainstream society. Some of our finest poets came forth during this time to enthrall audiences with their varied messages of hope, praise, love, and defiant racial confidence—Yusef Komunyakaa, Ntozake Shange, Thulani Davis, Sherley Anne Williams, Quincy Troupe, Nathaniel Mackey, Ai, Michael S. Weaver, Cornelius Eady, E. Ethelbert Miller, Cyrus Cassells, Elizabeth Alexander, Patricia Smith, Michael Harris, Akua Lezli Hope, and Lucinda Roy. Poet Rita Dove duplicated the groundbreaking feat of Gwendolyn Brooks decades earlier by winning a Pulitzer Prize for her 1987 collection *Thomas and Beulah*.

"Poetry is a journey, a vocation, a way of being in the world," says Cassells, an award-winning poet who spends an average time of three years to produce a volume. "For me, it's a process of self-revelation, where I learn who I am through the writing of my books. By the time my books are published, I'm living out elements of what I've written."

As the new millennium settles in, some say the militancy and creativity of that time can still be heard in the hip-hop singers and musicians of today. It can also be found in the new poets of this generation: Saul Williams, Jessica Care Moore, Carl Hancock Rux, Ras Baraka, Tracie Morris, Kevin Powell, and Asha Bandele. In their words and rhymes, one can detect the full range of influences: jazz and blues, gospel, folk songs, hip-hop even the "dozens." They understand that poetry is the most intimate of dialogues between the speaker and reader, an enticement of the imagination, of image and language. With this new crop of poets, there comes a unique poetic style, spoken and written rants that bridge feeling and thinking, that marry rhythm and style, and go deep into the consciousness of the reader. Whether it's the Nuyorican Poets Cafe in New York, or Chicago's Guild Complex, poets of the new generation are writing and singing their poetry with a verve and fierceness not seen since the late 1960s.

"Poetry is a way of offering someone a lesson, a way of understanding a person without a book," says Asha Bandele, an acclaimed New Generation poet and author of the memoir *The Prisoner's Wife*. "Poetry is such a humble craft. It allows you to say so much between the spaces, between the lines, of those private moments. Toni Cade Bambara once said art is about salvation. Either you're going to tell the truth or not in your work."

# SELLING POETRY IN THE MARKETPLACE

Getting published as a poet is not an easy thing. Some of our best poets have never found their way into print, yet they continue to work on their craft. Remarkably, African American poetry has never been widely taught in the nation's public schools. Most students get only varying doses of Whitman, Frost, Eliot, Yeats, or Sandburg. Rarely will the works of Sanchez, Baraka, Hayden, Giovanni, or Brooks be used for instruction during those early classes in rhyme, meter, and verse.

However, an audience for African American poetry has been growing since the late 1960s and continues to expand. If you want to get into print, first send your work to any number of black literary magazines, such as *Callaloo* and *African American Review*, or to any number of university literary publications. However, sometimes your remuneration may consist only of copies of the publication that printed your work. The amount of money from a sale to a major magazine can be substantially more. Still, get your work out there and build a readership. If your poems are accomplished, you will not be overlooked, because editors and other poets are always looking for something new and original.

"Publish wherever you can, read whoever you can," says Cornelius Eady, a noted poet and educator. "Good poetry will find its way into print. The reader needs to be transported to the moment of the poem. If the poet has constructed that moment and it's powerful, the reader is there with him on the page. It's a magic trick. Editors and publishers are looking for that kind of poetry."

Several first-rate poetry anthologies exist, and they serve to showcase established and new poets. An entry in any anthology assures a poet of a larger audience than that of a reading at a local café. Correspond with the poets you admire. Seek their advice. Ask for contacts.

"I never got into the habit of sending my poems out," says Lucille Clifton, an internationally known poet and writer. "They were published in anthologies because someone saw my work and loved it. I concentrate on the writing. Poems come to me from sound, memory, or dreams. I try to stay open. There is a music in the language, and this is what brings forth the words. Poetry will always be here because it fills a human need."

Remember that the slot reserved for poetry books at mainstream publishing houses is very limited. Usually the larger houses publish the more renowned, older poets with strong academic ties, but that leaves little access for the younger ones. Do not give up. Identify the poetry editor at the house and ask for the guidelines for submission; they will vary with the house. Indeed, try the large houses and the smaller ones as well. Go to the bookstores, both chains and independents, and see which university presses or small imprints publish poetry similar to what you are doing. Contact the poetry editor at that house. Often, determination and a strong commitment to the work pay off in the end.

THE POET and novelist Thulani Davis remembers submitting her first poems, each of them a stunning hybrid of lyrical images and prose, to Elizabeth Hardwick, then a teacher at Barnard College. Hardwick, a highly reputable writer in her own right, scrutinized the young woman's work and said: "Well, this isn't poetry. I don't know what it is, but keep writing it."

# DUDLEY RANDALL

## PUBLISHER, POET

On January 14, 1914, Dudley Randall was born in Washington, D.C., but his family moved from the nation's capital to Detroit in 1920. He first showed promise as a writer when he was thirteen, after one of his poems was published in the *Detroit Free Press*. In his after-school hours, his time was spent reading and dissecting the work of the Romantic poets Keats and Shelley before he discovered the verve and imagination of the influential Harlem Renaissance writers Jean Toomer, Langston Hughes, and Countee Cullen.

Like many of his contemporary Americans, Randall served in the military during World War II. Later, he tried to make sense of the experience in many of his postwar works. He found time to complete studies for degrees in English and library science between 1949 and 1951 before taking a job as librarian for five years at Morgan State and then Lincoln University. His affection for his adopted hometown, Detroit, prompted his return to the Motor City for another library post in 1956, where he worked until assuming a short-lived assignment in Wayne County in 1969. Following his abbreviated time in the classroom, Randall accepted an assignment as librarian and poet-in-residence at the University of Detroit, where he performed his duties until 1974.

His greatest achievement as a poet and publisher came in his establishment of Broadside Press in 1965, a move to publish his well-received poem "Ballad of Birmingham," a tribute to the four little girls killed during the 1963 bombing of an Alabama church. The press was launched with its first formal collection, *Poem Counterpoem*, a 1966 collaborative effort between the poets Margaret Danner and Randall, using the singular visions of both writers to explore common themes. Another acclaimed Broadside effort, *For Malcolm: Poems on the Life and Death of Malcolm X*, edited by Randall, attracted immediate notice. Several broadsides and chapbooks by a growing number of important African American poets and writers made Randall's press a leading outlet for black expression in the late 1960s and 1970s. As an independent African American book publisher, Randall led the way by bringing to print such a significant group of writers as Sonia Sanchez, Nikki Giovanni, Etheridge Knight, and Haki Madhubuti. His work, contemporary and stylistically refined, was highly respected, with a number of exceptional collections including *Cities Burning* (1968), *More to Remember: Poems of Four Decades* (1971), *After the Killing* (1973), and *A Litany of Friends* (1981).

In 1977, Randall sold Broadside Press, and a few years of emotional challenges ensued. His spirits were lifted when, in 1981, he was named the first Poet Laureate of the city of Detroit. Presently, Randall is still writing, advising young poets, and acting as consultant with the current owners of his African American literary legacy.

## IN HIS OWN WORDS

*On the founding of Broadside Press:* "The whole idea originated when a folk singer wrote me for permission to set my poem 'Ballad of Birmingham' to music. A broadside, a single sheet of paper with a printed poem, is an old idea, but it had not been used for some time. Also, it was an economical way to make poems available to the people. I wanted to publish poems people liked, so I started selling poetry broadsides at fifty cents to a dollar in 1965. I got the idea to publish books after attending a writers' conference at Fisk in 1966. I was so pleased to get poets like Sonia Sanchez, James Emmanuel, Don L. Lee [Haki Madhubuti], and Etheridge Knight to submit poems for the press. I asked Etheridge, who was in prison, if he had enough poems for a book, which he did."[1]

*On his idea of quality poetry*: "I wanted to be a publisher of good poetry. It didn't have to be a certain style. I wanted the poet to have a powerful, expressive voice. The poetry didn't have to be radical. I stayed away from anything I thought was vague or obscure. The reader should read the work and come away with some kind of emotion or information, touched in some way by the words on the page."[2]

*On the current trend of slam and performance poets*: "I think I like some of the older poets better. Many of the younger poets do not seem to be able to write as well. They do not seem to be as serious about the craft. You don't need to read poetry to write poetry, but you should write poetry because you must. It should be in your blood. You can study on your own and still be a good poet. So many of the great ones did it just that way."[3]

---

1. Personal interview with writer.
2. Ibid.
3. Ibid.

# NAOMI LONG MADGETT
## POET, PUBLISHER, EDUCATOR

Born July 5, 1923, Madgett was the daughter of a Baptist minister, possessing a facile mind and a hunger for books. Her first poetry collection, *Songs to a Phantom Nightingale,* was published when she was only fifteen years old. Later, she graduated from Virginia State College, married, and raised her daughter. A stint as a reporter at the African American weekly *Michigan Chronicle* followed, and in the mid-1950s she joined the Detroit school system as an English teacher. As a teacher, she was a tireless activist for the inclusion of more black literature classes in the city curriculum. In the 1960s Madgett collaborated with other local poets for a series of readings and workshops, which many have called the beginning of the Detroit School of Poets, including such talents as James Thompson, Oliver LaGrone, Dudley Randall, Alma Parks, and Gloria Davis. Frustrated with the reception of black poetry by mainstream publishers, Madgett, with her husband, Leonard Patton Andrews, and several friends founded Lotus Press. Madgett and Andrews assumed control of the press after two years, publishing many extraordinary poets including Toi Derricotte and Gayl Jones. In 1993, the overworked publisher negotiated distribution rights of Lotus Press with the Michigan State University Press, ending a successful seventy-six-title run. The university established the Lotus Press Series and granted Madgett the post of senior editor. During her tenure at the helm of Lotus Press, Madgett continued writing some of her finest, most deeply personal poetry, examining the challenges of urban life, family, and womanhood. Her 1972 collection, *Adam of Ife: Black Women in Praise of Black Men,* earned acclaim for its appreciation of the African American male, his accomplishments, his contributions to family and community. A self-described workaholic, Madgett still travels occasionally, giving readings or appearing at conferences, while continuing to write. Much of her joy, since the death of her husband a few years ago, comes from her work with her local congregation, both as a choir member and church historian.

## IN HER OWN WORDS

*On Lotus Press:* "I learned the business the hard way, and the press grew and grew. By 1984, I was doing everything by myself, with occasional help from volunteers from Wayne State University. But I understood the significance of Lotus Press through the enthusiasm of the young poets who sought it out. When I was first published, there were no outlets for black poets. Today, all but twelve of the original titles are still in print."[1]

*On her own poetry:* "The kind of poetry I wrote was not popular. I possessed my own way of seeing things, my creative vision. I'm not a trend follower."[2]

*On Dudley Randall and Broadside Press:* "Dudley was a pioneer with his Broadside Press, opening the way for so many young voices. It was an exciting time. He told me once that he chose poets by what he thought would sell. We differed there, because I chose my poets on their literary merits. Possibly I didn't always agree with the political messages, but I fought for their right to express them. Still, I published a lot of angry poets."[3]

1. Personal interview with writer.
2. Ibid.
3. Ibid.

*On slams, performance poetry, and young poets:* "Performance poetry is very popular, especially among the young
people, but I'm not optimistic about literary poetry. The performance variety is entertaining and easy to grasp. It's bringing
a lot of young talents into the world of poetry. Literary poetry, I
believe, may become the sole domain of the elite, poets writing for one another. Still, I have much hope for the young
poets. I always advise them to keep writing, keep persisting.
It's much easier to get into print than ever before, but young
poets should prepare themselves so they can take advantage
of the opportunity. Remember, just because you write from
deep emotion does not mean the poetry is necessarily good.
Read good poets and poetry. Join a writers' group and study
your craft."[4]

## Selected Classic African American Poetry Anthologies

*The Book of American Negro Poetry*, edited by James Weldon
    Johnson (1922)
*Negro Poets and Their Poems*, edited by Robert T. Kerlin
    (1923)
*An Anthology of Verse by American Negroes*, edited by
    Newman I. White (1924)
*Four Negro Poets*, edited by Alain Locke (1927)
*Caroling Dusk: An Anthology of Verse by Negro Poets*, edited
    by Countee Cullen (1927)
*Golden Slippers: An Anthology of Negro Poetry*, edited by
    Arna Bontemps (1941)
*The Poetry of the Negro, 1764–1949*, edited by Langston
    Hughes and Arna Bontemps (1949)
*Beyond the Blues: New Poems by American Negroes*, edited by
    Rosey Pool (1962)
*New Negro Poets*, edited by Langston Hughes (1964)
*Black Expressions: An Anthology of New Black Poets*, edited
    by Eugene Perkins (1967)

4. Ibid.

*Kaleidoscope: Poems by American Negro Poets*, edited by Robert Hayden (1967)

*The New Black Poetry*, edited by Clarence Major (1969)

*Soulscript: Afro-American Poetry*, edited by June Jordan (1970)

*Black Out Loud: An Anthology of Modern Poems by Black Americans*, edited by Arnold Adoff (1970)

*Dices or Black Bones: Black Voices of the Seventies*, edited by David Adam Miller (1970)

*Black Voices from Prison*, edited by Etheridge Knight (1970)

*We Speak as Liberators: Young Black Poets*, edited by Orde Coombs (1970)

*Natural Process: An Anthology of New Black Poetry*, edited by Ted Wilentz and Tom Weatherly (1971)

*Three Hundred and Sixty Degrees of Blackness Comin' at You*, edited by Sonia Sanchez (1971)

*Poetry of Soul*, edited by A. X. Nicholas (1971)

*Jump Bad: A New Chicago Anthology*, edited by Gwendolyn Brooks (1971)

*Black Spirits: A Festival of New Black Poets in America*, edited by Woodie King Jr. (1972)

*Modern and Contemporary Afro-American Poetry*, edited by Bernard Bell (1972)

*You Better Believe It: Black Verse in English From Africa, the West Indies, and the United States*, edited by Paul Berman (1973)

*The Forerunners: Black Poets in America*, edited by Woodie King Jr. (1975)

*Every Shut Up Ain't Asleep: An Anthology of Poetry by African Americans Since 1945*, edited by Michael S. Harper and Anthony Walton (1994)

*In Search of Color Everywhere: A Collection of African-American Poetry*, edited by E. Ethelbert Miller (1994)

*Listen Up!: Spoken Word Poetry*, edited by Zoe Anglesey (1999)

# WRITING CHILDREN'S BOOKS

Often you will hear someone say that they are going to write a children's book since that will be an easy way to get something published. But getting a children's book published is hardly effortless. First, you need to know what the editors are seeking, whether the work you may want to write is fiction or nonfiction. Your simply "creating" a chocolate version of Goosebumps or The Baby-Sitters Club will not suffice as a way of getting into print; you must be informative, original, and entertaining.

The history of African American children's books may not be a long one, but it has produced a memorable collection of work for youngsters from birth through the early teens. Black writers and illustrators have shown a deep awareness of the importance of these books to the mental and emotional development of our children. They know that the books, in all of their varied forms, provide keys for learning and mastering arithmetic as well as reading and verbal skills, bolstering racial pride and self-confidence, and building socialization skills.

There was a large boom in children's books during the 1980s, but that has receded somewhat as independent stores that specialized in such books have either closed or reorganized their inventories. Many mainstream publishers have scaled back their lines and imprints and are printing fewer copies of new releases.

Several influential educators have complained that this retreat in the industry may further indicate a lack of commitment to literacy in our public schools, noting that there could be dire consequences if the enjoyment of reading is not encouraged in the early years. This warning has not been lost on

African American writers, artists, and publishers of children's books. In recent years, they have increased their efforts to produce quality books about African culture and history, African American social and political experience, and African American achievements in science, arts, and sports.

Children's books are thriving in the African American community. Answering the demand of black parents for relevant books for their youngsters, African American publishers are creating every type of book for our young: story and board books, picture books, biographies, fables, fairy tales, fiction and nonfiction. The writers display a keen respect for the imagination and intelligence of their impressionable audience: babies/preschoolers, kindergarten to grade three, middle graders from grades four to six, and the young adult (YA) readership, from grades seven to nine. Some of the African American community's finest writers are now writing for the younger audiences. They include such writers as Nikki Giovanni, Virginia Hamilton, Walter Dean Myers, Joyce Carol Thomas, Delores Johnson, Cheryl Willis Hudson, Eloise Greenfield, Nikki Grimes, Angela Johnson, Debbi Chocolate, and Valerie Wilson Wesley.

"I saw my contribution in writing these books as a way of encouraging our children to read and write," says Wesley, author of *Freedom's Gifts: A Juneteenth Story* and *Where Do I Go from Here?* "For a long time, there was nothing out there for our children except negative images, but that is changing now. Our books are full of affirming, healing images that will strengthen our children and community."

That commitment informs the artistry of many of the writers who have chosen to alter, through their literature, the warped perception of African American youngsters. Tonya Bolden, author of several children's and young-adult books, says that writing the books is more than an opportunity to hone her craft or make a living; it is a way of giving something back to her community. "This is the part of the literary life I enjoy most. Writing books for our children is something you cannot take lightly. I know how a single book can make such a deep impact on a young life and transform it forever."

Yes, these writers seek to write books that will impact the mind of the African American child for a long time to come. They have teamed up with a stellar group of artists to create a growing legacy of African American literature that will stand the test of time, with exceptional illustrators such as Larry Johnson, Tom Feelings, Leo and Diane Dillon, Faith Ringgold, Cheryl Hanna, Pat Cummings, Ashley Bryan, the late John Steptoe, George Ford, James E. Ransome, Carole Byard, Jerry Pinkney, Jan Spivey Gilchrist, and Synthia Saint James.

Publishers, writers, and artists have seen the African American children's books soar to nearly 15 percent of the overall market, of which the YA market is the most lucrative. YA titles offer age-appropriate material to many of the genres found in the market for grown-ups, such as mystery, horror, and action. Boys in the YA category are often falsely labeled as being aloof toward reading, but they love the horror and action books. The taboo for YA readers is explicit romance, because of their tender age and impressionability.

The growing market for African American children, for the most part, follows the same literary rules as the adult market. Manuscripts for children in the middle grades and YA manuscripts should tally 25,000 to 40,000 words. Here are some tips for writing for this audience:

· An author should not write any children's book that talks down to the child or treats the child as a miniature adult.

· The story line, even if dealing with a bothersome topic, should be clear, well organized, and emotionally balanced.

· Kids are looking for fun, surprises and twists, not lectures or sermons.

· Focus your attention on the children in your book and let the action revolve around them.

· Get into the heads of your young audience and give them characters they can identify with.

· If the story is one of mystery or suspense, remember not to be *too* terrifying or scary.

· Nothing works better than strong characters, originality in language and vision, thoughtfulness, and a compelling narrative voice.

· Avoid cliches.

· Pay attention to descriptions and details.

· Kids love positive, happy endings that result from the young characters' having overcome a series of challenges.

Writers of children's books know the awesome responsibility of penning stories for the younger set, from birth to eight, where the learning curve is at its strongest and a foundation of the inner self is formed. Books serve as an aid in child rearing, and they help prepare the child to function, later in life, as an adult.

If you are truly interested in writing children's literature, check out the market:

· Familiarize yourself with the best authors and artists in the field.

· Order the catalogs from the best publishers in the field.

· Find an original story or idea and take the time to produce a rich, engaging narrative.

· If you're having trouble polishing your manuscript, join a workshop or an on-line group where you can experience the scrutiny and support to make your work a stronger candidate for publication.

While African American representation in the young-readers book market remains small, its percentage of the market is growing along with the responsibility of the publishers and writers. That is the word according to Wade Hudson, who, with his wife, Cheryl, runs Just Us Books in New Jersey, which publishes the acclaimed Afro-Bets series and other children's titles. The company, based in East Orange, New Jersey, started in 1988, with sales increasing 25 to 30 percent annually.

"What we are showing the African American community is that we are willing to bear part of the responsibility in the education of our children," Hudson said in a recent *Quarterly*

*Black Review* interview. "Each of us plays a part in the education of our children. We accept being role models of inspiration and encouragement to others."

A classic book on the subject of African American children's books, released in 1998 by John Wiley & Sons, should be of great interest to parents, educators, and writers seeking to publish in the field. It's titled *Black Books Galore! Guide to Great African American Children's Books*, by Donna Rand, Toni Trent Parker, and Sheila Foster. The book includes an informative foreword by Dr. James P. Comer, a renowned African American child psychiatrist and associate dean of Yale University's School of Medicine.

# PART V

▼▼▼▼▼▼▼

# READING GROUPS AND
# COMMUNITY-BASED ORGANIZATIONS

▼▼▼▼▼▼▼▼▼▼

# READING GROUPS: GATHER YE
# TOGETHER TO DISCUSS THE WORD

Call them what you will: book clubs, book groups, or reading groups. The fact remains that bibliophiles and people who just enjoy sharing the delights of reading African American books are coming together more than ever before to form literary societies. The number of reading circles now meeting in apartments, churches, and libraries across the country has skyrocketed as publishers offer a wider variety of literature celebrating the African diaspora. Rachel W. Jacobsohn, the author of *The Reading Group Handbook*, recently estimated the number of reading groups at 500,000, conservatively, with others placing the number even higher. Black reading groups especially seem to be growing in a rapidly accelerating trend, coalescing wherever a handful of people can locate a quiet spot to chat about their favorite books. A current estimate of African American reading groups, according to a 1990 *New York Times* article, put the total at slightly more than 100,000 nationwide.

Black people have had a love affair with books for a very long time. The history of African American literary societies begins in the 1800s, when freed blacks organized the groups to plan action for the antislavery movement. Blacks living in slavery were punished if they were caught reading or carrying a book. Often the penalties for such an offense could be quite severe, since many slaveholders saw reading as the first step to a possible rebellion. Southern states prohibited blacks from socializing in even small numbers, but northern societies fully utilized their opportunities to gather, to read the latest abolitionist tracts, and to exchange news of their oppressed brethren living below the dreaded Mason-Dixon line. They read the Bible, performed their own poetry or narratives, and laid the groundwork for community newspapers, clubs, and free schools.

Books and reading were viewed as essential ingredients in the struggle to "uplift the race." In fact, the African-American Female Intelligence Society organized in Boston around 1830 "for the diffusion of knowledge, the suppression of vice and immorality, and for cherishing such virtues as will render us happy and useful to society." Other reading groups were formed during the 1830s to encourage reading and education as tools to combat prejudice. Black women in New York started a Colored Ladies' Literary Society. Black men in Pennsylvania founded both the Young Men's Literary, Moral Reform Society, and the Philadelphia Library Company of Colored Persons, which built libraries for their book-starved communities.

These societies reflected the political and artistic climate of the nation. In the post–Civil War era, they hit membership peaks as many former slaves sought to capitalize on their newly won freedom. The groups hit a decline during the roller-coaster ride of the American economy in the first half of the twentieth century. That trend slowly reversed itself. With the resurgence of black pride and the Afrocentric movement of the 1960s and 1970s, African Americans of all ages sought out books that strongly reinforced positive images of themselves and their communities. This momentum continued through the lean 1980s, as reading groups grew and more books were published by African American writers.

Today, growing numbers of black men and women across the country gather once or twice a month in libraries, restaurants, homes, and apartments to discuss books. Over sixty black literary societies meet regularly, according to Sandra West, who recently wrote the first major study of these groups. This number greatly increases when an additional tally of more than 300 informal gatherings is factored in.

West, founder of the Frances E. W. Harper Literary Society, one of the country's most respected reading groups, says that its success after its formation in 1987, in Newark, New Jersey, was no fluke. "I'm very aware of the tradition of the black literary societies," she adds, thinking of her second creation, the Paul Robeson Reading Group, in Savannah, Georgia. "They served us well during our struggle with slavery. I think there are several reasons why there has been a resurgence of the groups. The new black middle class who went to college in the sixties and seventies loves to read. They are supporting black writers and buying books from black bookstores. We have wonderful writers currently on the scene and there are so many good books out there. Also, some groups have become multicultural, embracing the works of writers from Africa, Asia, and South America. I don't agree with people who believe we should read books just by African Americans. There are so many worlds, so many writers out there to be explored."

Not all black reading groups are so liberal in their selections. Lana Turner, founder of the New York Literary Society, feels black writing must be a priority with African American reading groups. There are more than one hundred members in her society, meeting monthly except during the summer. Started in 1982, the group is renowned for its annual "Read-In," featuring prominent writers, held during February—Black History month.

"We cover all genres, all literature from African writers to our own authors," Turner says. "We do not read Europeans. We're strictly Afrocentric in our reading. We want to support our authors who may not get the attention. There is a hunger now for good writing. Our people are just waiting to hear these words read. They want to talk about these words. It's affirmation and discovery. There is still a need to come together and talk about who you are. It's our history and we haven't forgotten it."

Book-lovers come from all walks of life: students, professionals, blue-collar types, and members of fraternities and sororities. Michelle Paynter, a psychotherapist in Kansas City, Missouri, created Bookmates, an ingenious mix of book-lovers and chess players. "We love the written word and what it does for our imaginations," she says. "I, like so many readers in our group, am an escapist. We live in our heads. The words trigger our imaginations, our dreams, our goals. We get lost in the characters, situations, and the overall drama. Books nourish us and our lives."

It seems that the common aim of these groups is to make the African American community more aware of its treasured writers and their wonderfully diverse creations while expanding its taste beyond the limits of the bestseller lists. Without a doubt, black literary societies are here to stay.

ZORA NEALE HURSTON was a major literary influence on the novelist Tina McElroy Ansa, the gifted author of *Baby of the Family* and *The Hand I Fan With*. Ansa's second novel, *Ugly Ways*, sold more than 200,000 copies. Ansa, like Hurston, believes in the power of folklore to strengthen a community's resolve and resilience. "We've got to stop jettisoning parts of our heritage that are important—whether it's the blues, what we call superstition, folklore. These are the things that got us through the horrors of the Middle Passage into this country, delivered us to these shores, and got us through slavery. And I think that's what I want to do in my novels, to remind us of our connection to spirit."

# ORGANIZING A READING GROUP

Putting together a reading group can be fun if you consider all of the essentials that will unite your collection of personalities. Here are some key points:

1. In choosing the composition of the group, consider the issues that may be discussed in relation to the members' age, gender, education, religion, and politics.

2. Wisely choose the number of members in your reading group. Bigger is not always better. A smaller group can sometimes produce a sense of intimacy and intellectual stimulation that can be very positive.

3. Decide on the location of the meetings. More than one site will give the gatherings variety.

4. Settle on a meeting format. Vary moderators to add spice and depth to the discussions.

5. Decide whether a meal should be included at the meetings. Some prefer to omit this element, the better to maintain the focus of the group.

6. If safety is a major concern, arrange to see that every member gets home safely. Carpooling or traveling in groups is always a good idea.

7. Open up book selections to cover all genres and a wide range of authors. Your reading list can include the contemporary or the classic, poetry or prose, fiction or nonfiction, an essay or a short story. Some groups even indulge in a combination fiction-film night, which allows for discussion of the merits and demerits of interpretions by moviemakers.

8. Inquire whether a local bookstore, church, or library will sponsor your group.

9. An effective group leader can keep order while sparking genuinely thought-provoking discussions. The leader can also set the tone of the exchanges with wit, humor, and insightful remarks.

10. The success of a reading group comes in its ability to exchange ideas and to participate fully in the analysis of numerous subjects arising from the selected material. Members should be generous, informed, and polite. Rudeness should not be tolerated. But do have fun!

## LANA TURNER ON THE RIGHT MEMBERS AND THE RIGHT TALK

"Each person brings their own personality to the discussion. Some people summarize and throw out ideas, while others set up the basic themes to get the ball rolling. It's all up to the moderator. Sometimes we'll get stuck on a question until the moderator gets the flow going. Some groups come together as friends. They talk about children and families. That is not the case with our group. We're there to discuss the book. We save the socializing until we've dealt with the book."

## MICHELLE PAYNTER ON PROPER READING GROUP ETIQUETTE

"In order to ensure that your group will be of a high standard, you want to make sure that everyone is truly committed, very motivated, and literate. You want people who are curious and love reading and words. Everyone does not have to be friends, but they must be focused on the discussion. You want to keep pets, music, cigarettes, and children out of the room while the group is in progress. No moving around. No telephone. You want people who will listen and respond with an articulate reply."

# THE BLACK LITERARY CLUB

## A BOOK CLUB FOR AFRICAN AMERICANS

Annette Leach's idea of starting a major African American reading club began while she worked as an ad writer with the Mingo Group, a black New York advertising agency. As an avid reader, she was deeply distressed that she could not find books that appealed to her among the offerings of the leading white commercial book clubs such as Book-of-the-Month Club or the Literary Guild. Even the most fully stocked bookstores, the sprawling chains and the customer-friendly independents, carried only a small selection of works by black writers.

Seeking to remedy this problem, Leach attended the American Book Association's annual fair in 1993, going from booth to booth, asking for a list of black writers. The stark fact that many representatives of the major publishers did not know the names or titles of their African American writers troubled her greatly, so she gathered all of the available catalogs with the notion of starting a book club featuring serious fiction and nonfiction by scribes of her tribe. Not wanting to court controversy, she steered away from subjective areas like poetry, New Age books, or self-help volumes.

The following year, the Black Literary Club was born. "It was a one-woman operation," Leach recalls. "I did the business of the club at night after work. There was so much to learn. Getting a handle on the direct-mailing business was my first task, compiling mailing lists from friends and supporters. We started with 5,000 names and now, eight catalogs later, we have reached a peak of 20,000 subscribers, with more than 200,000 items mailed out. It's all so hectic but deeply rewarding."

## THE CLUB'S MEMBERSHIP

Who are her customers? Leach says her customers are African American professionals, college-educated, with a lot of disposable income. They are older readers, not on the Internet, from their thirties to their late sixties. Her customers consist of people who love to read, have time to enjoy a good book, and, usually, are trying to build a library.

Every good enterprise must find a way to publicize itself, to bring in fresh consumers, to perpetuate the business. With her advertising background, Leach took her company to her potential markets with several innovative approaches, most notably the club's literary cruise. In January 1998, the club sponsored a three-day cruise to Nassau, Bahamas, with three popular authors in an intimate setting. The response was overwhelming and thoroughly positive, and the endeavor was repeated in the fall, aboard the luxurious *Queen Elizabeth* 2.

## AN ENTERPRISE STRUGGLING TO PROSPER

Followers of the Black Literary Club recognize Leach's staunch efforts to maintain the business on a growth curve despite some significant business challenges. She has cut back on the costly publication and mailing of the club's once-quarterly catalog, reducing its release to three times yearly and thus also minimizing postal costs. In recent months, she explored the Internet as another avenue to prospective readers, not disheartened by the users' sometimes fickle literary tastes.

"I'm very optimistic," Leach says. "We've gone through

some hard times but our commitment to the Black Literary Club has never wavered. We believe that many of the books offered by publishers fall into the mire of sex and violence. There is a new standard emerging, a higher standard of excellence, civility, and sophistication. That is what we want to offer our readers. This is the audience we are seeking."

# THE GO ON GIRL! BOOK CLUB

## A NEW STANDARD IN BOOK CLUBS

Established in 1991 by three women as a reading group in New York City, the Go On Girl! Book Club has blossomed into twenty-nine chapters in ten states with 350 members, according to one of its founding members, Monique Greenwood. The national organization, now with a growing clout in the publishing industry, has far exceeded the original dreams of its framers—Tracy Mitchell-Brown, Lynda Johnson, and Greenwood, growing in small, faithful chapters across the country. The GOG! founding trio often came together for lunch to discuss their favorite books and authors in the early days, with their first shared reading being Steven Corbin's ambitious Harlem Renaissance novel, *No Easy Place to Be*.

Now, as the group's national coordinators, the women have created a unique chapter format, with each having a membership cap of twelve women. Despite the membership limitation, there is no restriction on the number of GOG! chapters that can operate in a city. In fact, eight chapters are active in the hub of the publishing world, New York City. Some of the other GOG! locations exist in Philadelphia, Washington, D.C., St. Louis, Seattle, Chicago, Oakland, and in states such as New Jersey, Maryland, and Virginia. A survey of the book club's membership finds women of all ages, from a diverse range of economic and professional backgrounds. Whether married or single, widowed or divorced, the women come together for one reason alone: to chat up a good book.

"As we state in our mission statement, we want to expand

the literary experience of our members by promoting quality works by our writers, mostly female," says Greenwood, currently editor-in-chief at *Essence* magazine. "We want to hear our stories. There are so many books out there and some of them not so good. We've put a few things on our lists that were very disappointing, so we are currently discussing ways to overhaul our selection process to make it stronger."

What makes this group so significant is that all of its members read a particular title at the same time. The members receive an annual reading list, a dozen books in all, and everyone is expected to finish the selection by the day of the monthly GOG! gathering, so lively, often probing exchanges can occur. By the way, the books are chosen from suggestions compiled by local chapters, and where fiction always gets a sizable percentage of support, GOG! members also appreciate good nonfiction as well, reading something from each genre every year. Each of the book club's meetings is held at a different member's home each month. Since the sisters love to show off their culinary expertise, often the meetings are dazzling showcases for exotic food and beverages. Refreshments aside, the club also distinguishes itself in its documentation of member responses to the discussed books, collecting questionnaires from the participants and passing on the results to publishers and authors. Every author loves good, constructive feedback from the audience after the book hits the stores — something apart from the usual critics and industry pundits.

## AUTHOR SUPPORT

"We back our authors and books in many ways by sending book reviews and letters of support to publishers," Greenwood continues. "We encourage our writers by recognizing their work with awards, supporting readings and signings. And most of all, we support them by buying their books in the stores. That's what really counts, support at the cash register. Some authors who want to make our list come to our conferences and lobby the members. Once we select an author, we support them all the way. Our members show up in full force at every stop of their tours."

The book club also publishes a quarterly newsletter, *Jambalaya: The Go On Girl! Gazette,* which publicizes the group's Author Awards, hosted each year by a different chapter. At the first awards presentation, in 1993, the recipients were Gloria Naylor, Barbara Summers, Barbara Neely, and Beacon Press in GOG!'s ongoing encouragement of the publication of quality writing. At the 1998 ceremony in Largo, Maryland, the group honored Diane McKinney-Whetstone as its author of the year for her novel *Tumbling,* and Virginia DeBerry and Donna Grant as new authors of the year for their sister-friend classic, *Tryin' to Sleep in the Bed You Made.* It also feted the legendary novelist Dorothy West with a lifetime achievement award. Past honorees include Valerie Wilson Wesley, Benilde Little, Connie Briscoe, Sonia Sanchez, Jill Nelson, Bebe Moore Campbell, and Brenda Lane Richardson.

According to Greenwood, the club will continue to grow across the nation. The proliferation of the GOG! Book Clubs can be linked to the relocation of former members and word-of-mouth endorsements from friends and relatives of members living in other cities. Its optimistic view of literacy and publishing is also a factor. The group is working to put together a college scholarship fund to aid young writers from the African American community. A few chapters are creating junior chapters to foster literacy in our inner-city schools. In the words of its founders, The Go On Girl! Book Club is on the move!

**Some Past Go On Girl! Reading Selections**
*The Street,* Ann Petry
*High Cotton,* Darryl Pinckney
*1959,* Thulani Davis
*Double Stitch: Black Women Write About Mothers &
    Daughters,* Mary Helen Washington and Patricia
    Bell-Scott (editors)
*Devil in a Blue Dress,* Walter Mosley

*The Isis Papers,* Frances Cress Welsing
*The Content of Our Character,* Shelby Steele
*Volunteer Slavery,* Jill Nelson
*Coffee Will Make You Black,* April Sinclair
*Parable of the Sower,* Octavia Butler
*The Souls of Black Folk,* W. E. B. Du Bois
*Sally Hemings,* Barbara Chase-Riboud
*Brothers and Sisters,* Bebe Moore Campbell
*Good Hair,* Benilde Little
*Where Evil Sleeps,* Valerie Wilson Wesley
*How Stella Got Her Groove Back,* Terry McMillan
*The Hand I Fan With,* Tina McElroy Ansa
*Don't Block the Blessings,* Patti LaBelle
*The Wedding,* Dorothy West
*What Looks Like Crazy on an Ordinary Day,* Pearl Cleage

# BLACK WOMEN IN PUBLISHING

Black Women in Publishing, Inc. (BWIP), the oldest support network for African American women (and men) seeking successful careers in publishing, was established in 1979. Through hard work and diligence, it has expanded into a group with a national and international membership. Open to anyone with a curiosity about the publishing industry, BWIP has members working in the business in such diverse areas as editorial and management, human resources, publicity, marketing, finance and production, art and design, and sales. Other members are writers, publishers, agents, attorneys, and business owners.

BWIP sees itself as an association with the mission of increasing the presence of African Americans in publishing. After two decades, the organization continues to offer conferences, workshops, and networking opportunities, using its diverse membership as a learning tool for those wishing to improve their career and their entrepreneurial potential.

"We are a resource and networking organization to encourage people wishing to go into publishing," says Valerie Dixon, BWIP president. "Our focus, however, is the African American community. We put the group together starting with a core of women employees in the industry who wanted to discuss the challenges of the business. We welcome all people, all races, all sexes. The common denominator is an interest in the media business and the world of words. We're going into the twenty-first century, and knowledge is so important. Knowledge is not just power; it's growth."

At the first BWIP meeting in 1979, organizers expected an

attendance of only fifteen people. But more than seventy-five black women appeared, and they decided on the spot to meet on a monthly basis; thus, the group was born. The organization set as its major goal to act as a resource for members desiring to move forward in two areas: personal development and professional achievement. A networking directory and a career and entrepreneurial opportunity bank were quickly established so that all members could take advantage of the support given by the association. Every member receives a monthly newsletter as well as a seasonal journal listing contacts nationally.

Dixon views publishing as an important arm of that influential machine known as "the media," stressing the need for greater black representation in its decision-making upper echelon. "The media has not been a great source of opportunity for us," she notes. "There is a glass ceiling for blacks in the media industry, especially publishing. Publishing is essentially a white business, and that has to change."

The fact of BWIP's devotion to excellence, initiative, and achievement by African Americans in publishing can be seen in its annual presentation of the organization's Recognition Award to employees working at the top of their game in a pressure-packed business. Dixon and the group's vice president, Patricia Byrdsong, make it a point to schedule time for working with young people aspiring to break into the ranks of the career-minded in publishing, addressing them in schools and gatherings held at halls and auditoriums across the country. Such a commitment, often done after school and on weekends, goes a long way toward encouraging *and preparing* black youth to try for entry-level slots at the publishing giants, a move that they would not otherwise have attempted. Also, the Anna Marie Muskelly-Bryan scholarship is awarded annually by BWIP to a promising college junior pursuing an editing career.

Concerning African American writers, an increasingly vital component of the fuel propelling the industry, Dixon offers some sage advice: "Our writers must do their homework, learn where the grants are, where the writing programs are, where the writers' organizations are. And get involved. Go to the library and find out what is available to help you achieve your goal."

There is a sliding scale of BWIP membership fees for student, regular, and corporate members eligible for the many benefits offered by the organization. For more information, write:

Black Women in Publishing
P.O. Box 6275
FDR Station
New York, NY 10150

# AFRICAN AMERICAN WOMEN ON TOUR

## AN EFFECTIVE NETWORK FOR BLACK WOMEN WRITERS

Maria Dowd, executive producer of African American Women on Tour (AAWOT), expresses nothing but pride for the nine-year-old organization that has served as one of the premier support networks for black women writers, providing rare opportunities for forums, workshops, book signings, and conferences. The group, according to Dowd, presents writers with a chance to market themselves and their books to far-flung audiences. This increasing exposure of good books to readers hungry for more news and deeper insights into themselves, as well as the pleasure of meeting the authors up close, has African American Women on Tour officials pleased with the results of their gatherings across the country, in such locales as Los Angeles, New York, Chicago, Detroit, Atlanta, Philadelphia, Houston, and Dallas.

Not a membership organization, AAWOT opens its services to any woman writer serious about bringing her book to the public. The group offers venues for workshops and signings, followed by an evening with the author. Authors who have taken advantage of these occasions eagerly note that the chance to network with other writers while meeting their fans is an experience that cannot be beat.

"Our success is judged by our growing attendance and our increased respect in the book industry," Dowd explains. "We are in the business of healing black women through the power of the word. There have been copycats, but we were the first."

On the ongoing wave of strong African American women

authors gaining a sizable percentage of the nation's readership, Dowd says: "Maya, Alice, and Toni have been around for
years, but the popularity of personal empowerment books
opened the floodgates for the more established authors. Much
of the credit must be given to Iyanla Vanzant for sparking the
current interest in black women writers with her positive perspective. Iyanla gradually built her following for several years
in the black community with her appearances and signings.
Furthermore, she constructed an effective and profitable industry around her work, and her books are regularly on the
bestseller lists. People buy her books like crazy, and the big
publishers noticed the strong market among women and
came calling."

Vanzant was one of the headliners of the star-studded 1998
AAWOT tour, which included the author Maya Angelou, the
motivational speaker Byllye Avery, the former talk show host
Bertice Berry, the vocalist Gladys Knight, and the actresses
Sheryl Lee Ralph and Phyllis Yvonne Stickney. Susan Taylor, editor-in-chief of *Essence* magazine, remains a major at-
traction on the tour. At each conference tour stop, a large,
centrally located hotel, a well-tailored, tightly run program
consistently lives up to the organization's motto and its con-
stituency: "For women of color who need to recharge and take
charge."

"We keep our eyes open because trends change, but we're
careful not to let the corporate influence overrun our goals,"
Dowd adds. "We take it a season at a time, examining the
ebb and flow of the marketplace, and then we act accordingly. We're passionate about what we do because our
women are passionate about the books and the messages they
bring."

For more information, write:

African American Women on Tour
3914 Murphy Canyon Road
Suite 216
San Diego, CA 92123

PART VI
▼▼▼▼▼▼▼

# WRITERS RESOURCES
▼▼▼▼▼▼▼▼▼▼

# WRITERS WORKSHOPS

Can writing be taught? Some controversy surrounds the issue of whether writing can be effectively taught in workshops and seminars, or even in a university setting. Currently, there are more than 3,000 writers workshops active and at least 100 M.A. and M.F.A. writing programs being offered at leading universities and colleges. In fact, those numbers have soared in recent years. Supporters see instruction in creative writing as something entirely possible, given the right environment, teacher, and willing student. Workshops, classes, and seminars, according to some writing gurus, offer a chance for a novice writer to evolve and develop into a better practitioner of the craft. These opportunities permit writing teachers to serve as guides and mentors through the use of exercises designed to produce, in many cases, the maturation of a salable manuscript.

However, detractors are adamant in their belief that a real writer cannot be produced through rote group instruction. Some critics believe that the kind of support and exchanges usually found in workshops, seminars, or classes may yield a safe, positive setting in which the novice writer can sharpen latent skills, but nothing can be done to create a fine writer if there is no talent at the start.

Al Young, poet and novelist, has mixed feelings about the importance of workshops, but says they may serve to provide young writers with an outlet to get their work critiqued. "While M.F.A. programs don't make you a writer, such workshops can provide writers with the tools to get their poetry and prose published. You see a lot of their work published in literary journals. It's very well represented there, and that can give them a big boost in their confidence. Possibly the workshops' greatest value comes in getting a response to your work from people who are as passionate about writing as you are."

In reality, the structure of a workshop may help the young writer find the discipline to confront the blank page on a daily basis. Many writers use this option to discover whether they do indeed possess the commitment necessary to forge ahead as a professional writer. With these individuals, the personal attention and encouragement of one's peers stoke the creative fires, resulting in the surge of confidence so vital to producing quality work.

Another consideration cannot be overlooked. That is the significance of meeting published writers with both expertise and valuable contacts in the publishing world. Many books have found their way to editors at mainstream publishing houses through the referrals and recommendations of instructors at workshops and seminars. These veterans not only offer hope, they also provide inside information that can assist beginners in avoiding many of the pitfalls of getting into print.

"By meeting editors and other writers at workshops, you start to think of yourself as a professional writer," says Anita Diggs, editor at Warner Books. "I agree that basic talent can't be taught, but you can learn discipline and much about the fundamentals of the writing process. That new attitude can go a long way in giving a young writer the devotion to craft which will make it easier to get published."

In the setting of the workshop or seminar, critical lessons about writing can be learned, such as technique, revision, and grammar. Some say you can accomplish everything that could be taught in a class or workshop by taking a page of poetry or prose, diagraming it, and imitating every adjective and verb. However, line-by-line imitation can carry the learning process only so far.

"It's tough for a young writer just starting out," says John A. Williams, author of twelve novels including the classic *The*

*Man Who Cried I Am.* "If you're going to be a writer, you'll need to do the work, regardless of the odds. For so many writers, the library was their first workshop, opening the doors of imagination and perception. Read the great literature and study our history. Literature lives in history. Don't confine your study to just one thing. As a writer, you cannot afford to have a narrow focus, so don't limit your study to your own culture and history."

When someone chooses the workshop setting, care must be taken to utilize fully the time and expertise available, according to bestselling mystery writer Valerie Wilson Wesley, who attended workshops such as the Harlem Writers Guild and writing seminars at The New School. "It's helpful to be around writers, to be in that community and enjoying the exchange of ideas," she says. "There is a time to talk, socialize, and there's a time to write. If you're there with a project in mind, you must remain focused on the work. It's easy to talk a book away. This is why young writers often do not produce the works that possessed them in that environment. You must make the most of workshops and all that they offer."

Overall, workshops and seminars can provide benefits only if there is a full commitment and dedication on the part of the participant. Otherwise they are a waste of time and money. A writer must enter the workshop environment with his or her goals and objectives clearly in place to truly benefit from what is offered.

The following is a partial list of sources providing information on writers workshops and seminars open to both young and established writers:

*AWP Official Guide to Writing Programs*
Associated Writing Programs/Dustbooks
P.O. Box 100
Pasadena, CA 95967

*Encyclopedia of Associations*
Deborah M. Burck, Ed.
Gale Research
P.O. Box 33477
Detroit, MI 48232-5477

*Guides to Writers Conferences*
Shaw Associates
625 Biltmore Way
Suite 1406
Coral Gardens, FL 33134

*Literary Market Place*
R. R. Bowker
121 Chanlon Road
New Providence, NJ 07974

List of Writer Residences and
Retreats
*Poets & Writers Magazine*
72 Spring Street
New York, NY 10012
212-226-3586

*Networking at Writers
Conferences: From Contacts to
Contracts*
Steven D. Spratt and Lee G.
Spratt
John Wiley: New York, 1995

Annual Writers Conferences and
Seminars Listings
*Writer's Digest*
1507 Dana Avenue
Cincinnati, OH 45207

# WRITERS ORGANIZATIONS

Academy of American Poets
584 Broadway, Suite 1208
New York, NY 10012
212-274-0343

American Society of Journalists
and Authors
1501 Broadway, Suite 302
New York, NY 10036

Associated Writing Programs
Tallwood House MS1E3
George Mason University
Fairfax, VA 22030

Association of Authors
Representatives
10 Astor Place, 3rd floor
New York, NY 10003
212-353-3709

Association of Desktop Publishers
3401-A 800 Adams Avenue
San Diego, CA 92116-2490
619-563-9714

The Authors Guild
330 W. 42nd Street, 29th floor
New York, NY 10036
212-563-5904

The Authors League of America
330 W. 42nd Street
New York, NY 10036
212-564-8350

International Associations of
Crime Writers Inc.
North American Branch
JAF Box 1500
New York, NY 10016
212-243-8966

International Women's Writing
Guild
Box 810
Gracie Station
New York, NY 10028-0082
212-737-7536

National Writers Association
1450 S. Havana, Suite 424
Aurora, CO 80012
303-751-7844

National Writers Union
113 University Place, 6th floor
New York, NY 10003
212-254-0279

PEN American Center
568 Broadway
New York, NY 10012
212-334-1600

Poetry Society of America
15 Gramercy Park
New York, NY 10003
212-254-9628

Poets & Writers
72 Spring Street
New York, NY 10012
212-226-3586

Romance Writers of America
13700 Veterans Memorial,
Suite 315
Houston, TX 77014-1073
281-440-6885

Science Fiction and Fantasy
Writers of America
532 LaGuardia Place, #632
New York, NY 10012-1428

Society of Children's Book
Writers and Illustrators
345 N. Maple Drive, Suite 296
Beverly Hills, CA 90210
310-859-9887

Volunteer Lawyers for the Arts
One E. 53rd Street, 6th floor
New York, NY 10022
212-319-2787

Writers Guild of America
East Chapter
555 W. 57th Street
New York, NY 10019
212-767-7800

# THE INTERNET FOR WRITERS

Many writers, frightened of the technology and its demands, somehow manage to overlook the Internet as a tool and forum for their work. In the past, the struggling writer could plead poverty as the reason for not being plugged into the system that puts a wealth of university libraries, newspaper morgues, wire services, and national archives at your fingertips. All you need is a PC with a modem or a connection to the system through any one of a number of Internet Service Providers (ISPs). America Online remains the most popular of the lot, but shop around to find the service that fulfills your needs; there are many, such as Prodigy.

## THE TOOLS OF THE TRADE

You need a computer with as much RAM, or memory, as your wallet can bear, and a generous hard drive, paired with a monitor that will not damage your eyes. In either a home or an apartment, you may need to install a second telephone line that will not interfere with your primary line, so calls can avoid interruption. Once you've set up your operation, an unbelievably wide range of information on the Internet, on any topic under the sun, can be yours with the stroke of a few keys.

## RESEARCHING AND EXPLORING THE WEB

If research is the chief reason for your interest in the Internet, you will need an effective browser, or software, to explore the various websites. Using any of the most commonly used browers, such as Netscape or Internet Explorer, you can save much time and energy while you surf, searching for data and information. The research capabilities of the Internet are enhanced by the possibilities it offers for the inquisitive writer to enter chat rooms for lively discussions with other authors and experts on any field. Just point and click at a site, and you're there, exchanging dialogue on the very topic of your work with someone knowledgeable in that area.

One cautionary note: Although a vast world of information will be available from these sites, be certain to check and double-check the sources and the material before incorporating this input into your work. Two indispensable tools for electronic research remain Gopher, a program for locating and retrieving files on the Internet, and FTP, or File Transfer Protocol, a system used to transmit files. Both of these items will permit you to take full advantage of on-line information services, allowing you to write up to your potential.

Promotionally, the Internet opens an entirely new set of options, prompting a growing number of writers to establish sites complete with attractive home pages and full support documents on their work. This move alerts the on-line literary community and others to their presence, providing essential advertising to entice would-be readers to seek out the writers' books. Try it with *your* book. And the contacts made during your Web search can be extremely valuable. By joining in discussions about the writings of others, you let your peers experience your opinions about the art and craft of writing.

There's nothing like some hypertext bonding. Post messages and queries on the more popular on-line sites, and sources will often come forward with the desired information. Presto! One single source can open the floodgates to areas of research that you never even considered. However, exercise some decorum:

· Don't make a pest of yourself.
· Always treat others on the Internet as you would want to be treated.
· Excessive displays of ego and overzealous acts of self-promotion can backfire, and your research effort could be made that much harder.


## USING SEARCH ENGINES FOR RESEARCH

Since finding information on the Web can be an awesome task, the need early arose for some type of system to cut time spent in wading through the countless pages constantly arriving and departing on-line. It was dizzying—sheer madness. All of that changed with the development of search engines, computer programs that scanned for a particular key word or subject. The search engines work by homing in on the specific term or topic after you type it into the system. Click the "search" button on the screen, and the program does the work. What you get is a list, offering you several options toward your goal. If one search engine cannot provide you with the answers, then you can switch to another, and again another, until your quest is rewarded.

Among the most frequently used search engines are Yahoo!, HotBot, Internet Sleuth, Excite, InfoSeek, Alta Vista, Northern Light, and Lycos. Even with the able assist of a competent search engine, you will quickly realize that a lot of the material found on the Web is pure fluff, too abstract or vanity-driven for use. In your search for data, your ability to narrow your focus can only improve with practice and experience. Instinctively, your skill in finding the crucial words and terms to ferret out the right information becomes sharper with each passing day. Several approaches can unlock that elusive fountain of facts, using a specific date or a series of dates or maybe a key word, and clicking on the appropriate link. It's all there. You just have to be patient and let your search engine do the digging for the right index.

For the writer and book-lover, the Web offers everything in terms of booksellers, publishers, publications, workshops, and book reviews. Book buyers can now browse through any of the on-line book outlets for their choice of the latest and even the most obscure volumes. In fact, prices of books list significantly lower on-line than at neighborhood stores, which must charge higher rates to pay for overhead. Amazon, an on-line bookstore, discounts 20 to 40 percent off list price, while boasting a huge selection of over 1.5 million books and rapid mail delivery of all orders. Its chief competitor, Barnes and Noble, which opened a bookstore on America Online in 1997, counters with cutting the cost of hardcover books by 30 percent and paperbacks by 20 percent.

## AFRICAN AMERICANS IN CYBERSPACE

African Americans have charged into cyberspace with a host of websites for writers and readers—computer watering holes that spout news, author chats, art and film updates, literary gossip, insider job scoops for writers, and research and reference information. Black representation, like the other segments of the Internet, keeps growing at an incredible pace, with new sites appearing daily. Remember: Constantly update your list of favorite websites, as they are subject to change without prior notice.

### On-Line Resources for Books and Writers
Amazon.com (www.amazon.com) The superstore of books on-line.

Advanced Book Exchange (www.abebooks.com) Five hundred book dealers for anyone seeking out-of-print and rare books.

American Booksellers Association (www.amerbook.org) Any

fact, topic, or news about books, booksellers, resources, writer support sites, and the publishing world.

Barnes and Noble (www.bn.com) The nation's largest bookseller.

Bibliofind (www.bibliofind.com) Full-service source for rare book searches.

Book Wire (www.bookwire.com) Everything you want to know about books, authors, signings, readings, and gossip.

Book Zone (www.bookzone.com) Publisher home pages, book listings, contests, prizes, awards, author and book news.

Inkspot Writers' Forum (www.inkspot.com) Author forums, market chat, sites for young writers, author classifieds, and book news.

Library of Congress (www.loc.gov) A massive collection of resource materials on every topic and category possible.

National Writers Union (www.nwu.org) Writer bees unite! Information on legal issues, conferences, seminars, and contract rights for writers.

rec.arts.books News group listings, postings, and info for book lovers and writers on the Net.

Title Net (www.titlenet.com) Search site for author, title, and subject information.

The Write Page (www.write page.com) On-line news and chat for fans and authors of genre lit.

**Cyber-Soul Websites for African American Writers**

African American Literature Book Club (www.aalbc.com) On-line book site, in partnership with Barnes and Noble, writer resource information, reviews, author chat, and readings.

The Amistad Research Center (www.arc.tulane.edu) One of the finest African American archival resources available in the nation.

Black Voices (www.blackvoices.com) Cultural news, chat rooms, book information, and gossip.

Drum and Spear Books (www.drumandspear.com) African American literature on-line discount at 20 percent, new books, reviews, young adult and children's titles, and calendars.

EverythingBlack (www.everythingblack.com) Current events, cultural tidbits, job information, and more.

Mosaic Books (www.mosaicbooks.com) New book releases, bestsellers, and full-service information on black bookstores.

Netnoir (www.netnoir.com) The best networking site with interesting cultural and literary chat.

Schomburg Center for Research in Black Culture (gopher.nypl.org.research/sc/sc.html) One of the premier research centers on African American culture, based in Harlem.

# GRANTS AND AWARDS

Look below for a short but very important list of some of the major institutions offering grants-in-aid and awards or information about them. If you are interested in finding contact names or information on entry fees or on deadlines, write the organization, including a self-addressed, stamped envelope, and request all specific details available about the particular contest or award of interest to you. Once you get the guidelines, take time to read the materials carefully to confirm that your work or situation qualifies you to apply.

A trip to your local branch library can yield several resource books, full of information on grants and awards, that can make your quest that much easier. So there is no reason to despair, with the financial support available that most writers need at some point in a career, in order to advance toward the goal of getting into print. The following twenty-one listings are among the leading organizations offering a wide range of information on how to pursue the grants and awards you desire.

The Academy of American Poets
584 Broadway, Suite 1208
New York, NY 10012

American Academy of Arts and
Letters
633 W. 155th Street
New York, NY 10032

American Library Association
50 E. Huron Street
Chicago, IL 60611

The American Poetry Review
1721 Walnut Street
Philadelphia, PA 19183

Associated Writing Programs
Award Series in Poetry, Short
Fiction, the Novel, and Creative
Nonfiction
Tallwood House, MS-1E3
George Mason University
Fairfax, VA 22030

The Authors League Fund
330 W. 42nd Street
New York, NY 10036

Carnegie Fund for Authors
1 Old Country Road
Carle Place, NY 11514

The Chicago Tribune
c/o The Nelson Algren Award for
Short Fiction
435 North Michigan Avenue
Chicago, IL 60611

The Cleveland Foundation
1422 Euclid Avenue
Suite 100 — Hanna Building
Cleveland, OH 44115-2000

The Foundation Center
79 Fifth Avenue
New York, NY 10003-3050

The Foundation Center
1001 Connecticut Avenue NW
Suite 938
Washington, DC 20036

The Foundation Center
312 Sutter Street
San Francisco, CA 94108

John Simon Guggenheim
Memorial Foundation
90 Park Avenue
New York, NY 10016

Robert F. Kennedy Awards for
Fiction and Nonfiction
1206 30th Street NW
Washington, DC 20007

National Endowment for the Arts
1100 Pennsylvania Avenue NW
Washington, DC 20506

The National Poetry Series
P.O. Box G
Hopewell, NJ 08525

PEN American Center
568 Broadway
New York, NY 10012-3225

Poetry Society of America
15 Gramercy Park
New York, NY 10003

Poets & Writers
72 Spring Street
New York, NY 10012

Mary Roberts Rinehart Fund
MSN 3E4
English Department
George Mason University
4400 University Drive
Fairfax, VA 22030-4444

Writer's Digest
1507 Dana Avenue
Cincinnati, OH 45207

# REFERENCE GUIDES FOR WRITERS

Appelbaum, Judith. *How to Get Happily Published.* New York: HarperCollins Publishers, 1998.

Balking, Richard. *A Writer's Guide to Book Publishing.* New York: Plume Books, 1994.

Boswell, John. *The Insider's Guide to Getting Published.* New York: Main Street Books, 1997.

Bykofsky, Sheree, and Jennifer Basye Sander. *The Complete Idiot's Guide to Getting Published.* New York: Macmillan, 1998.

Greenfield, Howard. *Books: From Writer to Reader.* New York: Crown Books, 1989.

Holm, Kirsten, and Donya Dickerson (eds.). *2000 Writer's Market: 8,000 Editors Who Buy What You Write.* Cincinnati: Writer's Digest Books, annual.

*Literary Market Place: The Directory of the American Book Publishing Industry.* 2 vols. New Providence, NJ: R. R. Bowker, annual.

National Book Award authors. *The Writing Life.* New York: Random House, 1994.

Page, Susan. *The Shortest Distance Between You and a Published Book.* New York: Broadway Books, 1997.

Potter, Clarkson N. *Who Does What and Why in Book Publishing.* New York: Birch Lane Press, 1990.

# INDEX

Atkinson, Pansye, 140
Attaway, William, 28, 170,
187, 197
audio rights, 59
Authors Guild, 92
autobiography/memoir, 20,
21, 25; classic African
American, 183–85
autographed books, 101
awards, literary, 4, 114,
190–96; African American
awardees, 192–96; most
important, 190–92;
resources, 323–24

Bailey, Pearl, 193
Baker, Augusta, 187
Baker, Houston A., 172, 181,
188
Baker, Josephine, 184
Baldwin, James, 25, 30, 105,
114, 135, 171, 172, 173,
180, 187, 197, 203, 208,
209, 234, 265, 268
Ballantine, 15, 16, 97, 99
Bambara, Toni Cade, 5, 175,
177, 181, 188, 244–46, 273
Bandele, Asha, 185, 272, 273
Banneker, Benjamin, 167
Baraka, Amiri, 30, 140, 171,
181, 183, 188, 271
Baraka, Ras, 272
Barnes, Steven, 267
Barnes & Noble, 119, 123,
124, 320
Beatty, Paul, 31, 88, 189
Bell-Scott, Patricia, 184, 302

Bennett, Gwendolyn, 187
Bennett, Lerone, 171, 179
bestsellers, 4, 13, 14, 15, 78,
111–21; lists, 112–19, 156;
race issues, 111–19; road
to, 120–21
Billingsley, Andrew, 180
biography, 20, 21
births of notable African
American authors, 186
Black Arts Movement, 30–31,
139–40, 146, 171, 271, 272
Blackboard list, 118–19, 156
Black Classic Press, 90,
140–44
Black Literary Club, 297–99
Black Women in Publishing
(BWIP), 304–6
Bland, Alden, 28
Bland, Eleanor Taylor, 255,
256
Bolden, Tonya, 284
Bontemps, Arna, 147, 176,
179, 187, 211, 270, 281
book clubs, 59, 113,
291–303; Black Literary
Club, 297–99; Go On
Girl!, 300–303;
organizing, 295–96
booksellers, 4, 94, 95, 118,
122–26; African American,
122–26, 127; bestseller
lists, 118–19; independent
vs. large chain, 13, 96,
100, 118, 119, 122–24,
127, 159; on-line, 71, 98,
100–2, 123, 159, 320

# ABOUT THE AUTHOR

Robert Fleming, a freelance journalist and associate professor of writing at the New School for Social Research, formerly worked as a reporter for the *New York Daily News* where he earned several honors, including a New York Press Club Award and a Revson Fellowship in 1990. His articles have appeared in publications including *Essence*, *Black Enterprise*, *The Source*, *U.S. News and World Report*, *Omni*, and *The New York Times*. He is the author of *The Wisdom of the Elders* and two books for young adults, *Rescuing a Neighborhood: The Bedford-Stuyvesant Volunteer Ambulance Corps* and *The Success of Caroline Jones, Inc.: The Story of an Advertising Agency*. His poetry and essays have appeared in *UpSouth*, *Brotherman*, *Sacred Fire*, and *In Search of Color Everywhere: A Collection of African-American Poetry*.